HANDBOOK OF

ZERO to HERO

(New Edition)

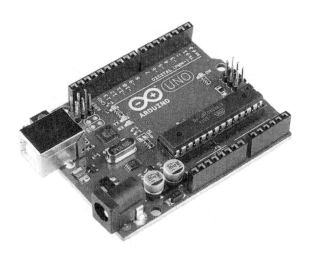

ARSATH NATHEEM S

WHY I WROTE THIS BOOK

When we think about the word '**Education**', we often think of the formal schooling that happens in primary, secondary and high schools and colleges. Although, this is not the only way of education, tacit and practical knowledge is something that we often can't learn by reading books; it is achieved by addressing real world problems and practice, it relates to experience, intuition, ideals, creative thinking, emotions, values, skills and attitudes. Arduino Education makes the next generation of STEAM programs and tacit knowledge that empower schoolchildren on their creative learning journey through secondary school, high school, and university and help them succeed.

Arduino has been used in thousands of unique projects and various development applications. The Arduino software is simple-to-use application for beginners, and now flexible enough for advanced users, teachers and scholars and use it to build cost efficient scientific devices, to demonstrate chemistry and physics principles, or to get started with programming and robotics, Project based learning will lead to cooperating education and create a deeper impact on the student. It also builds the understanding part more enjoyable as students are able to understand more while learning it in a group. Consequently, let us focus on a plethora of simple projects related to Interesting Arduino sensors that will enhance student's innovative mindset. The Arduino project works at all times and makes improvements to the existing system, and for that reason, Ultimately, students can develop a forward-thinking practical mindset and way   of   thinking.

"Tell me and I forget, teach me and I may remember, involve me and I learn" -- Benjamin Franklin

WHY YOU SHOULD READ THIS BOOK

This Arduino Handbook will help you learn all about making projects with Arduino, and beneficial for novice to expert level students, and research scholars. This handbook is written for those who is enthusiastic in innovative projects with the help of open source tools and technique, and it is a huge collection of ideas to do some creative projects, to create something new to society, This book consists of six chapters starting from Arduino basics, electronic components, Arduino boards and their sensors, to getting started with Arduino programming, then you can practice 33 step by step projects by doing, and the book ends with more than 100 fascinating project-ideas and finally Troubleshooting Arduino. I believe this Arduino handbook will be helpful for students and research scholars for their mini projects. Also includes operative basics in case of open-source electronics, for college, school students and hobbyists to learn Arduino from the basic to expert level through practical schematic diagrams. I hope this would be a wonderful project guide for science fair projects and their new innovative works.

TABLE OF CONTENTS

CHAPTER 1:

ARDUINO: EVERYONE NEED TO KNOW

Introduction

The first ever Arduino controller board was born in 2005, at the teaching space of the Interactive Design Institute in Ivrea, Italy. An article about a wiring design submitted by a Colombian scholar named Hernando Barragan can be found in the Interactive Design Institute. The name of the proposal thesis was **"Arduino - The Revolution of Open Hardware".** Of course, it sounded a slightly different from the typical proposal but nobody would have make-believe that it would be carve a niche in the domain of electronics.

The Arduino software IDE was developed by David Mellis and was based on Wiring. Previously, Gianluca Martino and Tom Igoe joined the development of Arduino mission, as well as the five are well-known as the actual creators of Arduino board. They needed a controller should be straightforward, easy to associate with different kind of module and components (such as LED, motors, relays, and sensors), considerably weightless, also easy to accessible in the open-source community, and simple to program. It also wanted to be cost efficient, easy to available, because as students and artists aren't known for rich in cash. They choose the AVR type of 8-bit microcontroller (MCU or μC) devices from Atmel and aimed a self-sufficient circuit board with easy-to-use connections, put pen to paper bootloader firmware for the microcontroller, and finished it all into a basic integrated development environment (IDE) which used programs entitled as **"sketches."** The result was the Arduino Hardware.

Microcontroller

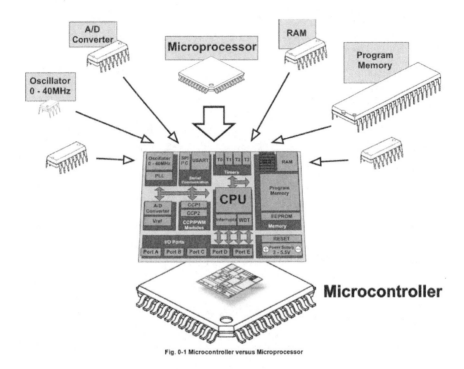

Fig. 0-1 Microcontroller versus Microprocessor

A minicomputer on a single chip, having a processor, input/output memory, Analog to digital converter (ADC), and Digital to analog converter (DAC) generally "embedded" inside some micro device which they control, a microcontroller is often small and cost efficient.

Development Board

A printed circuit board contain a microprocessor and tiny or no hardware is dedicated to a user interface, which designed to facilitate work with a specific microcontroller is called development board.

In development board typical components include:

- Power circuit
- Simple input; usually buttons and LEDs
- Programming interface
- I/O pins

Here are some popular development boards listed:

- Arduino
- BeagleBone Black
- Raspberry Pi
- Intel Galileo
- Goldilocks
- pcDuino
- Uruk
- ExtraCore

What is the Arduino?

The word "Arduino" can mean 3 things

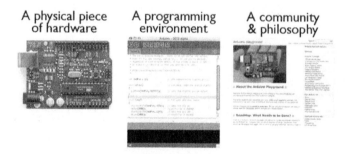

A physical piece of hardware   A programming environment   A community & philosophy

Why Was Arduino Developed?

- Physical Computing - by means of components which able to interact with people, besides by the world around us
- The Arduino was initially developed for artists, inventors and designers, to make prototype interactive displays
- Intended for non-scientists, less knowledge required to learn.
- Minimalist programming

- **"Forgiving"** microcontroller board which able to handle a widespread of wiring connection errors.

What can Arduino be used to Teach?

- To understand preliminary electronics (voltage, current, resistance)
- How electronic components, sensors and actuators works.
- Elementary programming and troubleshooting
- Design of simple scientific devices and equipment
- Overcome the challenges of interactive with users via a DIY project (e.g., messages, formatting numbers, ease of use, etc.)
- Statistics and difference in data collecting and visualization

DIFFERENT TYPES OF ARDUINOS

 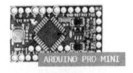 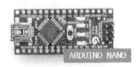

The microcontrollers used in the various models of Arduino.

Name	Processor	Operating/Input Voltage	CPU Speed	Analog In/Out	Digital IO/PWM	EEPROM [kB]	SRAM [kB]	Flash [kB]	USB	UART
101	Intel® Curie	3.3 V/ 7-12V	32MHz	6/0	14/4	-	24	196	Regular	-
Gemma	ATtiny85	3.3 V / 4-16 V	8 MHz	1/0	3/2	0.5	0.5	8	Micro	0
LilyPad	ATmega168V ATmega328P	2.7-5.5 V / 2.7-5.5 V	8MHz	6/0	14/6	0.512	1	16	-	-
LilyPad SimpleSnap	ATmega328P	2.7-5.5 V / 2.7-5.5 V	8 MHz	4/0	9/4	1	2	32	-	-
LilyPad USB	ATmega32U4	3.3 V / 3.8-5 V	8 MHz	4/0	9/4	1	2.5	32	Micro	-
Mega 2560	ATmega2560	5 V / 7-12 V	16 MHz	16/0	54/15	4	8	256	Regular	4
Micro	ATmega32U4	5 V / 7-12 V	16 MHz	12/0	20/7	1	2.5	32	Micro	1
MKR1000	SAMD21 Cortex-M0+	3.3 V/ 5V	48MHz	7/1	8/4	-	32	256	Micro	1
Pro	ATmega168 ATmega328P	3.3 V / 3.35-12 V 5 V / 5-12 V	8 MHz 16 MHz	6/0	14/6	0.512 1	1 2	16 32	-	1
Pro Mini	ATmega328P	3.3 V / 3.35-12 V 5 V / 5-12 V	8 MHz 16 MHz	6/0	14/6	1	2	32	-	1
Uno	ATmega328P	5 V / 7-12 V	16 MHz	6/0	14/6	1	2	32	Regular	1
Zero	ATSAMD21G18	3.3 V / 7-12 V	48 MHz	6/1	14/10	-	32	256	2 Micro	2
Due	ATSAM3X8E	3.3 V / 7-12 V	84 MHz	12/2	54/12	-	96	512	2 Micro	4

Arduino LilyPad

The LilyPad Arduino is a microcontroller board intended for wearables and e-textiles. LilyPad is well known for its clothing-based projects. It can be stitched to textile material, fabrics, cloth and likewise mounted power source, sensors and actuators with conductive textile fiber.

Arduino BT

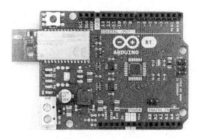

The Arduino BT is an Arduino board with built-in Bluetooth module, utilized for various types of wireless communication, and remote-control application.

Arduino Esplora

Esplora is an Arduino board intended for gaming enthusiast for hassle-free gaming experience and used as a Gaming Controller.

Esplora Arduino board consist of joystick, linear potentiometer (slider), microphone, buttons control, temperature sensor, light sensor and three-axis accelerometer, not the typical set of input/output pins.

Leonardo

- Compared to the Arduino Uno, Leonardo is a minor upgrade.
- It has built in Micro USB compatibility
- Utilized to PC as a mouse or keyboard

Arduino Due

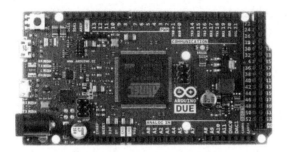

- Arduino Due has much faster processor, and plethora of analog, digital pins compared then Arduino Uno.
- Due is similar to the Arduino Mega
- Moreover, its works on 3.3 volts as well as 12v.

Arduino Nano

Arduino Nano is a superficial mount little microcontroller breadboard embedded model with integrated Micro USB Port.

It is a tiny, full-fledged microcontroller, breadboard friendly, and cost-effective device, it has everything like same as Die/Due/Uno board has (electrically) with extra digital and analog I/O pins and onboard +5V AREF jumper.

Arduino Micro

- When size matters: Micro, Nano, and Mini, smallest board ever made by Arduino developers.
- Arduino Micro comprises all functionality of Uno and Leonardo
- Arduino micro is simply working on a breadboard

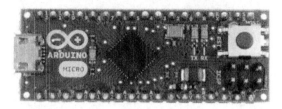

Why use Arduino UNO?

- Arduino is an open-source electronic prototyping boards based on flexible easy to practice hardware and software.
- Reasonably priced, we can buy Arduino less than $10.00, Provided assemble your own Arduino board, or buying clone for more less than in that.
- Cross Platform IDE (Support in common Operating System such as Windows, MAC, and Linux), Open-source IDE and extensions.

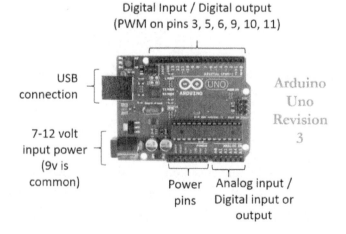

Fig. Overview of Arduino UNO

What Approach Have I Follow to Learn Arduino?

1. **Start simple** - build confidence **learn by doing** with small project before going difficult one.
2. Practice components that will capture the thoughtfulness and imagination of the students
3. Build a new project by modifying previous one.
4. Make a "problem" for pupils to resolve that THEY will understand through practical however not too complicated
5. Find problem in your society, gather knowledge from it, make an idea, then instantly do a development with it, and give a solution with your project.
6. Teach pupils just how to find required info from datasheets (e.g., tolerances, current limits, etc.) and, likewise learn from the internet

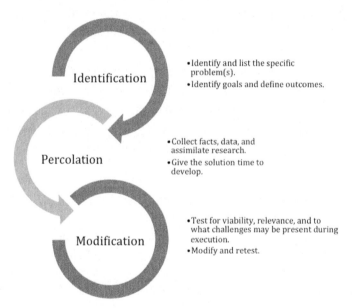

Identification
• Identify and list the specific problem(s).
• Identify goals and define outcomes.

Percolation
• Collect facts, data, and assimilate research.
• Give the solution time to develop.

Modification
• Test for viability, relevance, and to what challenges may be present during execution.
• Modify and retest.

Identification The first step to start a project is problem-solving process is to identify, define, and articulate the problem. The use of brainstorming and mind maps is valuable for some of the more difficult problems. **Percolation** Data collection, research, and idea exploration are next steps. The main reason that **innovation** is so difficult is because many ideas in a vacuum may not seem realistic or appropriate.

GETTING STARTED WITH ARDUINO

Arduino IDE (Integrated Development Environment)

The Arduino Software (IDE) is easy to learn, and so far, flexible enough for more creative people to take advantage of for educators, its user-friendly platform related on the simple programming environment, therefore students able to learn by doing Arduino codes in that environment will be related with how the Arduino Microcontroller and its IDE workings.

A Computer for the Physical World:

The welcoming blue board in your hand (or on your workbench) is the Arduino. In earlier you may think of Arduino as the child of a typical PC and Computer system. By its origins, the Arduino is fundamentally a tiny portable controller or a computer. It is responsible of gathering inputs (such as push button or a sense from a LDR or light sensor) and understanding which data to handling a number of outputs (Such as blinking an LED or an electronic DC motor). Consequently, the term "physical computing" was born - an Arduino is clever of interpretation the domain of electronics and linking it to the physical world in a genuine and tangible approach. Trust me - this will absolutely make more sense as early as possible you practice Arduino.

Installing Arduino IDE with Arduino Uno R3 board

STEP-1: Download the Arduino IDE (Integrated Development Environment) from the official website link given below summary.

Access the Internet: with the purpose of get your Arduino controller functioning, and before getting started, you have to download Arduino IDE first from Official website www.arduino.cc (Arduino is Open Source, hence need not to pay for it, it's free!). This Application, well-known as the Arduino IDE, you can always ready to start write your own code for the Arduino to do really what you want. Which is similar to a WordPad for writing Arduino sketch.

With an internet accessible PC, open up your default browser and type in the below URL into the web search bar: Download the newest version of Free **Arduino IDE** from this page: http://arduino.cc/en/Main/Software

For dissimilar OS platforms, the method of using Arduino IDE is not the same. Kindly ensuring to the following links:

Windows User: http://www.arduino.cc/en/Guide/Windows

Mac or Linux User:

http://www.arduino.cc/en/Guide/MacOSXLinuxUser
http://playground.arduino.cc/Learning/Linux

For learn more about Arduino IDE, Kindly checkout to the Link: http://www.arduino.cc/en/Guide/HomePage

Arduino UNO SMD R3

Arduino Uno is one of the most widely used microcontroller boards, powered by the ATmega328. Its wide range of support network and versatility are the primary reasons for its popularity. In addition to the 14 digital I/O pins, the Arduino UNO board has 6 analog inputs, six of which should be PWM (Pulse Width Modulation) outputs. An ICSP (In-circuit serial programming) header, a 16 MHz crystal oscillator, a USB A/B port, and a reset button. It's all right, you'll understand later.

STEP-2: Connect your Arduino Uno to your PC or Laptop via Arduino cable, use the Type A/B cable to connect to one of your Laptop's USB inputs.

STEP-3: Installing Drivers

1. Depending on your laptop's OS, you have to observe some guidelines. Kindly checkout the official website URLs mentioned below for particular guidelines on how to add or install the drivers on your Arduino boards.
2. For Installing Arduino IDE for **Windows** Visit the official website mentioned below to access the steps for Download Software on a Windows Supported PC or personal laptop http://arduino.cc/en/Guide/Windows
3. For Installing Arduino IDE for **Mac OS X:** Mac doesn't need to install drivers. Visits the below web link if you have a query http://arduino.cc/en/Guide/MacOSX
4. **Installation Arduino IDE for Linux:** Visit to the same web address under the Linux categories mentioned below URL to access the web pages to download Linux supported Arduino IDE. https://www.arduino.cc/en/guide/linux

Afterward, continue with the installation and please allow the driver installation step if needed,

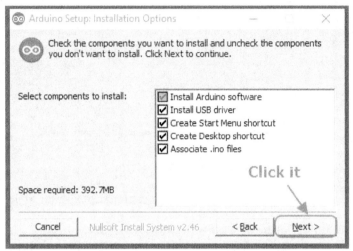

Select the tools or components to install and click "**next**" button to continue

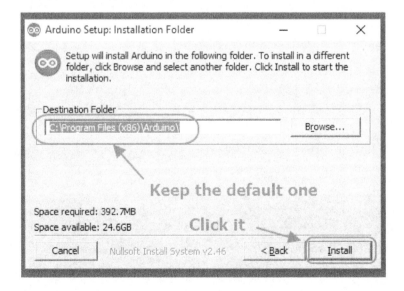

Browse and **Select Destination** folder or the installation directory

The procedure will extract and install all the necessary files to execute accurately the Arduino Software (IDE) on system.

Step 4: How to open examples sketches or program on Arduino IDE.

Open Arduino IDE Software >File >Examples >Basics > **Blink**

Step 5: Choose your Controller board

For choosing board, you have to follow this entry in the **Tools > Board** list of options which match up to your Arduino board.

Choosing an **Arduino/Genuino Uno.**

Step 6: Select your serial port

Choose the serial port of the board from the **Tools > Port** menu. This is mostly to be COM3 or upper (COM1 and COM2 are commonly kept for hardware serial ports). To discover, you be able to disconnect your board and do the previous steps again, I mean re-open the menu; the entry which disappears must be the Arduino board. Reconnect the board to the PC via Arduino cable and choose that serial port.

TTL logic levels (5V or 3.3V depending on the board) are used for serial communication on pins TX/RX. This pin should not be connected directly to a serial port as it operates at +/- 12V and could result in damage to your Arduino board.

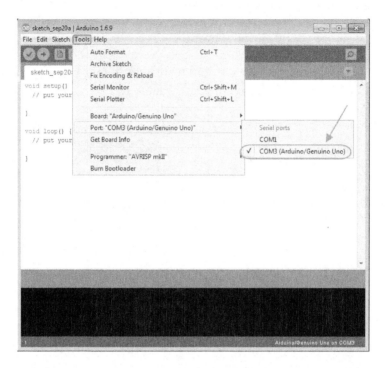

Serial communication allows the Arduino board to communicate with a computer or other devices. Serial is the name of one of the serial ports on all Arduino boards (also called a UART or USART). In addition to USB connections, digital pins 0 (RX) and 1 (TX) are used for communication. Thus, digital input or output cannot be used on pins 0 or 1 if these functions are used.

An Arduino board can be communicated with via a serial monitor that comes with the Arduino environment. In the toolbar, click the serial monitor button to select the same baud rate as calling begin ().

The Arduino Mega has three additional serial ports: Serial1 on pins 19 (RX) and 18 (TX), Serial2 on pins 17 (RX) and 16 (TX), and Serial3 on pins 15 (RX) and 14 (TX). Because this board does not have a USB-to-serial adapter, you will need a separate USB-to-serial adapter to communicate with your PC. Connect the TX pin of your Mega to the RX pin of your external device, the RX pin to the TX pin of your device, and the ground of your Mega to the ground of your device to send and receive TTL serial data.

In addition to Serial1 and Serial2, it also has Serial3 on pins 15 and 14 (RX) and on pins 17 and 16 (TX). Likewise, an ATmega16U2-TTL Serial chip is connected to pins 0 and 1, which is connected to the USB debug port.

Furthermore, the SAM3X chip has a serial port that is compatible with USB, SerialUSB. The Arduino Leonardo board interfaces with TTL (5V) serial communications via pins 0 (TX) and 1 (RX) of Serial1. A serial connection can only be used for USB CDC communications

Arduino IDE Interface

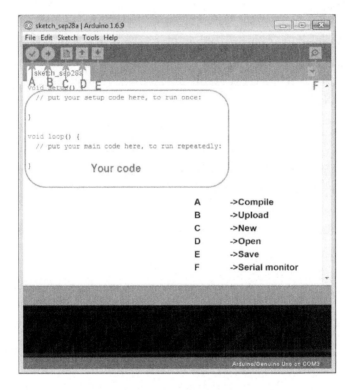

In the Arduino Integrated Development Environment - or Arduino Software (IDE) - users can input code, view notifications, create text consoles, use a toolbar with buttons for common functions and delve into menus. Connected to the Arduino and Genuino hardware, it allows programs to be uploaded and communicated with.

Step 7: Upload the program

Here and now, just click the "Upload" button in the Header IDE Icons. Wait just a second - you can see the RX and TX leds on the board flashing. Once the upload is finished, you may see the message **"Done uploading."** will seem in the status bar.

Step 8: Result

A couple of seconds later once the upload done, you could be able to see the pin 13 (L) LED built-in on the Arduino board, it will **ready to start blink** (in orange color), If it done... well done! You've understood basic Arduino interface.

Arduino Libraries

- The Arduino platform can be emerging into the next level through the utilization of libraries, much like most programming environment.
- Libraries offer an additional value meant for benefit in programming, e.g., functioning with hardware or handling data. Large number of Arduino libraries comes with built-in the software IDE, nevertheless you can be able to download on websites or make your own.
- You can express an Arduino Library is such a Class with Methods/Functions. This is a great method to construct your sketches
- There are three places where Arduino libraries are stored: inside the IDE installation folder, inside the core folder, and inside your sketchbook's libraries folder. Libraries selected during compilation are designed to allow for updating of libraries present in the distribution

For Instances:

- ❖ Stepper Motor Library for an Arduino is written like
     #include <Stepper.h> **'.h'** is an extension for the library header.
- ❖ SD card library: Which means permits for reading from and writing to the SD cards, for example on the Arduino shield for an Ethernet and Wi-Fi modules
     1. Ethernet Library for the Arduino is **#include <Ethernet.h>**
     2. Wi-Fi library for the Arduino is **#include <WiFi.h>**

For writing your own libraries refer here:

Writing a good library is not an easy task. Developers have different perceptions about what the appearance of a library like this should be. In my opinion, developers should cover robust libraries with unit tests, as well as provide detailed documentation. In addition, an intuitive and easy-to-use interface is crucial for any decent library.

I have worked on several large software development projects most of my career. The frameworks we used were robust, and we wrote proper unit tests and integration tests for most of them. You'd probably spend more time debugging if you didn't have well-written tests.

The Arduino kit I have been using for about a year and a half is very intuitive to me. Aimed at hobbyists and self-taught programmers, Arduino was developed by its creators. The community of people interested in electronics is large; however, the quality of the published code is often very variable. I often check the code on GitHub for Arduino libraries I need, but the code is frequently unmaintained. Library materials were often not properly documented, even when they were maintained. Unit tests weren't present in most of them.

https://www.arduino.cc/en/Hacking/LibraryTutorial

https://www.arduino.cc/en/Reference/Libraries

How to add library files

Installing or adding Arduino libraries would be done by three different types of steps:

1. Manually Adding the Library files,
2. Importing a ZIP compression file,
3. Adding Libraries with the library manager.

These Two approaches should be done with drop down menu options. On the other hand, for the manual installation, we need to choose the libraries and place that into the Arduino "**libraries**" folder.

Step 1: Add library file: Sketch>Include Library>Add.ZIP Library

Procedure for utilize an existing library in an IDE, just refer the Sketch

Menu, select "Include Library or Import Library", and choose required libraries from drop down menu, Here **#include** is a supplement statement at the first line of codes for both header (.h) file in the library space. As you know these statements form the public functions and constants distinct by the library existing to codes.

Step 2:

Choose your library file as zip format on the sample programming file, as shown:

Step 3: Finish, Congratulation! You have learned how to install Arduino libraries. For next session we will learn hello world of Arduino (Blink an LED) program.

Hello World of Arduino (Blink an LED):

In this lesson, we will begin the journey of learn by doing with Arduino, let's start your first Arduino Project, this is simple to get started, how to run blink an LED.

Component Required:

- 1 x Arduino UNO
- 1 x LED
- 1 x USB Cable
- 1 x 220Ω Resistor
- 2 x Jumper Wires
- 1 x Breadboard

Principle:

In this project, we will program the Arduino's General-Purpose Input Output (GPIO) HIGH level (+5V) and LOW level (0V), and before make sure the LED that is linked to the Arduino's GPIO, which is blink by a certain frequency.

What is the LED?

The LED is stand for Light Emitting Diode. LED is generally made with gallium arsenide, gallium phosphide both are semiconducting materials. The LED consist of two electrodes: a positive and a negative electrode. This is illuminating only after a forward current passes, then it will glow red, green, blue, yellow, etc. The color of the LED is depending on the material that is used.

Generally, 5-20mA is drive current of the LED. So in actuality, it generally require more resistor for limiting current, because of protect the LED from the high current.

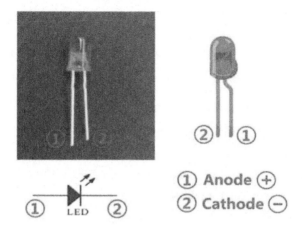

(1) Anode (+)
(2) Cathode (−)

What is resistor?

The important role of the resistor is used to limit currents. In general, electronic circuit, the letter 'R' denotes resistor, moreover the unit of resistor is ohm (Ω).

Writing an Arduino sketch

Before developing an Arduino code, we have understood some basic Arduino C functions, we may learn in upcoming lesions…

```
/* FILE NAME:  BARE MINIMUM CODE*/

    void setup() {
    // put your setup code here, to run once:


    }

    void loop() {
    // put your main code here, to run repeatedly:


    }
```

Basic Arduino C functions:

Here is some essential Arduino functions, and commands everyone need to know before write a code.

setup()

The setup() function is known for what time a code starts. Useful to initialize variables, start utilizing libraries, pin modes, and more... The setup function may simply run once at a time, afterward to each activate or reset of the Arduino microcontroller.

loop()

When making a setup() function, that initializes and use the initial values, the loop() function do from exactly what its label recommends, in addition, loops repeatedly, letting your sketch to change and respond. Utilize it to dynamically regulate the Arduino board.

pinMode() / pinMode(var1, var2)

Arranges the definite pin to work each as an input or an output. Set the mode of assumed pin is pinMode functions. **Var1** is known as the number of the pin and **var2** is known as mode (I/O).

digitalWrite() / digitalWrite(var1, var2)

digitalWrite alters the status of the pin. **Var1** is known as the number of the pin and var2 is the status (HIGH, LOW).

delay()

delay() Function can be used for **pauses** the codes for the certain amount of duration (in milliseconds) stated as parameter. (1 seconds is equal to 1000 milliseconds.)

Procedure of Blink an LED Projects:

Step 1: Build the circuit for blink an LED as shown below:

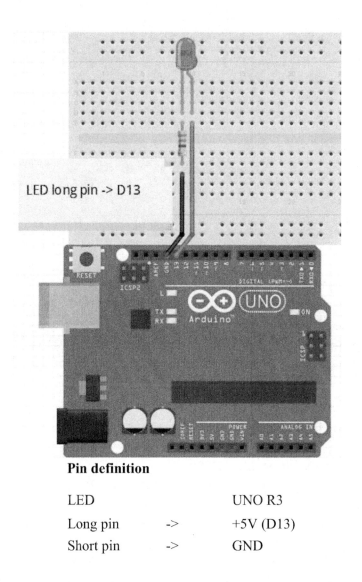

Pin definition

LED		UNO R3
Long pin	->	+5V (D13)
Short pin	->	GND

Note: The lengthy LED pin is linked to the digital signal port 13(D13).

Step 2: LED Blink: Write your first code on Arduino IDE.

Uploading the Sketches

- Before Uploading sketches make sure you are connected your Arduino board to the USB cable (Types A/B).
- Make sure if you choose right Arduino Board on tools menu follow these steps to choose desired controller board **Select Tools→Board→Arduino Uno** to find your board in the drop-down menu. You be able to choose various types of microcontroller boards from this list, such as the Arduino Nano, Arduino Uno and Arduino Mega.
- Also, the essential stages are select the right serial port for your Arduino board. You can see all the existing COM serial ports by

selecting **Tools→Serial Port→ comX,** In IDE, once you have recently connected your Board to Computer, the COM port may typically be the bigger number, for e.g. COM 3 or COM 15.

- **Click Verify** Button for the code is checked once before uploading
- **Click Upload** Once Click the upload button, then the code is dump to the Arduino Microcontroller board.

Step 3: Compile the sketch and upload to Arduino board. Congrats! Finally, you finished your Arduino Project Blink an LED. Let's see the Question-and-Answer Session about Arduino Platform.

Arduino Q & A Section

1) What is the Arduino used for?

Arduino is an open-source electronic prototyping boards utilized for flexible easy to practice hardware and software. An Arduino microcontroller board can read inputs (a light on a sensor module, a tweet on Twitter, a finger touched a switch), and use that data to trigger a motor, blink an LED, and broadcast data to the internet.

2) Who invented Arduino?

Massimo Banzi

In 2005, Hernando Barragán (maker of wiring), Massimo Banzi and David Cuartielles are building upon the work on developing open-source microcontroller, finally Arduino born. Their goal was to develop a collaborating art design module that could be easily accessed via a programmable interface at the Interaction Design Institute Ivrea in Ivrea, Italy.

3) Who uses Arduino?

Arduino developed for student, hobbyists, artists, designers and any person fascinated in building interactive project or environments.

4) Is Arduino based on C or C++?

Primarily, the Arduino IDE or compiler support C and C++. Actually, most of the Arduino libraries are written by C++ Programming. Most of the fundamental structure is not object oriented, however it could be. Therefore, "The Arduino IDE language" is C++ or C.

5) Is Arduino good for beginners?

Yes, Arduino is good for beginners, which they able to buy on a budget, an Arduino Uno is a worthy choice. There are several basic programming/ sketches that will support on the Uno, Novice learner also allowing to evaluate Arduino and practice as a wonderful knowledge gaining platform, and most of the mini projects can be designed with an Arduino Uno.

6) How does the Arduino work?

An Arduino board is connected to your laptop by a USB type A/B cable, in order to connect with the Arduino software since it's nothing but the Arduino IDE (Integrated Development Environment). This is done using an IDE that creates sketches and code, which is then sent to the Arduino microcontroller for execution. Afterwards, the application interacts with sensors, electronic components, motors, and lights.

7) What is the difference between Arduino and microcontroller?

Many of the board often use Atmel types of **AVR** microcontrollers. Arduino UNO is an **ATMEGA 328** based microcontroller series. Most commonly Microcontroller is a well suited than a microprocessor to whatever needs the recognizing of inputs.

8) How do I start Arduino?

+ Getting Started with Arduino UNO, Nano and Mega.
+ Practice your Arduino Uno on the Arduino web/online IDE.
+ Use your Arduino on the Desktop software IDE. Install or choose the board drivers. Start your initial sketch. Choose your controller board type and port. Upload the Sketch/program, furthermore study on the Software IDE Tutorials.

9) Is Arduino software free?

Yes, Arduino is an **open-source** hardware and software, almost all the open-source product is free, and Therefore Arduino is a free platform, we can able to modifying Arduino module without getting any license from Arduino developers.

10) How do I power an Arduino?

- We able to power-up the Arduino with power supplied from the laptop through a USB type A/B cable or by utilizing external power sources, such as power bank, li-ion batteries up to the 12V.
- Plugged into the barrel connector with Arduino by using an AC to DC adapter.

- Powering up Arduino by using all types of 5V DC input. ...
- Moreover, we can use batteries higher than 5V.

11) What is the programming language of Arduino?

The Arduino language is just a set of C/C++ functions which can be so-called from your sketch. Your code feels minor modifications (e.g., automatic creations of function prototypes) as well as then is accept straightly to a C/C++ compiler (avr-g++).

12) What chip does Arduino use?

Arduino uses **ATMEGA328** Microchip, which contain 14 digital input/output pins, 6 analog inputs, 6 pins can be utilized for Pulse-width Modulation (PWM) outputs, also includes a 16 MHz quartz crystal, a power jack, a USB connection support, an ICSP (In-Circuit Serial Programming) header, and a reset push button.

13) Does Arduino have a CPU?

The Arduino Uno doesn't have a CPU, but it uses a microcontroller named ATMEGA328. In an Atmega328 microcontroller include the processor core, programmable I/O and memory, peripherals are incorporated into a single **System on Chip** (SoC). However, the microprocessors possibly will have integrated registers, nevertheless it will depend on outward RAMs and peripherals.

14) Which is better Arduino or Raspberry Pi?

A microcontroller is a portable easy-to-use computer which be able to run one sketch/program at that moment, over and over again. Microcontroller is extremely straightforward to use. A Raspberry Pi is a general-purpose credit card sized motherboard, also utilized as a portable computer, generally Raspberry Pi is support by Linux OS, and it have the capability to run various programs. It is further more complicated to learn than an Arduino.

15) How is Arduino different from C?

The primary dissimilarity of Arduino vs Traditional C would be the **file**

associations. An Arduino software development is associated to the IDE (Integrated Development Environment) of Arduino, which is ultimately a C/C++ compiler that creates machine sketch for the Arduino boards.

16) Can an Arduino run 12v?

Arduino Power pin labeled as Vin, it is a input voltage in Arduino board (As an alternative of utilizing the barrel adaptor or USB cable). The Arduino voltage should be 9V to 12V, and which is regulated inside by the board to 5V.

17) What is the best Arduino?

Arduino Uno: Provided you are a novice learner, entering into the field of Arduino, the great choice for you would be the Arduino Uno R3, which costs around $20. Moreover, you can also buy clone boards such as Freeduino which cost around $5, you may also get started from this too.

18) Why Arduino Uno is best for beginners?

Arduino Uno is the most popular and standard board available in the market and most likely the primary option for the student. For the reason that, it has a major benefit is, that we able to use the board to the computer through a USB cable which does a dual purpose of delivering power to the board and performing as a Serial port to interface the Arduino microcontroller and the laptop.

19) Is Arduino difficult to learn?

The worthy information is that Arduino programming is merciful. It still has a learning curve, and writing an Arduino code it's not just simple, however it will be much simple than write sketches for your initial projects, to be sure, Arduino should be a stress-free technique to wet your feet in coding.

20) Is Arduino a PCB?

For dumping code to microcontrollers, for simple user interface the Arduino Environment provides an IDE, which is created for making right code for project, Arduino IDE integrated with C and C++, that's to say, a

PCB is not the similar as an Arduino, but a PCB is portion of Arduino.

21) Can Arduino run without computer?

So, we have a query… Can we run Arduino as a portable device and no computer needed? Yes, Laptop only sufficient to program it, after dumbing the code, Arduino can work as portable device with power source. Yes, Here Wi-Fi module and Ethernet also existing for connecting it to a network. ... But the Arduino is not effective to run software for that.

22) Can we use Java for Arduino?

We able to use Java SE Embedded or Java ME on a Raspberry Pi, on the other hand, the Arduino is a slightly too forced to execute Java directly. Though, with the support of serial port communication IDE, we able to communicate with java also control an Arduino from Java running on a different PC.

23) What is Arduino in IOT?

At the present time a buzzword field and fastest growing area is Internet of Things (IoT), IoT project is nothing but, all the physical things such as home appliance, sensors, and gadgets are linked together with an internet structure. IoT utilized in Plethora of Application such as Home Automation, Smart Agriculture system, and Smart-Health monitoring system.

24) What is the smallest Arduino?

Arduino Beetle is the smallest Arduino microcontroller available in the market. It has **AtMega32u4** 8bit AVR Microchip, It has 10 digital pins, 5 analog pins and 4 Pulse with Modulation pins, Beetle board functioning with 16MHz clock time.

25) What can the Arduino beetle do?

Beetle intended to make a Cost-efficient microcontroller, it should be simple and straightforward to use, and to afford a cost-efficient solution for reusable projects, Like DIY STEAM projects, electronic workspaces, E-Textiles, gift projects, and Practical Education. Aimed for students, research scholar and creators those who can't afford too much on controller module purchasing, Beetle should be a wonderful solution for them.

26) What is the difference between Arduino Uno and Leonardo?

The Primary modification between Uno and Leonardo is which Leonardo has an ATmega32u4 Microchip that contain inbuilt micro-USB port, but the Arduino UNO has ATmega328 Microchip which doesn't have the inbuilt micro-USB onboard. However, the UNO needs an added microcontroller to provide the USB capability. Cost wise Leonardo is 20%. Cheaper than UNO.

27) Which is better Arduino Uno or Nano?

As its name, Arduino Nano is a small in size and breadboard-friendly microcontroller board based on ATmega328 processor, as a replacement for the standard USB to connect to the PC, Instead Arduino Nano utilized the Micro USB but without the power cable for external power source which built on Arduino UNO.

28) What can the Arduino Nano do?

Arduino Nano is a more or less similar board to Arduino UNO in terms of functionality, but its small size makes it stand out from other boards. A breadboard-friendly, smaller-sized ATmega328 module built on the ATmega328, the Arduino Nano is small in size, wide-ranging, and breadboard-friendly.

29) Does Arduino have EEPROM?

In the Arduino Microcontroller boards, the EEPROM area is emulated and is 1024 bytes in size. Microcontrollers on Arduino boards are AVR-based and include EEPROM memory, allowing them to retain their values after being turned off (such a small hard drive). These EEPROM bytes can be read and written with this Arduino library.

30) What is the use of EEPROM in Arduino?

This memory type is referred to as electrically erasable programmable read-only memory. On the majority of Arduino boards, the microcontroller is built with EEPROM capacity of each 512 bytes, 1024 bytes, or 4096 bytes. Memory storage on this board is non-volatile, which means once the board goes down or loses power, the information does not disappear.

31) Can Arduino save data?

Provided Arduino is interfacing to the PC, the information can be stored by reading the serial output and saving that in a file. Provided a Micro SD card insert to the Arduino, the files or information can be stored straightly to the SD card.

32) What are the Different Types of Arduino Boards?

- Arduino Uno (R3)
- Arduino Mega (R3), Arduino Beetle
- Arduino Nano, Mini
- LilyPad Arduino, RedBoard Arduino
- Arduino Leonardo
- Arduino Shields and more...

Summary

This chapter introduces Arduino and shows you how you can get started with the microcontroller and addresses frequently asked questions. In the next chapter we will explore the basic components of electronics and different types of Arduino-compatible sensors and their functions.

CHAPTER 2:

BASIC ELECTRONIC COMPONENTS

In Arduino projects, major components typically included resistors, capacitors, transistors, integrated circuits (ICs), switches, relays, motors, etc. Usually, these components are used to build Arduino projects, so before we dive into Arduino sensors and projects, we need to learn about basic electronic components.

Resistors
A resistor impedes the movement of electricity over a circuit, resistors have a conventional value.

Since voltage, current and resistance are associated over Ohm's law, resistors are a simple technique to control voltage and current in your circuit.

Resistor color codes

1st band = 1st number
2nd band = 2nd number
3rd band = # of zeros / multiplier
4th band = tolerance

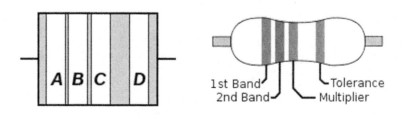

Color Code Number: (BBROYGBVGW)

Tolerance: Gold = within 5%

Black:	0
Brown:	1
Red:	2
Orange:	3
Yellow:	4
Green:	5
Blue:	6
Violet:	7
Gray:	8
White:	9

Unit

- To Identifying your units is significant
- Kilo & Mega are basic in resistors
- Milli, micro, nano & Pico can be utilized in additional components

K (kilo) = 1,000
M (mega) = 1,000,000
M (milli) = 1/1,000
u (micro) = 1/1,000,000
n (nano) = 1/1,000,000,000 (one trillionth)
p (pico) = 1/ 1,000,000,000,000 (one quadrillionth)

Capacitors

A capacitor is used to stores electrical energy. Here pool of electrons is obtainable for electronic components to usage.

Capacitance is measured in the unit of Farads. The mini capacitors typically used in electronics are often determined in micro-farads and Nano-farads. Some capacitors are polarized. Have to know the different length of terminals on one of the capacitors.

Polarity of capacitors

- The smaller terminal goes on the -ive side.
- The strip is on the -ive terminal sideways of the capacitor.

The panel is noted for +ive or -ive.

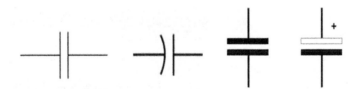

Applications of capacitors

- Capacitors can pass a ***pool of electrons*** for instant use.
- If a component wants an instantaneous supply of electrons, the capacitor can pass those electrons.

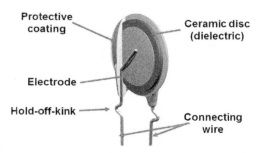

Protective coating

Ceramic disc (dielectric)

Electrode

Hold-off-kink

Connecting wire

Capacitors can **smooth out a signal** - remove the waves or spikes in DC voltage. The capacitor can attract the peaks and fill in the vales of a waved signal.

Inductors

An inductor is a passive electronic component which is stores energy as a magnetic field. In its minimum tough form, an inductor includes of a wire loop or coil. The inductance is straight proportional to the amount of turns in the coil. Inductance similarly relies upon the distance of the coil and on the kind of material about which the coil is wound.

An inductor, similarly called a coil, choke or reactor, is a passive two-terminal electrical component which stores the current in a magnetic-field once electric current pass through it. An inductor usually includes of an insulated wire twisted into a coil about a center.

Transformer

A transformer is a static-electrical device which exchanges electrical current among at minimum two circuits over electromagnetic acceptance. A changing current in one coil of the transformer makes an opposing magnetic field, that thusly prompts a shifting electromotive force (emf) or "voltage" in an instant coil. Energy can be exchanged among the two coils, without a metallic suggestion between the two circuits.

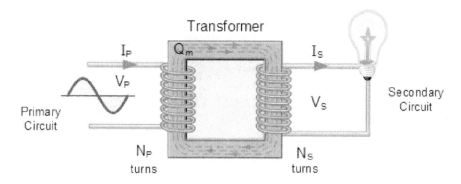

Faraday's law of inductance found in 1831 portrayed this influence. Transformers are utilized to increment or lessening the rotating voltages in electric energy applications.

Diode

A diode is a one-way controller (or gate) for electricity. Diode is a component by an irregular transfer characteristic.

A diode has little (preferably zero) resistance in one way, and high (preferably infinite) resistance in the other way.

Diodes will protect your electronics

Diode circuit protection

In a DPDT switch, if polarization is incorrect, the motor will run backwards. In an electronic circuit, if the polarization is incorrect, you can fry your components.

A diode in your scheme will assistance to avoid problems.

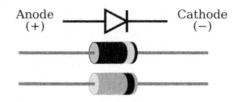

Light emitting diode (LED)
A light emitting diode (LED) is a semiconductor light source. Once electricity is flow through the diode, it produces light.

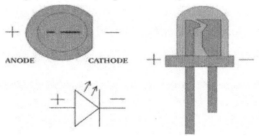

Variable resistor (Potentiometer)
A potentiometer is a variable resistor. As you physically turn a dial, the resistance variations.

How a variable resistor works

As the dial or wiper turns, electricity essential go through more or less of the resistive strip.

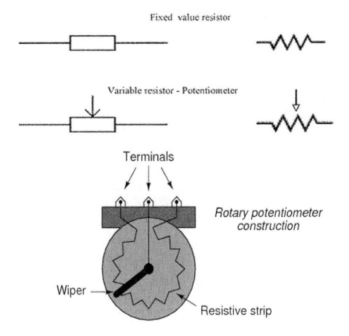

Fixed value resistor

Variable resistor - Potentiometer

Terminals

Rotary potentiometer
construction

Wiper

Resistive strip

In sequence, the variation in resistance means a variation in voltage, so as you turn the dial or wiper, you become a variation in voltage

Transistors

A transistor is a semiconductor device applicable to switch and amplify electrical power and electronic signals.

How a transistor works

- The passage of voltage or current between the terminals of a transistor varies the current over different pairs.
- Transistors are semiconductor elements arranged in a package with at least three terminals for the purposes of connecting to external circuits.

Transistors have 3 pins, there are five different types of transistors

1. Collector
2. Emitter
3. Base

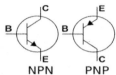

Bipolar Junction Transistor (BJT): There are two different types of transistors available in the market: NPN and PNP, presented in plastic cases or metal cans. Plastic casings have a flat front side and pins arranged in a serial manner on one side of the transistor. You can identify the pins by counting them as one, two, etc. by keeping the front flat side facing you. There will typically be three transistors in an NPN transistor: 1 (Collector), 2 (Base), and 3 (Emitter). Thus, the CBE. But in the case of PNP transistors, the condition is reversed. In other words, that's EBC.

Field Effect Transistor (FET): A Field Effect Transistor can be identified by starting counter-clockwise, keeping the curved portion facing you. The first one is the source, the next the gate, and the last is the drain.

MOSFET: Metal Oxide Semiconductor Field Effect Transistor: It is not uncommon for the pins of a MOSFET to be labeled as G, S, and D, which indicate the gate, source, and drain, respectively. The datasheet for the MOSFET may need to be consulted in some cases. As you make your way from left to right, normally you want to make sure the flat side of the pin is facing you.

IGBT- Insulated Gate Bipolar Transistor: With some practical IGBTs, like the GN2470, the raised surface faces the person holding it so that the short surface in the center acts as the cathode. Those on the left are Gates, and those on the right are Emitters.

Phototransistor: In a practical phototransistor like the L14G2, the collector is on the curved surface facing the person and the emitter is on the other side. The base is on the side opposite the emitter.

Schematic symbols

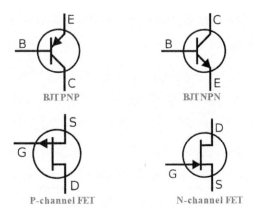

Integrated circuit (IC)

An integrated circuit (IC) is a group of transistors which is the controller or 'brain' of an electronic circuit. An input is received, an output is sent out.

Current microprocessor ICs can have billions of transistors each square inch, The majority of electronic devices contain some form of integrated circuit. A timer is an electronic device that functions as an amplifier, a logic unit, a counter, a calculator, a temperature sensor, and a radio receiver. Electronics have been revolutionized since integrated circuits are present in almost all modern equipment.

ICs are physically much smaller than discrete circuits. Contrary to discrete circuits, an integrated circuit is very light in weight. Compared to other systems, it's more reliable. It has a lower power consumption due to its smaller size. Failures can easily be replaced, but the failure can almost never be repaired

What an IC can do for us?

- Billions of electronically measured on/off switches (transistors) is how the microprocessor in a digital computer 'thinks' and purposes.
- A computer has a wide variety of tasks to perform.
- But other ICs can fully simpler, separate jobs. For i.e., an IC can take a voltage input and output instructions to a motor.

IC Terminology: Op-amp

An operational amplifier (op-amp) is a group of transistors inside the IC (Integrated Circuit). They frequently are the components doing the mathematical procedures.

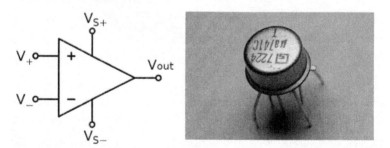

An operational amplifier amplifies weak electric signals by using an integrated circuit. Two inputs and one output are present in an operational amplifier. The input voltage difference between the two input pins is amplified and output by this driver.

The most common type of voltage amplifier is the Op-amp, which can be broadly categorized into non-inverting and inverting amplifiers.

H-bridge

An electronic circuit which allows voltage to be applied across a load in any direction.

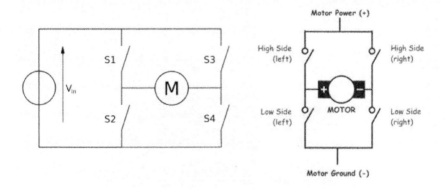

A DPDT switch also does this, but not electronically

Varying voltage

- A potentiometer or variable resistor permits you to variation the voltage input which goes into the integrated circuit (IC).
- Integrated circuit can now output change of pulse widths to the transistors on the H-bridge.

- This grouping of potentiometer, integrated circuit and PWM to the H-bridge *is **the key to speed controller.***

Printed Circuit Board (PCB)

The 'front' side of the board will have printed component information, such as resistor and resistance, diode type and polarity, Components are attached to a printed circuit board.

Holes go all the method over the board since one side to the other. Over hole soldering is needed to join components to the board.

Backside of Circuit Board

The 'back' side of the board will have lines indicating contacts between components. The lines on the back are alike to wires, Denser lines denote extra current (electrons) moving through, Components connect the lines.

Merits and its Application

Smaller size and less wire are required. PCBs with several electronic components are called characteristic PCBs. Copper tracks are used to connect components on a printed circuit board instead of a number of wires carrying current. This reduces the size of the interconnections.

Various electronic devices including **calculators**, **mobile phones, printers,** and **LCD televisions** utilize flexible circuits, Cameras, a heart monitor, a pace-maker, and hearing aids are made using these materials. Robotic arms, processing equipment, bar code equipment, etc., are among the products they manufacture.

WHAT ARE SOME GOOD COMPONENTS TO START WITH?

LED (Light Emitting Diode)

- Many of Light Emitting Diodes with range of colors (Make sure to similarly get two or more resistors for limiting current)
- LED has an illuminating feature which can be utilized for space as an actuator.
- Used for Flickering, blinking, dimming with PWM, "Adventurer Rider" result by 7 or more LEDs, strobe special effects, etc.
- Due to the fact, a Light emitting diode is a directional part, means that, which is stimulated simply if it is located in right direction with the circuit.

LCD (Liquid Crystal Display)

A LCD is a types of optical display most commonly utilized in electronic modules, in that a group of a liquid crystal is sandwiched among two transparent electrodes, this process play a vital role by making an LCD.

The LCD contains of 16 pins which are utilized for power, control, in addition data. It should follow a manufacturing standard Hitachi regulator therefore the basic functions of LCD are almost similar across the various kind of traders that sell them. They both have a 4-bit and an 8-bit parallel interface. We have been utilizing 4-bit parallel interface instead of 8-bit. Which means we will be transmit the upper nibble (1 nibble is equal to 4 bits) first, next to the lower nibble to transmit the byte of information essential for each command or character. LCD 16×2 or a 20×4 is most generally used in many projects that means which it can be show 16 characters on both 2 lines and 20 characters on both 4 lines, correspondingly.

LCD Pinout with an Arduino interface circuit shown below.

Why start with LCD?

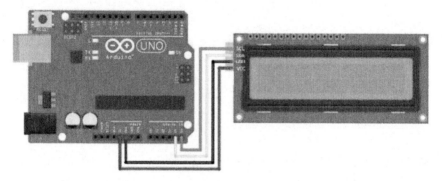

The LCDs support a parallel interface, significance which the Arduino has to handle numerous interface pins simultaneously to control the display. The parallel edition capable 4 digital pins for display, Learners definitely express vast degree of happiness from sending word to the LCD screen

DC Motor

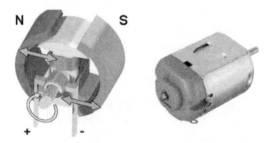

A DC (Direct Current) motor is one of the popular varieties of electronic motor. It generally consists of two terminals, which is positive and negative terminals. Once you connect these two terminals straightly to a power source, the DC motor will rotate. If you change the terminals, the motor will rotate in the reverse side.

Threat - Do not operate the DC motor directly from the Arduino board pins. This can be causes of Arduino circuit failure. Therefore, we should have used a driver circuit or a motor driver IC for before controlling all variety of motors.

Servo Motor

There are huge variety of servo motors existing in the marketplace and to each one has its unique characteristic, futures and usages. The upcoming lesson will assist you recognize the right type of servo motor for your mini project/invention.

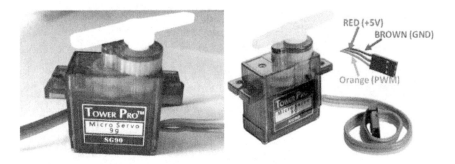

Many of the electronic servo motors operates from 4.8V to 6.5V, if we give high voltage, simultaneously we able to get high torque, However, usually an electronics Servo motors are functioned at +5V. More or less all hobby servo motors must be rotate just from 0° to 180° because of its gear placements therefore validate your mini project be able to work with help of the **half circle** if no, you be able to choose for a 0° to 360° motor or adjustment the motor to modify a **full circle**. In motors the gears are simply subjected to wear with tear, therefore if your project needs robust and long durable running motors, you can choose metal gears or else just go with typical plastic gear.

After picking the desired Servo motor for our project, the queries will come, how to use it. As we know already servo motor having three wires, there is power, ground, and a third wire to bring the signal. For rotating the servo motor, we want to connect the battery to at +5V with the Red and Brown wire as well as Transmit Pulse Width Modulation (PWM) signals to the orange wire. Therefore, we must rather that may produce Pulse Width Modulation signals to make the servo motor rotate well. We can able to utilize this hobby servo motor with any electronic development board such as 555 Timer or further more microcontroller environments such as Arduino, ARM, PIC, or even though a credit card sized computer or microprocessor such as Raspberry Pie.

Applications

- Hobby Servo motor utilized as actuators in various kind of robotic projects such as Robotic arm, Biped Robot, and Hexapod, and more….
- Frequently using in RC toys as steering control system,
- In Robots, doesn't required feedback for position control,
- Because of weightless, and little in size, as a result the servo motors utilized in multi-purposes DOF (Degree of Freedom) robotic application such as human-like robots.

Stepper Motor

A Stepper Motor or a step motor is a brushless synchronous Motor that splits a complete rotation into a small number of steps. Not like a brushless DC motor, that rotates constantly once a stable DC voltage is passing to it, subsequently a step motor will rotate in discrete step angles.

Stepper motors, because of its extraordinary design, which be able to control to a large degree of precision with no feedback system. The shaft in the stepper motor, attached by a sequence of magnets, which is managed by a group of electromagnetic coils which are electrified positive and negatively in a particular order, Accordingly, it exactly rotating it clockwise or anticlockwise in a little "step".

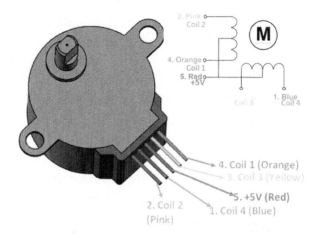

Here we can see two kind of stepper motor, Unipolar and Bipolar, and this is most essential to know which variety you are dealing with. For each of the stepper motor has unique design in structure. Many of the stepper motors are constructed or designed by steps per revolution of 12, 24, 72, 144, 180, and 200, subsequently steps moving angles is 30, 15, 5, 2.5, 2, and 1.8 degrees per step. We able to operate with or without feedback to the stepper motor.

Visualize a motor on a RC (Radio-controlled) aircraft. The motor rotations are extremely high in one direction or another. We be able to change the ROTATION of motor by change the level of voltage given, but we cannot convey to the propeller to END at a particular position. Now visualize a printer. Here is plenty of movable parts inside a printer, also consist of motors. Imagine those motor acts as the rotating rollers, paper-sheet feed which travel the slice of paper as ink is being printed on it. This motor should be able to run the paper-sheet an accurate distance it can be print the following line of word or the next line of a picture.

Stepper Motor Control

We discussed previously how to generate the magnetic field with which the rotor is going to align by energizing the motor coils in a specific sequence. It takes multiple devices to supply the coils with the necessary voltage, allowing the motor to run properly. Taking a look at the closest devices to the motor, we have:

- An electrical connection between the motor coils is physically controlled by a transistor bridge. The transistors can be viewed as electrically controlled interrupters, which allow an electrical current to pass through a coil when they are closed. For every motor phase, one transistor bridge is required.
- It is controlled by an MCU, with which it provides the voltage and current needed to trigger the transistors.
- The MCU is a microcontroller unit, which is typically programmed by a motor user, that generates specific signals to the pre-driver, allowing the motor to perform as desired.

How a Stepper Motor Works?

A typical DC motor can rotate simply in specific position; however, a Stepper motor be able to spin in exact steps.

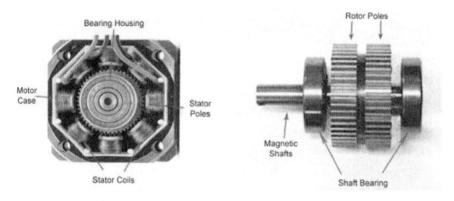

Stepper motors be able to rotate a precise number of degrees (or steps) as required. Which delivers total control to the motor, that permitting you to change it to a particular position, and grip that spot. Indeed, hence with electrifying the coils on inner part of motor aimed at precisely small time period.

Everyone have to know for nowadays is that, to spin a stepper motor, we have to give command it to spin a specific **number of steps** in one position or the another, and also convey it to the **speed** at which steps in that position. The drawback is which you have to always give the power supply to motor to retain it in the spot which you want.

There are many advantages to stepper motors

- In the right environment, stepper motors can be ideal, although not all applications will benefit from them.
- The first thing to note about stepper motors is that the torque they produce is full at standstill, and the direction of rotation is proportional to the input pulse.
- With stepper motors, you can control the speed, position, and repeatability of movement in excellent ways.
- Additionally, since stepper motors are not fitted with contact brushes, they are very reliable. Maximizing the motor's operational lifespan by minimizing mechanical failure is made possible by this technique.
- These motors are suitable for a wide variety of applications, as various rotational speeds can be achieved due to their inverse relationship with pulse frequency.

There are many uses for stepper motors, but here are some of the most common:

- Machines that print 3D objects
- Machines that produce textiles
- There are several types of printing presses
- A machine for playing games
- Imaging equipment for medical use
- Robotics for small spaces
- Milling machines that use CNC technology
- Stainless steel welding equipment

Despite the fact that stepper motors are most commonly used for these applications, they represent only a fraction of what they're capable of. In general, stepper motors can be used for any application that requires highly accurate positioning, speed control, and low speed torque.

LIST OF ARDUINO SENSORS AND MODULES

Sensors Input/Output

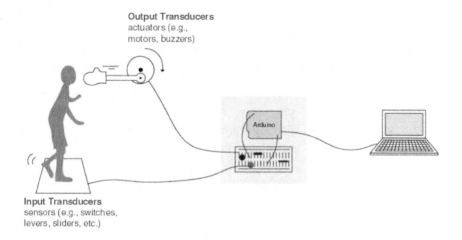

Fig. Theory and Practice of Physical User Interfaces

Ultrasonic Sensor Module

Ultrasonic Sensor - Utilize the ultrasonic waves to measure the **distance** between sensor and obstacle or any object, depending on time duration among **transmission** of ultrasonic wave and **Receiving** echo of it. HC-SR04 Ultrasonic module has four pins: there is Trigger, Echo, Vcc+, and Ground

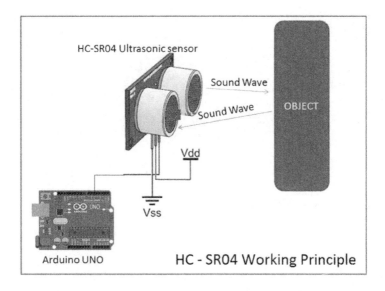

The ultrasonic module has built-in **transmitter** and a **receiver** which functioning at standard **40 kHz** operating frequency. This frequency is not including the hearing range of human and animals, Accordingly Humans be able to hear the sounds in a frequency range only from around 20 Hz to 20 kHz.

IR Infrared Obstacle Avoidance Sensor Module

IR Infrared sensor that will emits infrared radiation which bounced back by the obstacle or objects in proximity sensor. After sensed by a digital output is shown. Level of Sensitivity is might be adjusted by on-board variable resister or potentiometers. It will very effective for sensing a robot is around to interface with walls or other obstacles.

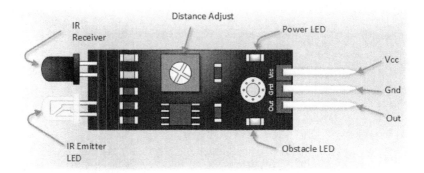

IR Sensor Module Features

- It will be operating at 5V DC.
- Input/Output pins are flexible at 5V and 3.3V.
- IR Sensor Module Range is up to 20cm
- Sensing range of IR Sensor can be Adjustable
- Module include Built-in Ambient Bright Sensor
- Support a Mounting hole
- Supply current is approximately at 20mA.

The IR LED or transmitter will be emitting an infrared waves or signals which, just in case of a **reflecting surface** such as white color walls, it should be spring back in opposite directions within that of the photodiode nothing but IR receiver that acquired the waves by sensing the obstacles or an object.

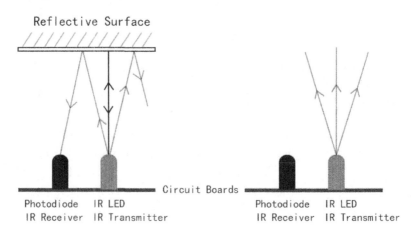

In case of an **absorbent surface** such as Black color walls, it can't be reflected and the object cannot be detected by the sensor. This result may come even if the object is absent.

IR Infrared Fire/Flame Detection sensor

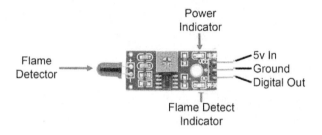

Fire Detection Sensor Module is much sensitive to the Smoke, flame nevertheless correspondingly can be sensing traditional light, and generally this is utilized as a fire alarm, Senses a smoke or else a luminance source of a wavelength in the range between 760nm-1100 nm.

IR Infrared Flame Sensor has difference characteristics such as Sensing point is nearly 60 degrees, mostly sensitive to the flame spectrum, steady performance, sensitivity is flexible.

Applications of IR Sensor

IR Infrared Fire Detection Sensors are applicable in various types of Emergency conditions which include the following.

1. Applicable in Hydrogen stations and identification for an Industrial heating
2. In the majority of fire detection projects, an IR sensor is used
3. Many industries use fire alarms as a fire emergency device
4. On firefighting robots, the flame detector module is used.
5. Detecting the presence of gas in kitchen devices powered by gas
6. Additionally, it is used in gas turbines, drying systems, and domestic heating systems

Soil Hygrometer Detection or Soil Moisture Sensor

Soil Moisture Sensors can be precisely sensing the amount of moisture or volumetric content available from the water in soils (such as from flower pots). These are much beneficial for Arduino agricultural projects.

The Soil Hygrometer is used capacitance to senses dielectric permittivity of the nearby range, at the soil dielectric permittivity is a role of the moisture level. Which a sensor makes a voltage relational to the dielectric permittivity, in addition as a result the moisture level of the soil.

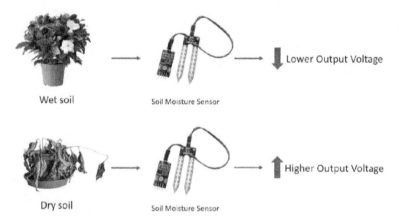

Soil-Moisture Humidity Sensing Module is utilized to identify the moisture content of the water. This module is extreme sensitive to the environment moisture. Once the soil is going to dry the sensor outputs will be in high level, or else outputs low. Soil moisture sensor is utilized in variety of an autonomous application such as automatic irrigation system, accordingly the plants in the farm can be automated without human assistance.

Humidity and Rain Detection Sensor

Humidity Detection Module also known as Rain Sensor that is engaged to sense the rain water and then trigger an alarm. Accordingly, we will preserve rain water to utilize it for future application. Here is plethora of techniques exist for save water such as Rain water harvesting. By using this way we be able to raise the level of ground water and utilize it's for crisis situation. Therefore, we can use Humidity and Rain water sensors for various kind of application such as Agriculture Irrigation, communication, automation, automobiles, etc.

What is a Rain Sensor?

A rain sensor is unique types of switching module which utilize to sense the rainfall. This sensor mechanism similar to the switch, as well as the operational functions of Rain water sensors, at whatever time there is rain, the switch can be normally closed.

Rain Sensor Module

The rain sensor module be made of **nickel coated** lines and that is based on the resistance principle. This module can be estimate humidity via analog output pins and that provides digital output whereas water level threshold surpasses, This sensor is analogical to the LM393 IC since which consist of electronic module and PCB board.

How does it Work?

In straightforward terms, the resistance of the collector board fluctuates according to the level of moisture taking place its surface.

While the Sensor is in Wet: the resistance will Surges, and the output voltage will decline.

While the Sensor is in Dry: the resistance is declines, and the output voltage is Surges.

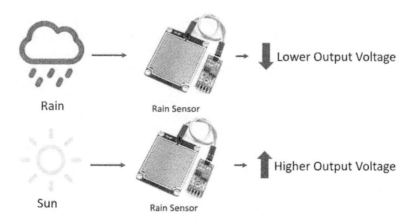

Microphone Sensor or Sound Sensor

Arduino Sound Sensor contains a sensitive capacitance mic for sensing sound and comes with built-in amplifier circuit, the digital output reacts as a key, and it will trigger, once the audio intensity has achieved a specific threshold level. The sensitivity threshold can be increase or decrease through variable resister on the module.

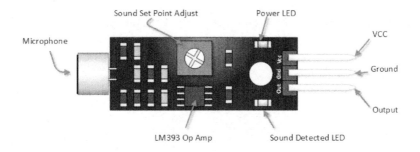

The analog output voltage is fluctuating by the intensity of sound acquired by the microphone module, we may connect this sensor output to Arduino analog pins and then we can able to process the output voltage, each microphone has digital and analog outputs.

AO: Analog Output, to output voltage signals from microphone in a real-time manner

DO: Once the audio intensity archives a specific threshold level, the microphone outputs will be high or low level.

There are two types of microphone sensor available in the market:

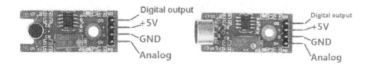

Microphone Sensor   High-sensitive Voice Sensor

1. Standard Microphone Module and
2. High-Sensitive Voice Sensor.

'**Sensitivity Level**' is the one and only dissimilarity for both microphones

Digital Barometric Pressure Sensor
The Barometric Pressure Sensor (BMP180) is one of the fascinating sensor modules available in the market, important role of this module is measuring the pressure and altitude, which can be used to forecast the

climate conditions, sense altitude, and estimate perpendicular velocity, it's a tremendously sensitive sensor on top. By means of you can realize in a second, it can be sensing the fluctuation in altitude of just a few inches.

This Barometric Pressure Sensor can be used in various kind of projects and innovation such as flying robots, weather stations, for enhancing day to day routine, autonomous vehicles, self-driving cars and much more...

Barometric Pressure

Barometric pressure is the pressure happened by load/weight of air pushing down to the ground, moreover it's called as atmospheric pressure, lets visualize a cluster of air rising from the ground's surface to the top of the sky. The air in the sky has huge mass, therefore gravity causes the weight of which cluster of air to exert pressure on the surface.

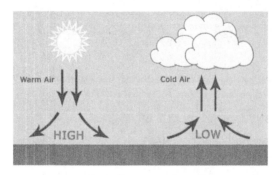

Atmospheric pressure or Barometric pressure consequences from the mass of the air on the ground. This pressure is around 1 kg per square centimeter on the sea level. Here are numerous units to indicate the barometric pressure which can be simply transformed to other one. The SI unit of measuring the pressure is **Pascal (Pa).**

Photoresistor Sensor (LDR)

The Light Dependent Resistor (LDR) is an electronic element that resistivity is differ from how much of lights received (the resistance will be declined while light is passing), Light dependent resistors also known as Photoresistors, are light sensitive sensors most frequently used to point out the presence or absence of luminance source, or used to estimate the intensity of light.

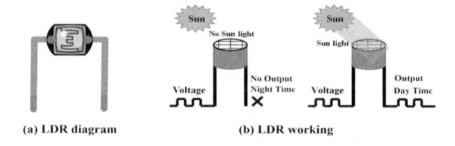

| (a) LDR diagram | (b) LDR working |

At the dark night time, LDR resistance is extremely high, the LDR is made-up of cadmium sulphide tape, a semiconductor. Once the photons passing through tapes, electrons can travel via the semiconductor. The significant role of Photoresistor is estimate the intensity of lights (most commonly used in street lights, night camera, detection systems, and automatic security lights).

The following are some of the advantages or benefits of photoresistor devices:

- In addition to being a replacement for variable resistance, it is also a light-dependent device.
- When light falls on it, its resistance drops, whereas in the dark, its resistance increases.
- There are many different types and sizes of photo resistors available at a low cost.
- They are very energy efficient and need very little voltage and power to operate.
- Simpler circuits can be created with it. Due to its bidirectional nature, all directions can be connected with it.

Applications of LDR

Low-cost and simple, light-dependent resistors can be readily used in a variety of applications. Devices such as these are used wherever it is necessary to know when light is present or absent. Light-responsive resistors are often used in lighting and light intensity meters, as well as burglar alarm circuits, as they act as light sensors. To provide more insight into this concept, here is an explanation of a live lighting project that uses LDR to conserve energy

Digital Thermal Sensor - Humidity Sensor

There are several types of temperature sensors compatible with Arduino, as you can see in the following image.

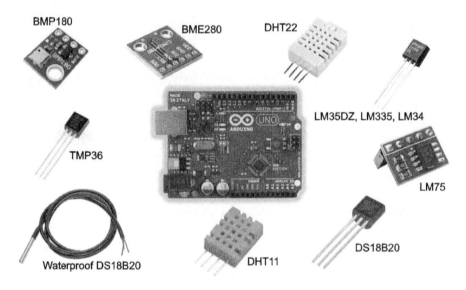

Measuring the temperature level with the Arduino is much straightforward and extremely useful task, here we can see widespread of temperature sensor module available in the market with specific characteristic that we can able to utilize in our upcoming projects, in this section, we can get through a several types of low-cost temperature sensors, this is Arduino friendly and also compatible with mini development module (Such as ESP32 or ESP8266 NodeMCU).

DHT11 Temperature and Humidity Sensor

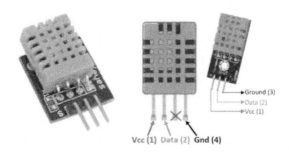

Vcc (1) Data (2) Gnd (4)

DHT11 is frequently used temperature sensor in Arduino platform, this will helpful for estimation of moisture content available in the surrounding air, nitrogen, argon or pure gas. The amount of temperature or moisture in air harmful for several physical, biological and chemical processes. In manufacturing enterprise applications, humidity may disturb the commercial rate of the products, safety, and health of the workers. Subsequently, in semiconductor field and control system manufacturing unit have estimation humidity or temperature is crucial one. There are two kind of Humidity sensors specific on their measurement units. They are listed here,

1. Relative humidity sensor and
2. Absolute humidity sensor.

DHT11 is a Relative humidity sensor, which is used measure the atmospheric air, this module also utilized as a thermistor and a capacitive sensor. DHT11 is developed as a sensor element and as a module the only dissimilarity of this sensor and module is the power-on LED and a pull-up resistor.

The DHT11 is a unique digital temperature sensor which measures temperature and relative humidity. This module includes a chip which can convert analog to digital as well as spit out a digital signal through the temperature and humidity. DHT11 is compatible with most electronic board and extremely simple to use at all microcontroller development board, as well as the Arduino.

DHT22

The DHT22 temperature sensor which most likely to the previous one. It similarly used to determine the humidity and temperature and the pin configuration is also same. DHT22 is considerably high cost, nevertheless it is reputed for its accuracy and it also have a broader humidity and temperature measurement range.

LM35DZ, LM335, LM34

The LM35DZ is a linear temperature sensor module which approaches commonly measured in Celsius. The temperature in Celsius is directly proportional to the analog output: 10mV for each amounts Celsius increase in temperature. This temperature sensor is most related with the LM34 (only difference is standardized in Fahrenheit), and by the LM335 (standardized in Kelvin).

BMP180

BMP180 is an atmospheric or barometric pressure sensor, as we know already in the previous section, correspondingly it can read temperature and much helpful for any weather station project.

TMP36

The TMP36 is one of the analog temperature sensors, it shows an analog output which is relative to the atmospheric temperature, and it's more or less same like LM35.

LM75

The LM75 sensor is a unique digital temperature sensor with an incorporated Sigma-Delta analog to digital converter with an I2C communication. Which functioning through I2C communication that means this can interface with the Arduino using the SDA and SCL pins.

BME280

The BME280 is a special type of atmospheric sensor which can be measures humidity and temperature. BME280 Temperature sensor could be interface with I2C or Serial Peripheral Interface communication protocol and the BME280 sensor might be powered by 3.3 or 5V.

DS18B20

The DS18B20 is a single cable digital temperature sensor, which means it just wants single data line with GND to interface with the Arduino. Every DS18B20 sensor module has an exclusive 64-bit serial code, this permits you can connect several sensors to the same data wire. Consequently, you can read temperature from various sensors with just single Arduino digital pin.

Waterproof DS18B20

The DS18B20 is correspondingly comes with waterproof model (Refer the DS18B20 manual), the single cable attached in the DS18B20 are secure with PVC waterproof coating that is supreme when you want to estimate the temperature of fluid, or provided the project wants to be exposed to liquid.

Application of Temperature and Humidity Sensor

1. Estimating moisture and temperature values in air conditioning systems, boiler, and other air circulation devices.
2. Meteorological department often utilized this module to forecast weather situations.
3. The temperature sensor is utilized for precautionary measurement in houses and wherever persons are troubled by humidity.
4. Utilize this module for detecting the amount of humidity level in safety measure application such as workplaces, museums, greenhouses and manufacturing units.

Rotary Encoder Module

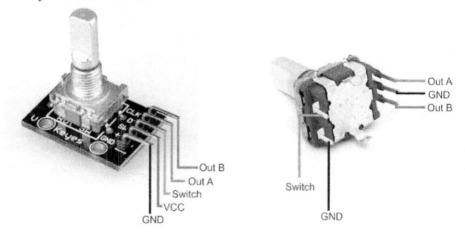

A rotary encoder is a unique kind of position sensor element that is utilized for measuring an angular position of a rotating shaft, rotary encoder be able to produce an electrical signal, for both analog and digital, based on the rotational movement.

Rotary Encoders are the advanced **Digital Equivalent** of the variable-resister and are more sophisticated than a variable-resister. It can be able to freely adjust or rotate until it reaches maximum level without end, breaks when a variable-resister to be able to rotate specific on 3/4 of the complete circle.

Variable Resister are good in situations somewhere you want to get the particular position of the knob. Though, rotary encoders are best in situations somewhere you want to get the adjustment in position instead of the particular position.

Rotary encoders are utilized in a widespread of application such as mechanical systems, with manufacturing controls system, photographic lenses, autonomous robotics, and PCs input devices such as optical mechanical mouse and trackballs, spinning radar devices, and controlled stress rheometers.

MQ-2 LPG Smoke Gas Sensor

The MQ-2 Gas sensor module can be detecting fire, smoke or gasses such as LPG, Hydrogen, Propane, Alcohol, Methane and also CO. The module series of this Gas sensor including with Digital Pin that makes possible this sensor to work even with no microcontroller support and that portable to use while we need to senses one specific gas.

At what time it comes to detecting the gas in ppm the analog pin must be used, the analog pin also TTL logic driven and operating at 5V and therefore it can be utilized with most reputed development board.

Accordingly in case you may searching for a sensor module to sensitive for fire or plethora of gasses then this sensor could be more suitable for you.

Application of MQ-2 LPG Smoke Gas Sensor

➤ MQ2 sensor module is used as a gas leakage alarm in Hospitals, Industries, and Home), and also used in air quality monitoring projects. It is right choice for sensing such as LPG, H2, Propane, Alcohol, and also CH4. Because of its great sensitivity and quick reaction, this sensitivity might be taken as early as possible. This sensor also used to identify the presence of gases in the atmospheric air.

➤ To detect toxic or explosive gasses and measure gas concentration, these devices are commonly used. Manufacturing facilities use gas sensors for detecting gas leaks as well as detecting smoke and carbon monoxide in homes. Various types of gas sensors have different sizes (portable or fixed), ranges, and sensing abilities.

SW-420 Motion Sensor or Vibration Sensor

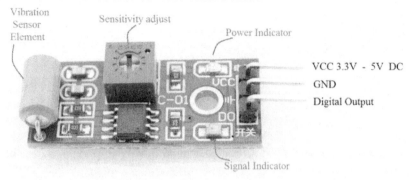

The vibration sensor based on the SW-420 Motion Sensor and LM393 Comparator that is utilized to sense the motion activity and vibrations, the sensitivity of vibration can be modify with a built-in variable-resister. If the time of without vibration or motion, the sensor will send command to the logic as **LOW** and once the motion or vibration is detected, the sensor will trigger to the logic as **HIGH.**

Vibration sensor has 3 pins there are VCC, Digital Output, and GND, The Digital Output pin is associated to the output pin of LM393 comparator IC. It extremely simple to interface Vibration sensor module with the any development microcontroller board like Arduino, Raspberry Pi and ESP8266.

The wiring connection of an Arduino with this SW-420 module is very straightforward, connect the DO pin of the sensor to any digital pin of Arduino and connect VCC and GND pins to 5V and GND pins of an Arduino board.

Applications of Vibration Sensor Module

- Shocks triggering
- Earthquake alarm
- Theft alarm
- Smart car
- Motorcycle alarm

Passive Buzzer Module

A buzzer is an electronic device which can be produce unique tones, most commonly utilized to provide loud response for the people. Buzzers are utilized in various kind of application such as emergency alarm clocks, calculator, keypads, hobby toys and several household appliances.

The Passive Buzzer Sensor contains a passive piezoelectric element. Which can be produce sounds from 1.5 to 2.5 kHz with changing it ON and OFF at a several frequencies whichever using PWM or Delays. On the other hand, an active buzzer sensor which have an on-board oscillating crystal, therefore that will make a unique sound once power-on. Nevertheless, a passive buzzer doesn't have this function, subsequently there is no beep-sound once given DC signal; as an alternative you should be apply square-waves which frequency is among 2K and 5K to operate it. The active buzzer sensor is slightly more expensive than the passive buzzer sensor, for the reason that, because it has numerous on-board oscillating circuits.

The buzzer module is extremely easy to wire up to the Arduino. Connect the left pin of the module to the pin that will drive it and the right pin of the module to Arduino GND. The module is driven by pin 8 in the circuit below. Several pins of the module are not connected, including the middle one.

Application

Passive Buzzer Sensor is used in various kind of application such as Detecting obstacles and gives warning, Burglar Alarm, Blind stick and also used as a Door knock alerts system.

Speed Sensor Module LM393

A speed sensor is similar to the **Tachometer** which is utilized to find out the speed of a spinning object such as fan, motor and a propeller, here is there are several kinds of Speed Sensor available in the market such as Hall-effect, Eddy Current, and Magneto-resistive Speed Sensor, etc.

Speed sensor is also known as **Hall Effect Sensor,** so that for estimate the speed of any spinning devices with Arduino, we may use LM393 Speed sensor. Speed Sensor Module consist of an IR Light Sensor combined with LM393 Voltage Comparator IC.

Applications

- LM393 Speed sensor most frequently used in Robotics.
- Motor Drivers
- Printers, Scanners, Copiers
- Contactless Switching,
- Measuring Speed, and used to find out an RPM.

This Infrared Hall Effect sensor with the Voltage comparator LM393, we be able to measuring the speed of spinning or rotation of the wheels in most of the robotic car projects. Provided we place a circle gear which rotates linked to our wheel. This will likewise be utilized as an optical switch.

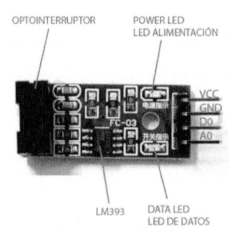

The simple working of this module is as follows; when anything is crossed between the sensor slots, that generates a digital pulse on the D0 pin. This pulse drives from 0V to 5V and is a digital TTL (Transistor-transistor logic) signal, finally, we be able to read this pulse with an Arduino.

Relay Module

A relay is primarily a **switch** that is activated by an electromagnet. The electromagnet just needs a little power to become triggered, and that we can send command from the Arduino and after once it triggered, this will pull the connection to produce the high voltage circuit, Relay module is an electrically activated switch, which can be switch on or off, allowing the current get through or not, and might be operated with minimal voltages as 5V given by the Arduino pins.

The following relay module has two channels (for those two blue cubes), and here we can see as of single to multichannel available in the market, there are one, two, four and eight channels. Most of the Relay module could be powered with 5V, which is applicable to work with an Arduino.

Here are other relay modules which are powered with 3.3V that is perfect for NodeMCU, ESP8266, ESP32 and other Development board.

The Arduino compatible relay consist of six pins: three pins on front side and another 3 pins on different side. In the lower side, here is there are 3 pins that are 5V, ground and signal. Accordingly, we can interface these pins with the microcontroller. Whereas, on the other hand here are normally open (NO), NC (Normally close) and C (Common), there are the output pins supporting for 5V relay. Consequently, we be able to associate the output device.

Most of the Arduino friendly relay module can be used in **two states** which are

1. Normally open state (NO)
2. Normally closed state (NC)

Normally open (NO)

In the normally open state, the beginning output of the relay should be minimal once that will be power on. Here in state, the **common** and the **normally open** pins will be used.

Normally closed state (NC)

In the normally closed state, the beginning output of the relay should be maximum once that will be power on. Here in state, the **common** and the **normally close** pins will be used.

The purpose of relays is to isolate low voltage circuits from high voltage circuits. Multi-circuit controllers are used to control multiple circuits. Automatically changeover can also be done with them. Controlling a heavy electrical load is done by microprocessors using relays

In real-world applications, relays are utilized in many areas. For instance, a cooling system could be an example. When the temperature in the room changes, the temperature-controlled cooling system will have to be able to switch the fan on or off accordingly. Thermometers are electronic devices with sensors inside them.

HC- SR501 Pyroelectric Infrared Sensor (PIR)

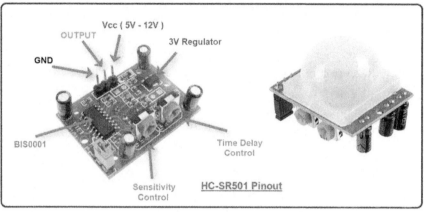

HC-SR501 is a modern motion detection module that is based on Infrared Technology, which is utilize an IR signal for sensing the object, which is include an autonomous control module, likewise having the functions of great sensitivity and reliability. This module consists of an auto-detection control modules, wherever we required to achieve motion. Pyroelectric IR Sensor is used in construction projects and industrials for security purposes.

Why use Pyroelectric IR Sensor, and Its Future

- HC-SR501 is also known as PIR (Passive Infrared) motion sensing module. Which is applicable for sensing the **moving objects**, specifically for the animals and human.
- This kind of sensor can be included as an element of a system which can repeatedly performs a task or alerts a human motion in that region.
- This module is made-up of an essential component of security, energy efficiency, automatic light control, house automation and many other valuable systems.
- PIR Sensor module also comprise time delay alteration and trigger selection that give permission for fine tuning with your various projects
- Every single living thing with a temperature directly above Absolute Zero (0 Kelvin / -273.15 °C), which can produce heat energy in the form of IR radiations.

- When a heat body alive can emit more radiation. Human body functioning on a same pattern and emits Infrared radiation via heat energy.
- A superior lens known as called **Fresnel lens** that focuses the IR Radiation onto the pyroelectric sensor.
- HC-SR-501 sensor module is intended to senses these types of IR radiation from living objects.
- Why PIR sensor to be extremely so popular because of main causes, is the fact that **Pyroelectric IR Sensor** is a most **versatile** which is much proficient all on its own way.
- By using PIR Module with other microcontroller like ESP8266, NodeMCU, and Raspberry Pi, you be able to develop upon its flexibility even more.

Accelerometer Module

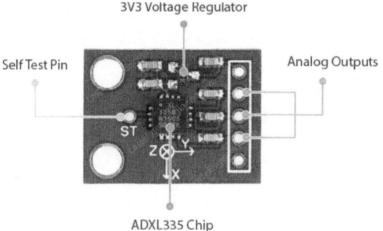

Before enter into the topics, you ever wondered how your mobile phone knows up from down! that is one of the interesting features of today's smartphone gadgets, now a days majority of smart devices includes a microchip called Accelerometer, which is built-in to the motherboard that make senses once you tilt it from right to left and up and down. That's how your smart gadgets immediately realizes while to change the screen position from landscape to portrait.

What is Acceleration?

The revolutionary scientist **Isaac Newton** well-defined in his 2nd law of motion or law of force, acceleration by connecting it to mass and force.

The acceleration is nothing but, the rate of change of velocity with respect to time, It have both magnitude and direction accordingly acceleration is comes under vector quantity. Which is the 2nd derivative of spot with respect to time or it is the 1st derivative of velocity with respect to time.

Here is the Examples of some real-time day to day life application of an acceleration:

1. While the vehicle is speeding up, and while the vehicle is slows down
2. When the vehicle turning at the bend is for e.g. of an acceleration for the reason that the direction is fluctuating. When the vehicle turning will be fast, the acceleration will be greater.
3. When you free fall form the bridge.

Force = Mass x Acceleration or (F = ma.)

Acceleration of an object is related on the mass of the object and the how much of force applied.

Acceleration = Force / Mass

This means that, acceleration is the amount of force we want to change each unit of mass.

- Accelerometer is an electromechanical module that involved the processes both electrical and mechanical that identify the force of acceleration by reason of gravity in g unit.
- The Accelerometer determining the acceleration laterally X, Y and Z axes and gives output of an analog voltage relational to the acceleration laterally these 3 axes.
- ADXL335 Module is most commonly used in the applications of tilt sensing.
- Many developments board like Arduino be able to process these

voltages by transforming them to digital signals via ADC.

- Accelerometer sensor module are broadly utilized in low power, cost sensitive, tilt sensing and motion detection projects such as Smartphone's gadgets, Gaming control systems Joysticks, Image, Video stabilization on gimbals cameras, Sports Fitness Gadgets & healthcare devices and Disk drive protection.

At the heart of the ADXL335 sensors is tiny in size, less power three axis MEMS (Micro Electro Mechanical System) accelerometer beginning Analog Devices through tremendously less noise. The module has overall detection range of ±3 g, which can be identifying the **static** acceleration caused by gravity in tilt-sensing projects, along with **dynamic** acceleration resulting from motion, shock or vibration.

This module functioning on voltage among 1.8V to 3.6V DC (3.3V ideal), and usually its takes just 350µA of current. Nevertheless, a built-in 3.3V regulator perform it a special choice for handling on 5V developments board like Arduino and Raspberry Pi.

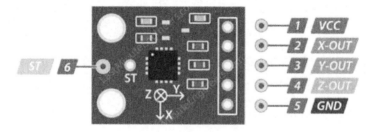

The breadboard friendly ADXL335 sensor module breaks out every single pin of the accelerometer to a 6-pin, 0.1″ pitch header. This contains three analog outputs for X, Y and Z axis estimation, there are two self-test pin and a supply pin that make you to clarify works of the sensor in the finishing projects.

Arduino Joystick Module

The joystick is more or less same function with two variable-resister (potentiometer) connected together, one for the horizontal movement (X-axis), and another one is vertical movement (Y-axis) variable-resistances are nothing but potentiometers and, in a technique, they react as a sensors module they deliver us with varying voltage relating on their spinning.

Mostly commonly the joysticks are utilized for gaming industries, aviation sectors and military applications.

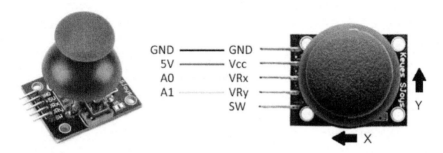

This Joystick controller module is an excellent input device for controlling stepper, servos motors, used as a video game joystick, and remote-control robotics applications. The Joystick have both digital (DO) and analog (AO) output options.

Piezo buzzer Sensor

Have you interested to make some tones with Arduino? Possibly a basic sound for an alarm, perhaps a beep to aware you after a particular input threshold level is achieved, or it could be to run and play the Super Mario Bro music to perform your young mind.

If any kind of sounds required for your projects, you may discover the simplest, fastest and probably the cost efficient way to generate your desired sounds with the **tone()** function and piezoelectric buzzer with your Arduino microcontroller.

Here is the two kind of piezo buzzers which are usually existing in the market. The one is present like a basic buzzer, once we give power source, that will produce a **Nonstop Beeeeeeppp**.... tones, another type known as a portable buzzer that appearance slightly bigger than traditional one and it will make a sound like **"Beep. Beep. Beep."** Why sound happening... Because of the internal oscillating circuit can perform there within. However, the first one is much often broadly utilized for the reason that, that can be personalized with help of customized circuits to easily compatible in our projects.

The buzzer is generally related with a switching circuit to turn ON or turn OFF, most of the buzzers required time and interval. We can just operate the buzzer with help of DC voltage ranging from 3V to 12V, and A basic 9V battery may be used, but then that is optional to usage a regulated +5V or else +6V DC power source.

Applications of Buzzer

- Most of the buzzers are audio signaling device which is utilized in various kind of application such as timer circuits, alarms and tone generating devices,
- Somewhere the people have to be alarmed about their project, and utilized in application like automobile electronics, communication devices, portable devices, because of its compact in size

Water Flow Sensor

YF-S201
WATER FLOW SENSOR

Powerful water management system take place in delivering water according to the actual necessity, and therefore assessing water level is play a vital role in aquatic management systems. Here are several methods to measure flow of water, and various kind of **water flow meters** utilized to estimate the amount of water-flow in pipelines, but these kinds of sensors available in the market are too expensive. Here, we only see the concepts for design & development of cheap water flow meters, with the support of easily accessible and cost-efficient sensor module for estimation the Flow of water.

YF-S201 Hall-Effect Water Flow Sensor

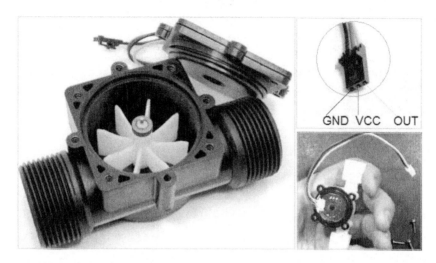

Precise water flow estimation is a vital step for both in circumstances of qualitative and cost-effective points of view. Water Flow meter is a standard sophisticated sensor module for estimate water flow, and this is simple to make a water flow controlling system, which utilizing the famous YF-S201 water flow sensor.

This sensor fixed in the pipe with the water line as well as includes a pinwheel module to estimate how amount of water have passed over it. Here is an advanced magnetic Hall Effect Water Flow Sensor which produce outputs an electrical signal by each revolution. The "YF-S201 Hall Effect Water Flow Sensor" consist of three wires: First one is Red/VCC (5-24V DC Input voltage), second one is Yellow/OUT (Pulse Output) and third one is Black/GND (0V). By counting the electrical pulses or signals from the output of the YF-S201 module, we can simply estimate the flow of water level (in litre/hour – L/hr) with a right conversion technique.

Magnetic flux leakage is used to determine magnetic fields, or to inspect materials (such as pipes or tubing) using hall probes as magnetometers. Devices that produce the hall effect produce a very low signal level and therefore require amplification.

Arduino Color Sensor

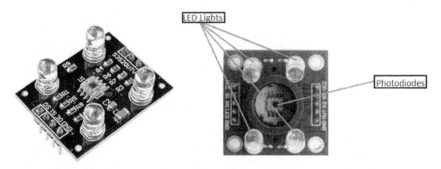

Arduino Compatible TCS3200/230 color sensor module can detect color and intensity of the light using photodiodes. This color sensor module converts data from the photo-detector into a square wave by through the light to frequency converter.

The frequency of the square waves is directly related to the intensity of light. At that moment the Arduino will process the square waves then show us the RGB color's values as an output. Accordingly, we can see the working diagram on interfacing controller with RGB Color Sensor TCS230 shown upcoming section.

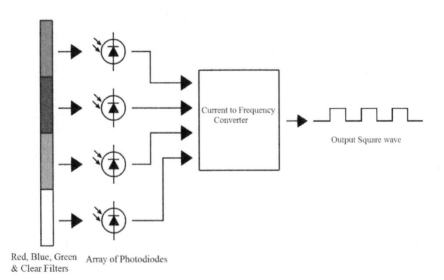

Red, Blue, Green & Clear Filters   Array of Photodiodes

Here we can utilize widespread of projects with color sensors module such as organize or separate a product by its color, Enhancing printer color, quality control systems and etc. Theoretically speaking, figments of our imagination is colors. When we see a green apple, which means that, it can reflect that specific wavelength (~550 nm for Green) of the EM Spectrum (EM - Electromagnetic).

This Electromagnetic wave is absorbed by the human eye and proportional on some biochemical reaction, consequently our brain says that specific wavelength is green color.

Optical Fingerprint Sensor

There are different kind of fingerprint sensors available in the market, from capacitive fingerprint technology utilized in recent smartphones, to optical fingerprint sensors frequently utilized in access control projects like smart attendance. In this lesson, we will learn about optical fingerprint sensor.

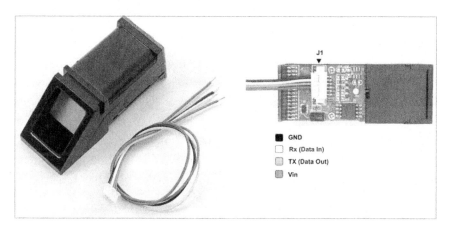

Fig. R305 Optical Fingerprint Sensor-Scanner

The Optical fingerprint sensor module is an extremely portable device. It come from embedded with an advanced DSP unit which stands for Digital Signal Processing unit, that is utilized to processing the input images of fingers captured and find out a match detect or not.

Once the fingerprint module acquired a fresh image, that is extracted and the characteristic features are separated. The memory board of the module is looking for a fingerprint with corresponding patterns and the consequence of that period is sent to the Arduino board through serial communication. This all process is finished within a second. The sensor module has the storage ability up-to thousand fingerprints model with its memory and its training accuracy rate is more than 99.8% which makes it more protected!

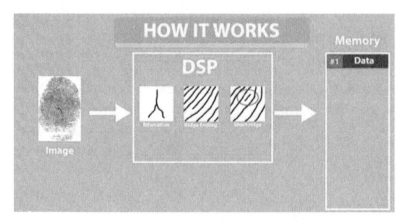

The Fingerprint reader is one of the safe and greatest technique to detect and identify the original person, as we know already which every fingerprint is unique even similar twins do not have unique fingerprints patterns. For utilizing this we can develop and fulfil most safety needs. To add multiple fingerprint authentication in Arduino like development board projects application, also we can able to develop this multipurpose optical fingerprint scanner-sensor (R305), which is make possible fingerprint sensing and authentication is super simple.

By utilizing this fingerprint sensor module, we be able to develop project like Biometric verification and Access control or smart attendance related security application easily. This optical fingerprint sensor module includes high powered AS601 Digital Signal Processing chip form Synochip which perform the task such as feature extraction, image rendering, processing, and searching. This also consist of TTL serial out consequently, we can link to any Arduino and Raspberry pi board or system. The DSP processor has built-in FLASH memory that can able to collect up to 120 fingerprints.

Heart Rate or Pulse Sensor

The Heart Rate Sensor is a plug-and-play pulse sensor for Arduino. Heart rate sensor is used to measure the electrical activity of heart such as **electrical pulse.** That can be utilized as a portable device and smart fitness gadgets by athletes, students, performers, working people, and game and mobile developers those who need to simply integrate a real time pulse-rate information into their healthcare projects and many applications. Principle which is an incorporated optical amplifying unit and noise removing unit in the circuit module. Fastener the Heart Sensor to your tin ear or fingertip and connect it into your Microcontroller like a Arduino and Raspberry Pi.

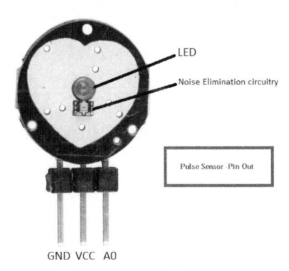

This Pulse rate sensor is pretty straightforward to use and activate it. Place or hold your finger on top of the sensor and that can sense the electrical pulse of heart is nothing but heartbeat by calculating the change in light from the development of capillary blood vessels.

Capacitive Touch Sensor

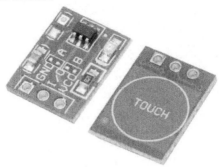

Capacitive touch sensors will be utilized as a replacement for of push buttons. The benefit is we don't necessary to apply force therefore we can just press a button. Similarly, we may activate a switch with no touching a capacitive sensor, obviously without touching it. Now a days we all using Touch screen gadgets and this technology is becoming famous progressively. You could be to interact with this day by day and every hour. Every smartphone these days has a touch screen or touch sensor.

In capacitive touch sensor when we bring human body nearby to the sensor module a capacitance or electrical flux is produced between the Human body and capacitive sensor. We assume the tip of finger and sensor body perform well, correspondingly the plates of the capacitor and a charge is created among the plates. This electrical flux or charge is chosen by the capacitive sensor module and this interpreted as a pressing button. For example, when we bring our finger back from the sensor plate the electrical flux or capacitance is lost and the circuit may break.

TTP223 Capacitive Touch Module IC is the best and well-known Arduino capacitive touch sensor available in the market. The corresponding circuit of the touch sensor module is specified in the below diagram. In the circuit of the TTP223 below, once we move our fingertip close to the touch plate, our finger and touch plate can be produced electrical pulse or capacitor like effects. This novel capacitor is in parallel to capacitor C1. Remember capacitor in parallel is enhancing capacitance. Consequently, the capacitance increases and an electrical flux is induced in the capacitor. This electromagnetic induction is chosen by the sensor such like pressing a button.

The principles of capacitive touch sensing.

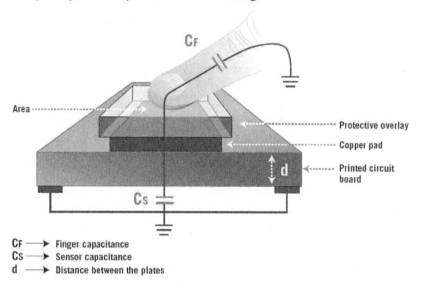

CF ——► Finger capacitance
Cs ——► Sensor capacitance
d ——► Distance between the plates

Note: We don't need touch our fingertip to touch pad. Capacitor can be produced by attractive our finger closed the touch plate. Subsequently the distance wanted to form capacitor is in Nano meters so typically we touch our finger to the touch plate.

Arduino Bluetooth Module HC-05 or HC-06

You ever assumed monitoring any of your electronic devices and smart gadgets with your smartphone? How about an autonomous robot or many other electronic appliances? Wouldn't it be simple to control it with your smartphone? Never mind, here is a cool sensor module for communicating an Android smartphone with Arduino through Bluetooth HC-05!

How Does It Work?

There are 3 Essential parts to this project. First one is Bluetooth supported smartphone, an Arduino and a HC05 Bluetooth Module.

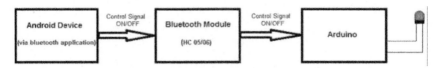

HC-05 or 06 functioning on serial communication. The Android application is intended to transmitting serial data to the Arduino board, HC05 Bluetooth module once a switch is pressed on the app. The Bluetooth module at the side receives the information and transmit it to the Arduino over the TX pin of the Bluetooth module (associated to RX pin of Arduino). Once the sketch is uploaded to the Arduino microcontroller verify the acknowledged information and relates it. If the acknowledged information is 1, the LED turns ON. The LED turns OFF once the acknowledged information is 0. You can open the serial monitor and be able to see the acknowledged information while connecting.

Arduino GPS Module (NEO-6M)

GPS stands for Global Positioning System this is a satellite-based location identification system which includes at least 24 satellites. GPS can able to function in all types of climatic situations, wherever in the world, GPS can work 24*7, we can utilize it with no maintenance fees, no installation and setup charges.

How GPS works

We all are known already; GPS is kind of satellites which spinning the

Earth double times a day in a specific orbit. Each satellite be able to send a unique signal and orbital parameters which permit GPS system to decode and calculate the exact places of the satellite

When your location has been identified, the GPS devices can calculate additional data, such as:

- Speed
- Distance to destination
- Bearing
- Trip dist.
- Trajectory.

What's the signal?

Global Positioning System satellites can send minimum of two little power radio signals. The signals travel by line of sight, which is nothing-but that will travel via clouds, plastic and glass however would not suffer from most solid things, like houses, tower and hills. Nevertheless, the latest receivers are more sensitive and generally it be able to track through building as well.

There are 3 different kinds of data existing in a GPS signal

1. Pseudorandom code is an I.D. code used to identify which satellite is sending data. The Pseudo Random signal is much complex which is exactly similar to the random electrical noise.
2. Therefore, the name came up as "Pseudo-Random." Consequently, we can see which satellites we are getting data from on our system's satellite page.
3. Ephemeris information is wanted to estimate a satellite's location and gives essential data regarding a status and health of a satellite, such as date and time.
4. Almanac data is representing that the GPS receiver where each GPS satellite device could be at any time all over the day and indicate the orbital data for that GPS device and many other satellites in the system.
5. Most of the satellite should be communicating the almanac

information for every satellite, almanac information contains a group of parameters for every satellite which might be utilized to estimate that approximate position in orbit.

NEO-6M GPS Chip

NEO-6M GPS chip is the heart of the GPS module is from u-blox. That be able to track more than 22 satellites on up to 50 channels and it can attains the industry's peak level of sensitivity, Such as For -161 dB level of tracking, it will consuming simply 45mA source current. The u-blox 6 locating machine correspondingly claims a Time-To-First-Fix (TTFF) of less than 1 second. Power Save Mode (PSM) is one of the greatest features that the chip provides. PSM is permits a decrease in device power consumption through selectively switching portions of the receiver ON and OFF. This will intensely cut the energy consumption of the device to just at 11mA building it appropriate for energy sensitive use cases, such as Fitness gadgets comes with built-in GPS. The essential data pins of NEO-6M GPS chip are fragmented out to a "0.1" field headers. This comprises the pins mandatory for transmission through a Arduino microcontroller over UART.

Note: - The GPS module and NEO-6M GPS chip can accept the baud rate from 4800bps to 230400bps with default baud of 9600.

RFID

What is an RFID reader?

RFID is stands for Radio Frequency Identification, which utilizes mini-RFID module for recognition and tracking purposes. An RFID tagging device contains the label itself, a read/write technique, and a host system use cases for data gathering, data processing, and data transmission.

In layman's words an RFID utilizes the electromagnetic fields to send information through minimal distances. RFID is beneficial to recognise people, to make possible transactions, etc...

We can utilize a Radio Frequency ID to open a door. For example, individual person with the unique code and right data on his RFID tag is acceptable to enter. An RFID system uses a tag linked to the data to be recognized, in this use cases we have an electromagnetic tag and a keychain. Tag has his own unique identification (UID).

RFID tags are pretty universal in our society that the average person perhaps meetings them day-to-day with no understanding it. Did you go to the library or bookstore today? The book you bought was possibly registered with RFID technology. Have you visited foreign in recent times? The authority can trace journey information with RFID chips in passports. Have you ever had suffering for searching a missing pet? Perhaps you should consider taking an RFID chip embedded in pet strap to support track her next time she once missed!

Application of RFID

- Identification
- Product Tracking
- Bookstores and Libraries
- Toll Gate Transaction
- Shipping and Logistics

By providing a low cost, powerful, and reliable technique to gather, accumulation and storage of information, RFID offers limitless opportunities for present-day and future use.

Turbidity Sensor

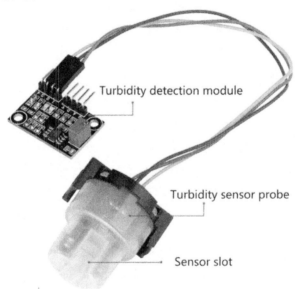

The Arduino based turbidity sensor module can sense water quality by calculating the level of turbidity. It can sense deferred particles in river or any kind of water resource by determining the light transmittance and scattering rate that variations by the amount of TSS (Total Suspended Solids) in aquatic Level. Once the TTS (Turbidity Threshold Sampling) Level increases, simultaneously the water turbidity level will increase.

This Turbidity sensor module both have digital and analog signal outputs.

We can choose the function which is based on to the Microcontroller Unit (MCU), by way of threshold is variable in digital signal method.

Turbidity sensors utilized in wide range of application such as estimation of water excellence in Ponds, Rivers, Wastewater, Watercourses, and used to identification the overflow of water, sediment transportation study, control instrumentation and research laboratory projects.

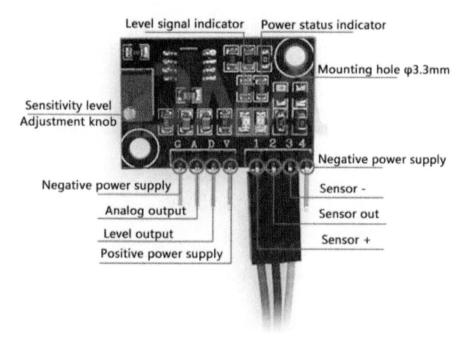

Fig. Turbidity Sensor Pinout

The significance Arduino turbidity sensor sense water standard by estimating the amount of turbidity, or the opacity. It used to sense suspended particles in liquid through light for calculating the light spread and sprinkling rate that variations with the level of total suspended solids (TSS) in liquid. As we knew already the TTS level is increases, the water turbidity level will increase.

Load cell Module

A load cell is an application of strain measurements associated to estimation of weight. A certain level of mass is given to a strain gauge, subsequently the gauge to strain a minimal level and production an electrical energy relative to the given load. This connection between strain and electrical energy is utilized in various use cases where estimation of mass is significant. Load cells are freely available in the market, for the reason that it's linear characteristics, cost efficiency, and their simplicity user interface.

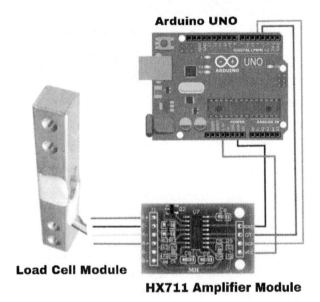

Arduino UNO

Load Cell Module

HX711 Amplifier Module

HX711 is an Analog-to-Digital Converter (ADC) for weigh scales comes with built-in preamplifier. This 24-bit ADC chip is known as the HX711, which produce the minor effects in strain gauge from the load cell into 24-bit changes in electrical energy or voltage (Arduino 0-5V).

HX711 is precisely intended for weight scales Arduino and such electronic projects. These kind of load cells that generally calculate weight deliver electrical outputs in millivolts. These results are much challenging to handle straightly by controllers, consequently we be able to utilize HX711 IC which obtain these electrical signals and deliver standard numerical data that might be utilized by a microcontroller, and consequently the chip has included preamplifier precisely to handle these low voltages.

PH Sensor Module
Arduino compatible analog pH sensor module is precisely intended to estimate the pH of the liquid and measure the alkalinity, or acidity. PH Sensor Module is most frequently utilizing in several kind of real-time use cases, such as environmentally friendly water testing, aquaculture, and aquaponics.

The **pH Sensor** looks like a glass tube generally made from a glass material contains a built-in tip known as "Glass membrane", which is include a buffer solution liquid of known pH (usually pH = 7). PH electrode structure validate surroundings with the continuous binding of Hydrogen ions on the existing of the glass tubes and glass membrane. Once the electrode probe is dipped into the liquid to be tested, H+ ions in the test liquid to start replacing with other positively electrified ions on the glass tubes or membrane, that can be generates an **electrochemical potential** through the glass membrane that is served to the electronic amplifier chip that calculate the voltage difference between both electrodes and converts it to **pH units**. The variance between these voltage differences can measure the pH value according to the Nernst equation.

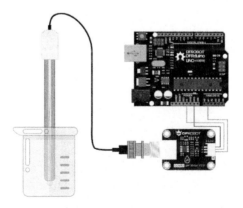

Fig. Analog pH Sensor Module SEN0161 Interfacing with Arduino

The pH is a level which determine the alkalinity or acidity of the Liquid. This is also known as H+ ion concentration index. The pH is a scale of H+ ion movement in liquid or any solution. The pH has a widespread range of application such as in agriculture, chemistry and medicine. Generally, the pH level is a digit between 0-14. Based on the thermodynamic standard conditions;

1. **pH<7**, that means the liquid is **acidic**;
2. **pH>7**, that means the liquid is **alkaline**;
3. **pH=7**, that means the liquid is **neutral.**

Pressure Sensor or Force Sensitive Resister (FSR)

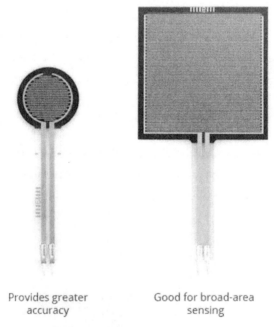

Provides greater accuracy

Good for broad-area sensing

In recent years, a force sensitive resistor (FSR) has become an indispensable sensor which is utilized in a wide range of industrial applications.

Nowadays we can see these sensors in handheld gaming devices, mobile phones, and other electronic instruments like electronic drums. These sensors can be easily used and are great for detecting pressure.

How does an FSR work?

Pressure applied to the sensing area determines how much resistance an FSR has. When you apply more pressure, the less resistance there will be. There is quite a large resistance range: greater than 10MΩ (at no pressure) to ~ 200 Ω (maximal pressure). The range of force that can be sensed by FSRs is nearly around 100g to 10 kg.

Basic construction

There are two membranes and one spacer adhesive in an FSR. An air gap separates the conducting membranes when no pressure is applied. The membrane contains two traces between the tail and the sensing area (rather round part). It's impossible to touch these traces as they are woven together, but not touching one another, consequently a conductive ink is coated on the other membrane. Pressing on the sensor shorts the ink between the two traces, the resistance of which is dependent upon the pressure applied.

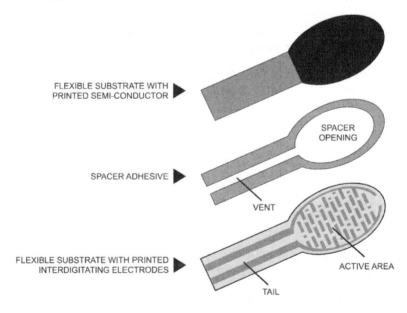

Force sensing resistors are used in various fields such as foot pronation systems, automotive sensors, electronic keyboards and controls, biomedical devices, as well as musical instruments, as well as mobile electronics and wireless communications.

Flex Sensor

A flex sensor is a different type of unique sensor that determines the amount of deformation or bending. Materials like carbon or plastic can be utilized in designing the sensor. The carbon surface is attached to a plastic strip. If you turn this strip away, the sensor's resistance will change. Therefore, it is also termed a bend sensor. Since its varying resistance directly correlates to the magnitude of the rotation, the bend sensor can also be employed as a goniometer.

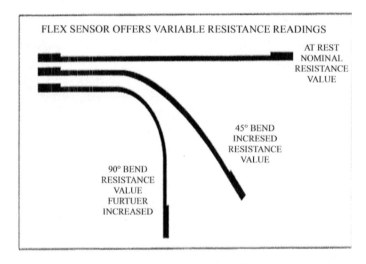

Most of the time, this sensor is mounted to the exterior, and you can adjust the resistance by adjusting the exterior. It is used by Nintendo in its power gloves, door sensors, robot whisker sensors, this also the key component in making alert stuffed animals.

Analog resistors are what are called Flex sensors. Variable analog voltage dividers are made with these resistors. There are carbon resistive elements inside the flex sensor, surrounded by a thin flexible substrate. Increased carbon content means a reduction in resistance. With a substrate bent, the sensor makes resistance which is relational to the radius of the bend. Flexible sensors are thin and flexible, which allows them to achieve high form factors. A sensor, as shown in Figure, produces a resistance output inversely proportional to the bend radius of the substrate, Consequently More resistance will be given by a smaller radius.

Flex-sensors are used for the following applications.
- ❖ Physical Therapy
- ❖ Healthcare Instruments
- ❖ Robotics motion
- ❖ Virtual Motion (Video Games)
- ❖ A computer's peripheral devices
- ❖ Musical Instruments

Summary

We have discussed the basics of electronic components in this chapter, the components you need to start with Arduino, and different types of Arduino Sensors and Modules. In the next chapter, we will explore the basics of Arduino programming and how to get started with Arduino programming

CHAPTER 3

ARDUINO PROGRAMMING

Introduction

A convenient, easy way to learn and use Arduino programming reference for understanding the basic Arduino commands and syntax can be found in this Chapter. Take it easy and keep things simple, some things have been left out that makes it a secondary reference. This is best used alongside other books, classes, websites, or workshops. Since then, the Arduino maker community has refocused attention on standalone use and, for example, excludes the use of arrays or more complex forms of serial communication. Starting with a description of Arduino's C derived programming language, the language's syntax and usage will be illustrated throughout this chapter with code fragments and some examples. An appendix includes many functions of the core library and sample schematics and starter programs. Where possible, this format complements O'Sullivan and Lgoe's Physical Computing.

Arduino code is written in **C++** and adds some special methods and functions, which will be discussed later. **Human-readable** programming languages include C++. The Arduino code file is compiled into machine language after being processed into a sketch (as it is called in Arduino parlance), which is a very simple hardware programming language. A sketch should be uploaded on an Arduino board after it has been written in the Arduino IDE.

Downloading and installing the Arduino IDE is the first step in programming the Arduino board. Linux, Mac OS X, and Windows are all supported by the open-source Arduino IDE. From the Arduino website, download the software (depending on your operating system) and follow the installation instructions.

Arduino programs follow a pretty straightforward structure. There are at least two blocks in an Arduino program, The preparation process and the execution of the plan The following statements are enclosed in curly braces in each block:

Structure of an Arduino Code:

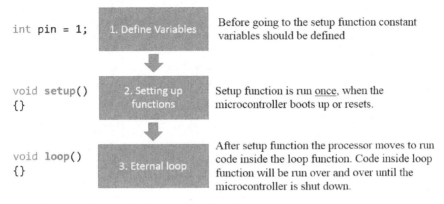

```
int pin = 1;
```
1. Define Variables — Before going to the setup function constant variables should be defined

```
void setup()
{}
```
2. Setting up functions — Setup function is run <u>once</u>, when the microcontroller boots up or resets.

```
void loop()
{}
```
3. Eternal loop — After setup function the processor moves to run code inside the loop function. Code inside loop function will be run over and over until the microcontroller is shut down.

- It's <u>required</u> to have both **setup()** and **loop()** functions in the code

Bare minimum code

```
void setup() {
  // put your setup code here, to run once:
}
void loop() {
  // put your main code here, to run repeatedly:
}
```

setup: The Arduino uses it only when powered on or when it's reset. It works in the same way as initializing variables and pin modes.

loop: Until the device is powered off, loop functions will run continuously. In this section, the logic of the program is defined. Microcontroller programming follows a similar pattern to while (1).

Arduino Data Types

Arduino C, a variable of data type **int** uses 2 bytes of information. When a sketch uses **int,** it tends to use it almost everywhere, unless it is very memory hungry. For tiny integer values or for Boolean values, even a single byte value could be used.

Table 1-1 Includes a complete list of available data types.

Arduino Data Types	Value Assigned	Value Ranges
boolean	8 Bit	True or False
byte	8 Bit	0 to 255
char	8 Bit	-127 to 128
unsigned char	8 Bit	0 to 255
word	16 Bit	0 to 65535
unsigned int	16 Bit	0 to 65535
int	16 Bit	-32768 to 32767
long	32 Bit	-2,147,483,648 to 2,147,483,647
float	32 Bit	-3.4028235E38 to 3.4028235E38

Analog to Digital Conversion

▶ What is analog?

It has a continuous voltage range (not just 0 V or 5 V)

▶ Why convert to digital?

We have a microcontroller that can only read digital input.

Converting Analog Value to Digital

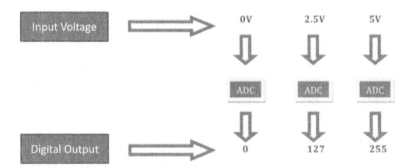

Quantization the signal

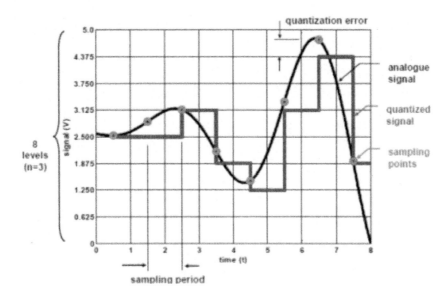

ADC in Arduino

▶ There are 6 ADC pins on the Arduino Uno board.
▶ Digital to analog converter with 10-bit resolution
▶ That means input voltages between 0 and 5 volts will be converted into integer values between 0 and 1024.

Reading/Writing Analog Values

▶ analogRead(A0); // The pin A0 is used to read the analog value.
▶ analogWrite(2,128);

Reading/writing digital values

▶ digitalWrite(13, LOW); // this will select the output voltage on pin 13 , 0V
▶ digitalWrite(13, HIGH); // It will select the output voltage on pin 13 , 5V

▶ int buttonState = digitalRead(2); // Reads pin 2 values from the buttonState

PinMode

▶ The pinMode function on the Arduino lets you choose an input and output pin.

▶ pinMode(13, OUTPUT); // pin 13 becomes an output pin.
▶ pinMode(13, INPUT); // pin 13 becomes an input pin.

ARDUINO PROGRAMMING BASICS

Structure

Arduino's basic structure isn't too complicated and works in two parts. Blocks of statements are enclosed between these two required parts, or functions.

```
void setup()
{
  statements;
}
void loop()
{
  statements;
}
```

Where **setup()** is the preparation, **loop()** is the execution. Both functions are required for the program to work.

At the very entry level of the program, the **setup** function has to follow the statement of any variables. A function that appears in the entire program runs only one time, and is utilized to initialize serial communication or set the **pinMode.**

Next comes a loop function, which contains the program to be run instantaneously, it reads Inputs, triggered outputs and much more. In most Arduino programs, this function is at the heart of the program.

setup()
When your program starts, setup() is called once. The pin mode is used to start a serial connection or initialize pin modes. This type of statement

must be included, even if they will not be executed.

```
void setup()
{
pinMode(pin, OUTPUT);  // sets the 'pin' as output
}
```

loop()

When naming the setup() function, the loop() function does specifically what its name recommends, and loops sequentially, enabling the code to modify, respond, and control the Arduino microcontroller.

```
void loop()
{
digitalWrite(pin, HIGH);   // turns 'pin' on
delay(1000) ;              // pauses for one second
digitalWrite(pin, LOW);    // turns 'pin' off
delay(1000) ;              // pauses for one second
}
```

functions

A Function is a block of code, wherever a function is called, a number of statements are executed. In an earlier lecture, we talked about the functions void set-up() and void loop() and others built-in will be explained later.

It is possible to write custom functions to simplify repetitive tasks and minimize clutter in code. The first step in declaring functions is specifying the type of function.

For example, 'int' represents an integer type function. A function's return type would be void, if it returns no value. Name the function after type and include any parameters that will be passed to it in parenthesis.

```
type functionName( parameters)
{
statements;
}
```

You can read the delay value from the potentiometer by using the function delayVal(). A local variable v is declared, then one of the potentiometer values is presented, The range for this number is 0-1023. Finally, it returns this value back to the main program by dividing by 4 for an additional value between 0 and 255.

```
int delayVal()
{
int v;                   // create temporary variable "v'
v= analogRead(pot) ;     // read potentiometer value
v /= 4;                  // converts Q-1023 to 9-255
return v;                // return final value
}
```

{} Curly braces

It is distinguished from "curly brackets" by its curly appearance, the void loop() function and for and if statements, and may contain blocks which are used to declare the beginning and end of function blocks and statement blocks.

```
type function()
{
statements;
}
```

{There must be a closing curly brace after an opening curly brace}, As a result of this, the braces are said to be balanced. Cryptic is often caused by unbalanced braces, often impenetrable compiler errors occur in a large program that are difficult to find.

An Arduino ecosystem has a feature to check whether curly braces are balanced. The logical companion of a brace is highlighted if you choose it, or if you click the entry point quickly following a brace.

; Semicolon

A semicolon must be utilized to separate sections of a program and to end a statement. For loop elements are also separated by semicolons. The integer 13 is declared for variable 'x'.

Note: The compiler will generate an error if you forget to end a line with a semicolon. A semicolon may or may not be missing, making the error text somewhat obvious. It's always important to check for missing semicolons, near the line where the compiler complained, in response to an impenetrable or seemingly illogical compiler error.

/*...*/ block comments

Multi-line comments, also known as block comments, or parts of text that are ignored by the sketch, a large text description is used to help others understand a piece of code or comments. The syntax will start with /* and finish with */ and it can span numerous rows.

> *Do not forget to add the closing comment to the enclosed block comment – it has to be balanced!*/

The program ignores comments, so they do not take up any memory, It's okay to use them to "comment out" portions of code or to use them to fix bugs.

Note: A single-line comment may be enclosed in a block comment, but two block comments are not allowed.

// line comments

Each line of code in a comment starts with // followed by the subsequent line of code. They don't take up any memory, just like block comments.

// Such comments can be put in a single line.
In many cases, a single-line comment will be placed after a valid statement to provide more info about what the statement accomplishes or to remind the reader.

Variables

Variables are used by the program to name and store a mathematical value. As their name implies, variables are numbers that can be changed continuously as opposed to constants whose value stays the same. It is necessary to declare a variable and optionally assign a value to it with the goal of storing the value. An analog input pin is connected to a variable named as input Variable, and its value is assigned to that variable:

```
int inputVariable = 0;          // declares a variable and
                                // assigns value of 0
inputVariable = analogRead(2);  // set variable to value of
                                // analog pin 2
```

'inputVariable' is the variable itself. On the first line, it is declared to include an integer, or int. Upon passing the 2nd line (sequence 1), the variable is set to value at pin 2 of the analog system. The value of pin 2 can now be accessed from anywhere in the code.

You can test the value of a variable once it has been assigned, or reassigned, based on specific circumstances, or its value can be directly used. Three ways to use variables are demonstrated in the following example, In the following code, input variable is tested for whether it is below 100 and if true value 100 is assigned to input variable, and set the delay to a minimum of 100 based on inputVariable:

```
if (inputVariable < 100)       // If the variable is below 100, it will tested.
{
inputVariable = 100;           // the value 100 is assigned if true
}
delay(inputVariable) ;         // uses variable as delay
```

Note: A variable's name should describe what it does, making it more readable. It is important for the programmer to name variables like tilt Sensors and pushbuttons to make it easier for anyone reading the code to understand what the variables represent. On the other hand, variable names like var or value do little to make the code easier to read and are only utilized here as examples. Anything in the Arduino language can be named a variable, as long as it is not already an Arduino keyword.

Variable declaration

An integer, long, float, or float-like variable must first be declared in order to be used, specifying an initial value and optionally setting a name. One set of arithmetic functions and general assignments is all that is needed in order to change the value of the variable. Here, inputVariable is declared to be an integer, or int, and its original value is zero. This is named as a simplified assignment.

int inputVariable = 0;

There are numerous places in which variables can be declared across the program, and which part of the program uses the variable depends on where the variable definition is located.

Variable scope

In a program, variables can be declared before void setup(), locally in functions, and occasionally in for loops within statement blocks. It is determined where the variable is declared, which calculates its scope, which determines the program's ability to utilize the variable.

Any function in a program can see and use a global variable. An initialization variable is declared before the setup() function.

Typically, a local variable is one created inside of a function or within a for loop. The function declaration only allows it to be accessed and used within the context in which it was declared. So, you can have different values for the same variable if they are in various sections of similar program. Simplifying the program and reducing the potential for programming errors can be achieved by making sure only one function has access to its variables.

Various types of variables are declared and their visibility is demonstrated by the following example:

```
int value;          // 'value' is visible
                    // to any function
void setup()
{
                    // no setup needed
}
void loop()
{
for (int i=0; i<20;)    // 'i' is only visible
{                       // inside the for-loop
i++;
}
float f;            // 'f' is only visible
}                   // inside loop
```

byte

Bytes represent 8-bit numerical values without decimal points. They can range from 0 to 255.

```
byte someVariable = 180;   // declares 'someVariable'
                           // as a byte type
```

int

The integer data type is utilized to store numbers without decimal places and stores 16-bit data with a range of 32,767 to -32,768.

```
int someVariable = 1500;          // declares 'someVariable'
                                  // as an integer type
```

Note: As long as a variable isn't forced past its maximum or minimum value due to an assignment or comparison it will roll over. As an example, if x = 32767 and later x is added to by the addition of 1, then x will equal -32,768.

long

Integers stored in 32-bit format, without decimal points, are of extended size datatype, with a range between 2,147,483,647 to -2,147,483,648.

```
long someVariable = 90000;   // declares 'someVariable'
                             // as a long type
```

float

A type of floating-point number that has a decimal point. Integers have greater resolution than floating point numbers which are stored as a 32-bit value with a resolution of 3.4028235E+38 to -3.4028235E +38.

```
float someVariable = 3.14;   // declares ''someVariable'
                             // as a floating-point type
```

Note: It can be complicated to compare floating-point numbers, since they are not accurate. In addition, floating point math performs calculations much more slowly than integer math.

Arrays

Arrays are collections of data accessed by index numbers. Array values may be accessed using the array name and index number. Arrays start at index number 0, with the first value beginning at index number 0 in the array. To utilize an array, you must declare it and possibly assign values to it.

int myArray[] = {valueQ, valuel, value2...}

Similarly, arrays can be declared by declaring the array type and size, and later assigning values to an index position:

int myArray[5]; // declares integer array w/ 6 positions
myArray[3] = 10; // assigns the 4th index the value 10

Arrays are retrieved by assigning an index position and the array's variable.

x = myArray[3]; // x now equals 10

For loops also make use of array values in two-dimensional arrays, where the index position and increment counter for each array value are the same. Below is an example of flickering LEDs using an array, Within a for loop, the counter reads the value contained at index spot 0 in the array flicker[], the PWM pin 10 is set to 180, pauses for 200ms and the index position is moved to the next position.

```
int ledPin = 10;                       // LED on pin 10

byte flicker[] = {180, 30, 255, 200, 10, 90, 150, 60};
                                       // above array of 8

void setup()                           // different values
{
pinMode(ledPin, OUTPUT);               // sets OUTPUT pin
}
void loop()
{
for(int i=0; i<7; i++)                 // loop equals number
   {                                   // of values in array
analogWrite(ledPin, flicker[i]);

                                       // write index value
delay(200); // pause 200ms
   }
}
```

Arithmetic

These mathematical operations include addition, subtraction, multiplication, and division. Two operands are returned as a product, difference, sum(respectively) or quotient(respectively).

```
y = y + 3;
x = x - 7;
i = j * 6;
r = r / 5;
```

The operands of the operation are based on their data types. Therefore, the result of 9 / 4 is 2 instead of 2.25 since 9 and 4 are not decimal numbers and cannot be expressed as fractions. Additionally, if the result of the operation exceeds the capacity of the data type, the result will overflow.

The larger type is used for the calculation if the operands are of different types. The calculation will use floating point math if one of the numbers is of the type float and the other of the type integer.

The variables selected for your calculations should have a large enough size to hold the largest result. Understand when and how your variable will roll over, in addition to knowing what happens in the opposite direction e.g. (0 - 1) OR (0 to - 32768). For fractions to be used in math, float variables are preferable, but they are large and take a long time to compute.

Note: Convert a variable's type on the fly by using the cast operator, (int)myFloat is an example. For example, 1 = (int) 3.6 will set i equal to 3

Compound Assignments

Combining two arithmetic operations into one variable Assignment is compound assignments. For loops are generally used to create them as is discussed later. The most common compound assignments include:

```
x ++        // same as x = x + 1, or increments x by +1
x --        // same as x = x - 1, or decrements x by -1
x += y      // same as x = x + y, or increments x by +y
x -= y      // same as x = x - y, or decrements x by -y
x *= y      // same as x = x * y, or multiplies x by y
x /= y      // same as x = x / y, or divides x by y
```

Examples include x *= 3 which would triple the value of x, which would lead to a new value of x.

Comparison Operators

When a condition is true, if statements compare variables or constants to see if they match. On the following pages, the referring to a predicate is utilized to describe any of the following:

```
x == y      // x is equal to y
x != y      // x is not equal to y
x <  y      // x is less than y
x >  y      // x is greater than y
x <= y      // x is less than or equal to y
x >= y      // x is greater than or equal to y
```

Logical operators

There are logical operators that are usually implemented to compare expressions, and depending on the operator it will return TRUE or FALSE. If statements are commonly used with three logical operators, AND, OR, and NOT:

```
Logical AND:
if (x > 0 && x < 5)      // true only if both
                         // expressions are true

Logical OR:
if (x > 0 || y > 0)      // true if either
                         // expression is true

Logical NOT:
if (!x > 0)              // true only if
                         // expression is false
```

Constants

Several predefined constants are available in the Arduino programming language. Constants are arranged into groups to simplify readability of the programs.

True/false

Logic levels are defined by Boolean constants. Typically, TRUE is defined as one while FALSE is easy to decipher as zero (zero) but can also be anything other than zero. Therefore, in the Boolean sense, -1, 2, and -200 all have the same definition of TRUE.

```
if (b = = TRUE);

{

doSomething;

}
```

High/low

When reading or writing to digital pins, these constants are utilized to define pin levels as HIGH or LOW. HIGH is defined as logic level 1, ON, or 5 volts while LOW is logic level 0, OFF, or 0 volts.
digitalWrite(13, HIGH);

Input/output

The constants utilised to define a pin's mode will be either INPUT or OUTPUT with the pinMode() function.

pinMode(13, OUTPUT);

if

if statements are used to determine if a condition has been attained, it performs any statements inside the brackets if the statement is true, such as a certain analog value being greater than a certain number. If false, the program skips the statement. Here's what an if statement looks like:

```
if (someVariable ?? value)
{

doSomething;
}
```

Here, the variable someVariable is compared with another value, which may be a variable or a constant. The statements inside brackets are run if the condition inside the parentheses is true, A program taking care of the brackets skips them if they are not present.

Note: Make sure you never accidentally use '='. If (x=10), for example. x is defined to the value 10 and thus is always true, even though technically it is valid. It is better to instead use '==', as in if (x==10), which simply checks that the value x is the same as 10, Think of '=' as "equals" opposed to '==' being 'is equal to".

if... else

When used with if...else, a decision can be made either one way or the other. In other words, if you needed to test digital inputs and perform one thing if they were HIGH and another if they were LOW, you would write this way:

```
if (inputPin == HIGH)
{
doThingA;
}
else
{
doThingB;
}
```

if else tests can also be run before another if test, so that a number of tests relating to the same thing can be run simultaneously. Moreover, one can have a limitless number of these other branches. Although there are several statements, only one set will be run according to the conditions:

```
if (inputPin < 500)
{
 doThingA;
}
else if (inputPin >= 1000)
{
doThingB;
}
Else
{
doThingC;
}
```

Note: A conditional statement is a simple logic check that checks if the statement's terms are true. In the first example, if (inputPin == HIGH), this statement can take any valid C statement. If the input is indeed high, or +5v, then if statement verifies only if the input is truly a high-level input.

for

For statements are used to repeat either a single statement or an array of statements. The loop is typically terminated by using an increment counter. For loop header consists of three parts that are divided by semicolons (;):

for (initialization; condition; expression)

{

doSomething;

}

Only one time is the local variable initialized, or the increment counter initialized. A condition of the following is tested with each loop. The following statements and expressions are performed if the conditions remain true and the tests for the condition again. After a period of time, the loop ends, indicating that the condition became false.

Below, the integer is initialized to 0 and the test is run to see if i is still below 20. If so, then it is incremented by 1 and the enclosed statements are executed:

```
for (int i=0; i<20; i++)    // declares i, tests if less
{                           // than 20, increments i by 1
  digitalWrite(13, HIGH);   // turns pin 13 on
  delay(250);               // pauses for 1/4 second
  digitalWrite(13, LOW);    // turns pin 13 off
  delay(250);               // pauses for 1/4 second
}
```

Note: Some other computer languages include BASIC, but they offer significantly less flexibility than for loops in C. Although semicolons are required, any or all of the headers may be omitted. In addition, the statements for the statement initialization, the condition, or the expression can have any valid C statement that contains variables unrelated to each other. There may be some solutions to rare programming problems with these unusual statements.

while

While loops will continue to loop indefinitely until the argument within the parenthesis turns false. Unless something changes the variable being tested, the loop will never terminate. In your code, this can be internal, like an incremented variable, or outside the code, like testing a sensor.

```
while (someVariable ?? value)

{

doSomething;

}
```

In the example below, 'someVariable' is tested to see if it is smaller than 200 and loops until 'someVariable' becomes greater than 200 and executes the statements within the brackets.

```
while (someVariable < 200)  // tests if less than 200
{
doSomething;              // executes enclosed statements
someVariable++;          // increments variable by 1
}
```

do... while

do loops work similarly to while loops as they are bottom-driven, except that at the finish of the loop the condition is tested; therefore, the do loop will always perform at least once.

```
do
{
doSomething;
} while (someVariable ?? value);
```

Following is an example where readSensors() is assigned to the variable 'x', followed by a 50 millisecond delay, and then loops indefinitely until the value of 'x' stops being less than 100:

```
do
```

```
{
x = readSensors();        // assigns the value of
                          // readSensors() to x
delay(50);                // pauses 50 milliseconds
} while (x < 100);        // loops if x is less than 100
```

pinMode(pin, mode)

Following is an example where readSensors() is assigned to the variable 'x', followed by a 50 millisecond delay, and then loops indefinitely until the value of 'x' stops being less than 100:

```
pinMode(pin, OUTPUT);     // sets 'pin' to output
```

Inputs are default for Arduino digital pins, so pinMode() is not required to declare them as inputs explicitly. Impedance state is said to exist on pins designated as INPUTS.

The Atmega chip comes with 20KQ pull-up resistors which are easily accessible from software. There is one way to gain access to these pull-up resistors:

```
pinMode(pin, INPUT);      // set 'pin' to input
digitalWrite(pin, HIGH);  // turn on pullup resistors
```

Connectors such as switches are normally connected to pull-up resistors. Here, you see that pin does not become an output, but merely the means by which internal pull-ups are activated.

Those pins specified for OUTPUT are thought to contain low resistance and provide a current of up to 40 mA (milliamps) to other instruments / circuits. Neither current nor voltage are sufficient to run most relay, solenoid, or motor devices.

The output pin on an Arduino can be damaged or destroyed or the whole Atmega chip can be damaged and fried if they are short circuited or if they receive too much current. A resistor of 4700 or 1KO can be connected in series with the OUTPUT pin of a computer if it needs external connecting.

digitalRead(pin)

This method results in a HIGH or a LOW result from the value of a specified digital pin. You can specify pins either as constants or variables (0-13).

```
value = digitalRead(Pin);    // sets 'value' equal to
                             // the input pin
```

digitalWrite(pin, value)

Outputs the specified digital pin as either HIGH or LOW. Either a constant or a variable can be used to define this pin.

```
digitalWrite (pin, HIGH);    // sets 'pin' to high
```

Here's an example of an LED that's linked to a digital output that reads a pushbutton connected to a digital input:

```
int led = 13;           // connect LED to pin 13
int pin = 7;            // connect pushbutton to pin 7
int value = 0;          // Variable to store the read value
void setup()
{
pinMode(led, OUTPUT);   // sets pin 13 as output
pinMode(pin, INPUT);    // sets pin 7 as input
}
void loop()
{
value = digitalRead(pin);    // sets 'value' equal to
                             // the input pin
digitalWrite(led, value);    // sets 'led' to the
}                            // button's value
```

analogRead(pin)

This function interprets the value from a 10-bit analog pin. These functions only work on pins 0-5 in the analog input. There are a total of 1023 possible integer values.

```
value = analogRead(pin); // sets 'value' equal to 'pin'
```

Note: An analog pin is not required to be declared before it can be used as an input or output; it can be used either way.

analogWrite(pin, value)

An output pin marked PWM is used to write a pseudo-analog value utilizing hardware provided pulse width modulation (PWM). This function is available by default on Arduinos with the ATmega168 chip beginning at version 2.0. The ATmega8 chip used in older Arduinos only supports pins 9, 10, and 11. Variables and constants may be specified with values ranging from 0-255.

analogWrite(pin, value);   // writes 'value' to analog 'pin'

At 255, a steady 5-volt signal is produced at the specified pin while a value of 0 generates a constant 0-volt output. For values in When the value is 0 to 255, the pin alternates quickly between 0 and 5 volts. The greater the value, the fewer times the pin is HIGH (5 volts). The value 64, for example, will be 0 volts three quarters of the time, and 5 volts one quarter of the time; 128 volts equals 0 volts half the time and 255 volts the other half; and 192 volts equals 0 volts one quarter of the time and 5 volts two-thirds of the time.

As the pin is considered to be hardware, it will continue to generate a wave in the background until another analogWrite call (or another call to digitalRead or digitalWrite on similar pin) is received.

Note: Unlike digital pins, analog pins do not need to be stated as INPUT or OUTPUT beforehand.

This example outputs a PWM signal to a PWM pin when we read an analog value from an analog input pin, convert the value by dividing it by 4, and convert it back into an analog value.

```
int led = 10;              // LED with 220 resistor on pin 10
int pin = 0;               // potentiometer on analog pin 0
int value;                 // value for reading
void setup(){}             // no setup needed
void loop()
{
value = analogRead(pin);   // sets 'value' equal to 'pin'
value /= 4;                // converts 90-1023 to 0-255
```

```
analogWrite(led, value);        // outputs PWM signal to led
}
```

delay(ms)
A time period of 1000 milliseconds will pause your program.

delay(1000) ; // waits for one second

millis()
The time within milliseconds since the current program began running on the Arduino board as an unsigned long quantity.

value = millis(); // sets 'value' equal to millis()

Note: Within approximately 9 hours, this number will overflow and reset to zero.

min(x, y)
This function finds the smaller number between two numbers of any information kind and returns it.

```
value = min(value, 100);        // sets 'value' to the smaller of
                                // 'value' or 100, ensuring that
                                // it never gets above 100.
```

max(x, y)
A function that returns the largest number from a set of data types.

```
value = max(value, 100);        // sets 'value' to the Larger of
                                // 'value' or 100, ensuring that
                                // it is at least 100.
```

randomSeed(seed)
The random() function starts with the value, or seed, specified by random().

randomSeed(value) ; // sets 'value' as the random seed

The Arduino does not produce a truly random number, so randomSeed lets you place variables, constants, and functions into the random function, in order to increase the number of random numbers. Several different functions, or seeds such as millis() or even analogRead() can be utilized in this function to read an analog pin's electrical noise.

random(max)

random(min, max)

The random function executes pseudo-random computations based on the input values and returns a result.

```
value = random(100, 200);      // sets 'value' to a random
                               // number between 100-200
```

Note: You need to utilize this after you have utilized the randomSeed() function.

Below is an example that creates a stochastic value between 0-255 and outputs on a PWM pin a PVVM signal similar to that quantity.

```
int randNumber;                    // variable to store the random value
int led = 10;                      // LED with 220 resistor on pin 10

void setup() {} // no setup needed

void loop()
{
randomSeed(millis());              // sets millis() as seed
randNumber = random( 255);         // random number from 0-255
analogWrite(led, randNumber);      // outputs PWM signal
delay (500);                       // pauses for half a second
}
```

Serial.begin(rate)

Opens serial port and sets the baud rate for serial data transmission. The typical baud rate for communicating with the computer is 9600 although other speeds are supported.

```
void setup()
```

```
{
Serial.begin(9600);              // opens serial port
}                                // sets data rate to 9600 bps
```

Note: You cannot use two digital pins at the same time when using serial communication.

Serial.printin(data)

The printing commands include a carriage return and a line feed, followed by printing data on the serial port. Printing data on the Serial Monitor is easier with this command than the Serial.print() command.

```
Serial.println(analogValue);     // sends the value of
                                 // 'analogValue'
```

Note: Please refer to the Arduino website to learn more about the serial.printin() and serial.print() functions and their various permutations.

Below is a straightforward example transmitting information every 1 second from analog pinO to the computer.

```
void setup()
{
Serial. begin(9600) ;            // sets serial to 9600bps
}
void loop()
{
Serial.println(analogRead(0));   // sends analog value
delay(1000) ;                    // pauses for 1 second
}
```

Digital output

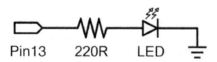

Pin13   220R   LED

It simply turns something on or off using a simple 'hello world' program. In this instance, an LED becomes visible by connecting pin13 to GND, which blinks every second. Due to the Arduino's built-in resistor, it is possible to omit the resistor on this pin.

```
int ledPin = 13;              // LED on digital pin 13

void setup()                  // run once
{
  pinMode(ledPin, OUTPUT);    // sets pin 13 as output
}

void loop()                   // run over and over again
{
  digitalWrite(ledPin, HIGH); // turns the LED on
  delay(1000);                // pauses for 1 second
  digitalWrite(ledPin, LOW);  // turns the LED off
  delay(1000);                // pauses for 1 second
}
```

Digital input

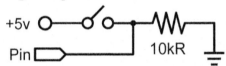

There are two possible states for this type of input: on or off. We're reading from pin2 a simple switch or pushbutton. Input pin HIGH turns an LED on when the switch is closed.

```
int ledPin = 13;             // output pin for the LED
int inPin = 2;               // input pin (for a switch)

void setup()
{
  pinMode(ledPin, OUTPUT);   // declare LED as output
  pinMode(inPin, INPUT);     // declare switch as input
}

void loop()
{
  if (digitalRead(inPin) == HIGH) // check if input is HIGH
  {
    digitalWrite(ledPin, HIGH);   // turns the LED on
    delay(1000);                  // pause for 1 second
    digitalWrite(ledPin, LOW);    // turns the LED off
    delay(1000);                  // pause for 1 second
  }
}
```

High current output

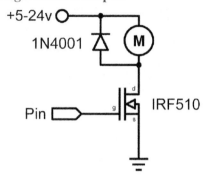

Controlling more than 40ma can sometimes be necessary with the Arduino. Switching higher currents could be achieved by utilizing MOSFETs or transistors. Using an instance, we can rapidly turn the MOSFET on and off five times a second.

Note: On the schematic the diode is shown only as a protection to the motor. But other eddy current devices would also be able to be utilized without the diode.

```
int outPin  =  5;          // output pin for the MOSFET

void setup()
{
  pinMode(outPin, OUTPUT);      // sets pin5 as output
}

void loop()
{
  for (int i=0; i<=5; i++)      // loops 5 times
  {
    digitalWrite(outPin, HIGH); // turns MOSFET on
    delay(250);                 // pauses 1/4 second
    digitalWrite(outPin, LOW);  // turns MOSFET off
    delay(250);                 // pauses 1/4 second
  }
  delay(1000);                  // pauses 1 second
}
```

PWM output

Pulse width modulation (PWM) can be used to reproduce analog signals by pulsing the output. Dimming and brightening an LED could result in servo motor control. A for loop is used to control the brightness and dimmer   of   an   LED   slowly.

```
int ledPin = 9;      // PWM pin for the LED

void setup(){}        // no setup needed

void loop()
{
  for (int i=0; i<=255; i++)  // ascending value for i
  {
    analogWrite(ledPin, i);   // sets brightess level to i
    delay(100);               // pauses for 100ms
  }
  for (int i=255; i>=0; i--)  // descending value for i
  {
    analogWrite(ledPin, i);   // sets brightess level to i
    delay(100);               // pauses for 100ms
  }
}
```

Potentiometer input

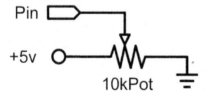

You can read values from 0-1024 using an analog potentiometer and an analog-to-digital converter (ADC) pin on an Arduino. An LED's blinking rate can be controlled by adjusting the potentiometer in the following example.

To connect the Arduino board, we connect three wires. Potentiometers have two pairs of pins, one of which is connected to ground.

A second connector connects the 5 volts to the outer pin of the potentiometer. Third, there is a potentiometer that goes from analog input 2 to the middle pin.

```
int potPin = 0;      // input pin for the potentiometer
int ledPin = 13;     // output pin for the LED

void setup()
{
  pinMode(ledPin, OUTPUT);  // declare ledPin as OUTPUT
}

void loop()
{
  digitalWrite(ledPin, HIGH);    // turns ledPin on
  delay(analogRead(potPin));     // pause program
  digitalWrite(ledPin, LOW);     // turns ledPin off
  delay(analogRead(potPin));     // pause program
}
```

Variable resistor input

Thermistors, thermistors, flex sensors and the like are all examples of variable resistors. In this example, the analog value is read using a function and the delay time is set using a delay function. LEDs can be dimmed by adjusting their brightness.

```
int ledPin    = 9;     // PWM pin for the LED
int analogPin = 0;     // variable resistor on analog pin 0

void setup(){}         // no setup needed

void loop()
{
  for (int i=0; i<=255; i++)  // ascending value for i
  {
    analogWrite(ledPin, i);   // sets brightess level to i
    delay(delayVal());        // gets time value and pauses
  }
  for (int i=255; i>=0; i--)  // descending value for i
  {
    analogWrite(ledPin, i);   // sets brightess level to i
    delay(delayVal());        // gets time value and pauses
  }
}

int delayVal()
{
  int v;                       // create temporary variable
  v  = analogRead(analogPin);  // read analog value
  v /= 8;                      // convert 0-1024 to 0-128
  return v;                    // returns final value
}
```

Servo output

Motors used in hobby products are self-contained and also able to move in a full circle. A pulse every 20ms is all that is needed. In this example, the motor is moved from 10° -170° and then back again, using a servoPulse function.

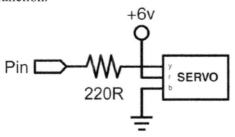

```
int servoPin = 2;     // servo connected to digital pin 2
int myAngle;          // angle of the servo roughly 0-180
int pulseWidth;       // servoPulse function variable

void setup()
{
  pinMode(servoPin, OUTPUT);    // sets pin 2 as output
}

void servoPulse(int servoPin, int myAngle)
{
  pulseWidth = (myAngle * 10) + 600;   // determines delay
  digitalWrite(servoPin, HIGH);        // set servo high
  delayMicroseconds(pulseWidth);       // microsecond pause
  digitalWrite(servoPin, LOW);         // set servo low
}

void loop()
{
  // servo starts at 10 deg and rotates to 170 deg
  for (myAngle=10; myAngle<=170; myAngle++)
  {
    servoPulse(servoPin, myAngle);     // send pin and angle
    delay(20);                         // refresh cycle
  }
  // servo starts at 170 deg and rotates to 10 deg
  for (myAngle=170; myAngle>=10; myAngle--)
  {
    servoPulse(servoPin, myAngle);     // send pin and angle
    delay(20);                         // refresh cycle
  }
}
```

Using Libraries

You'll find it helpful to only contain code that you'd actually use on the board, since Arduinos have a small amount of memory. By using libraries, this can be achieved. Libraries are used in Arduino, and by extension in C programming in general.

The Arduino IDE contains a library that contains instructions on how to use an LCD display. The program memory used here is approximately 1.5kB. If you don't use this library, there is no point in including it. It is "included" when required. A #include directive is used right at the start of your sketch for this purpose. Using the Sketch | Import Library... menu option, you can include the libraries installed by the Arduino IDE.

A significant collection of official libraries is included in the Arduino IDE, including:

- **EEPROM** for storing data in EEPROM memory

- **Ethernet** For system programming

- **Firmata** The serial transmission standard for Arduino to pc

- **LiquidCrystal** For alphanumeric LCD exhibits

- **SD** For reading and writing SD flash memory cards

- **Servo** For directing servo motors

- **SPI** The Arduino to peripheral transmission bus

- **Software** Serial For serial communication utilizing nonserial pins

- **Stepper** For handling stepper motors

- **WiFi** For WiFi network access

- **Wire** For I2C communication with peripherals

Some facilities are particular form of Arduino board:

Keyboard USB keyboard emulation (Leonardo, Due, and Micro)

Mouse USB mouse emulation (Leonardo, Due, and Micro)

Audio Audio playing utilities (Due only)

Scheduler For managing multiple execution threads (Due only)

USBHost USB peripherals (Due only)

Also, the Arduino community has contributed a vast number of libraries that are available on the Internet. Ones that are extremely popular include

OneWire using the 1-wire bus interface, Dallas Semiconductor's range of digital devices can be read.

Xbee For Wireless serial communication

GFX. A graphics library from Adafruit that plays efficiently on several various types of displays

Capacitive Sensing For proximity detection

FFT Frequency analysis library

The official Arduino website has a lot of the latest collections (http://arduino.cc/en/Reference/Libraries). You can also find them on the Internet. If you want to utilize these libraries, you must save them in your Arduino Documents folder Libraries. Please download the libraries and save them there. You must create the libraries folder if it does not already exist before adding a library. The Arduino IDE needs to be exited and restarted in order to recognize a library that has been installed.

Summary

It has been condensed very much in order to provide a condensed explanation of Arduino. At https://www.arduino.cc/, you can find free Arduino tutorials that you can refer to if you want to learn more about the Programming fundamentals. In the next chapter, we will get started with Arduino projects. Learn by doing more than 30 projects, we hope it will give you a fascinated experience.

CHAPTER 4

ARDUINO PROJECTS LEARN BY DOING

Project 1: Blink an LED

We will learn how to make an LED blink in this practical session

Components:

- 1 x Arduino UNO
- 1 x USB Cable
- 1 x 220Ω Resistor
- 1 x LED
- 1 x Breadboard
- 2 x Jumper Wires

Principle:

We are going to learn how to program Arduino's GPIO outputs at both high and low levels, and make an LED linked to Arduino's general-purpose input (GPIO) flicker with a specified frequency.

What is the LED?

The LED stands for light emitting diode. Gallium arsenide and gallium phosphide are the most common semiconductor materials in these devices. There are two electrodes in the LED: one positive, the other negative. Flashing red, blue, green, yellow and others, it only lights up when an electric current pass through it. Light varies in colour depending on the material it is made from. By using a lower value resistor, more current is allowed to flow, so the LED is brighter.

With higher resistor values, the LED will become dimmer because of the restriction in current flow. A majority of LEDs also have polarity, meaning that they need to be connected in the right directionless have just about the longest life span of any lighting solution when compared to traditional lighting solutions. A fluorescent or metal halide light will last only two to four times as long as a sodium vapor light.

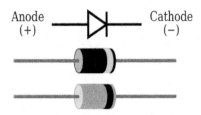

Procedure

Step 1: Build the circuit as below:

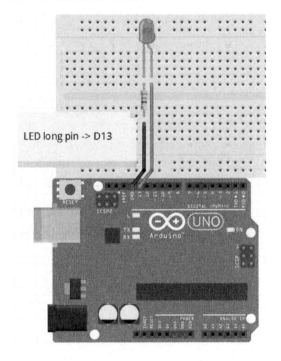

Pin definition

LED		UNO R3
Long pin	->	+5V
Short pin	->	GND

Note: Digital signal port 13(D13) is connected to the longest LED on the pin.

Step 2: Make an LED Blink Program using Arduino IDE.

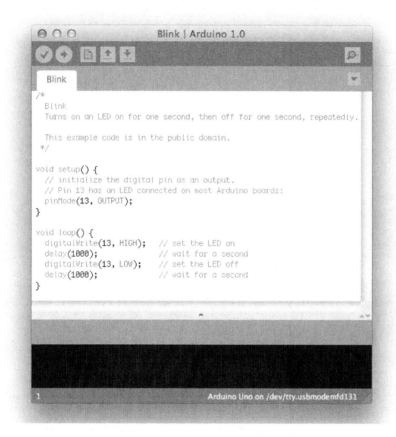

Step 3: Compile the sketch and upload to the Arduino UNO board. A Big Kudos. As a result, you can see the LED blinking.

Uploading the Program

➢ Please connect your Arduino to your PC with the USB cable before uploading code.

➢ **Select Tools→Board→** Identify your board in the Arduino menu by looking for Arduino Uno. You can also find the Arduino Mega, Arduino's smaller cousin, through this menu.

Please make sure that you are connecting to the correct serial port on your board, The list of accessible serial ports can be found by selecting, **Tools→Serial Port→ comX,** as soon as your Arduino is linked to a Windows laptop, it will take the largest number port, such as COM 3 or COM 15.

▸ **Click Verify** the LED Blink Sketch will be checked
▸ **Click Upload** Consequently, the program is sent to the Arduino microcontroller board

Project 2: Traffic Light 3 Way Controller

Overview:

The previous lesson covered how to get LEDs to light up when you program the Arduino. Here, we use the Arduino to control various LEDs, and the LEDs will be colored differently to make the lights shown in the traffic signal system

Components:

- 1 x Arduino UNO
- 1 x USB Cable
- 3 x 200Ω Resistor
- 3 x 5mm RED LED
- 3 x 5mm YELLOW LED
- 3 x 5mm GREEN LED
- 1 x Breadboard
- Several jumpers wire

Principle:

The experiment used in this lecture is very similar to the lesson in the previous lesson. Traffic light controller based on an Arduino is an easy project which is useful to know how traffic lights function in our everyday lives. The traffic light circuit has been shown in this post. In this circuit, three sides or ways have been demonstrated. Let's move on to the project.

One of the easiest Arduino projects to understand or code is the Traffic Light Controller. Traffic Lights are demonstrated on the three-way road using the LEDs on all three sides in the same method they would really work. This results in either one of the two sides having two red traffic light signals and one green light for their neighbour's side. In between changes from Red to Green, yellow light remains on, also for 1 second, but at progressively shorter intervals; in other words, the first 5 seconds are on Red, followed by 1 on Yellow, before the final second is on Green. The use of traffic control signals ensures the flow of traffic in an orderly manner. In addition, they are helpful in reducing the frequency of right-angle accidents. To allow other traffic to safely cross an intersection, they intercept heavy traffic.

Procedure:

Step 1: Build the circuit

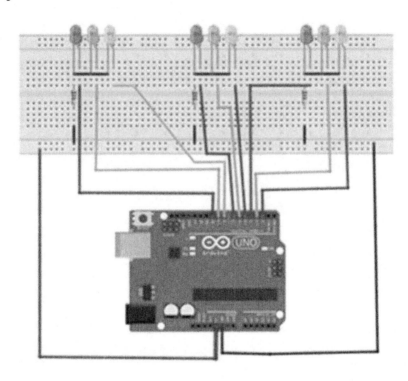

Step 2: Program code

```
/*********************************************************
TRAFFIC LIGHT 3 WAY CONTROLLER
LET LED BLINKS.
*********************************************************/
void setup() {
// configure the output pins
pinMode(2,OUTPUT);
pinMode(3,OUTPUT);
pinMode(4,OUTPUT);
pinMode(5,OUTPUT);
pinMode(6,OUTPUT);
pinMode(7,OUTPUT);
pinMode(8,OUTPUT);
```

```
pinMode(9,OUTPUT);
pinMode(10,OUTPUT);
}
void loop()
{
digitalWrite(2,1); //enables the 1st set of signals
digitalWrite(7,1);
digitalWrite(10,1);
digitalWrite(4,0);
digitalWrite(3,0);
digitalWrite(6,0);
digitalWrite(8,0);
digitalWrite(9,0);
digitalWrite(5,0);
delay(4000);
digitalWrite(3,1); //enables the yellow lights
digitalWrite(6,1);
digitalWrite(2,0);
digitalWrite(7,0);
delay(1000);
digitalWrite(4,1); //enables the 2nd set of signals
digitalWrite(5,1);
digitalWrite(10,1);
digitalWrite(2,0);
digitalWrite(3,0);
digitalWrite(6,0);
digitalWrite(8,0);
digitalWrite(9,0);
digitalWrite(7,0);
delay(4000);
digitalWrite(9,1); //enables the yellow lights
digitalWrite(6,1);
digitalWrite(10,0);
digitalWrite(5,0);
digitalWrite(4,0);
delay(1000);
digitalWrite(8,1); //enables the 3rd set of signals
digitalWrite(4,1);
digitalWrite(7,1);
digitalWrite(2,0);
```

```
digitalWrite(3,0);
digitalWrite(5,0);
digitalWrite(6,0);
digitalWrite(9,0);
digitalWrite(10,0);
delay(4000);
digitalWrite(9,1); //enables the yellow lights
digitalWrite(3,1);
digitalWrite(7,0);
digitalWrite(8,0);
digitalWrite(4,0);
delay(1000);
}
```

Step 3: The program was compiled and uploaded to the Arduino UNO board.

As a result, it is possible to keep the traffic flowing at a constant speed on a given route or route. In certain types of accidents or crashes, including right-angle crashes, it helps reduce their severity and frequency IIHS concluded that red-light cameras in all 79 large U.S. cities included in the study saved nearly **1,300 lives** since they were implemented through 2014.

As well as ensuring a smooth flow of traffic, traffic signals provide an opportunity for pedestrians and vehicles to cross an intersection and reduce conflicts between vehicles entering intersections from different directions. The use of traffic control signals ensures the flow of traffic in an orderly manner. As a result, there will be a decrease in the frequency of an accident of a special nature, such as an accident at **right angles**. As a result, heavy traffic can safely cross the road intersection while heavy traffic is stopped.

Project 3: Push button - LED Blinking

Overview:

We will learn in this lesson how to detect a button's state and toggle the LED's state based on the button's state.

Components:

- 1 x Arduino UNO
- 1 x USB Cable
- 1 x 220Ω Resistor
- 1 x 10KΩ Resistor
- 1 x LED
- 1 x Push Button
- 1 x Breadboard
- Several jumpers wire

Principle

Button

It is a common component of electronic devices to use buttons to control them. Connecting and disconnecting circuits is often one of their main functions. Despite the wide range of button shapes and sizes, we will use a single 12mm button in this experiment.

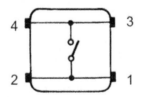

A normally open button is what we used. A button has two open contacts under normal circumstances; only when pressed are they closed. In an open state (unpressed), no electrical connection exists between the two legs of the pushbutton. Thus, we read a HIGH reading because the pin is set to 5 volts (through the pull-up resistor). The button closes (reaches a connection) when it is pressed, so when it hits a pin, it makes a connection to ground, so we read LOW. (The pin will still be connected to 5 volts, but the resistor in-between it will cause it to be closer to ground.)

It seems that the button jitters in the process of use. The jitter waveform can be seen here:

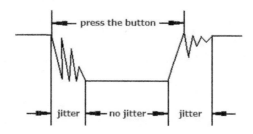

The Arduino will consider a press of the button as having been made many times since it will jitter. The jitteriness of the buttons should be dealt with prior to use. By using software programming, jitter can be eliminated. You can also solve the issue by using a capacitor. Here's an example of a software method. The first step is to determine whether the interface consists of low level or top buttons. If the level of the event is low, a delay of 510ms is needed. Then determine if you have a low or high level of button interface. With a low signal volume, you can surmise that the button has been pushed once. The jitter from buttons can also be avoided by using a 0.1uF capacitor.

Interrupt

A hardware interrupt was implemented to minimize the amount of time spent waiting for external events in polling loops. Their implementation may take the form of a distinct system with control lines, or they may appear within the memory subsystem.

Key functions:

attachInterrupt(interrupt, ISR, mode) Names one or more Interrupt Service Routines (ISRs) to be named when an interrupt happens.

Procedure:

Step 1: Build the circuit

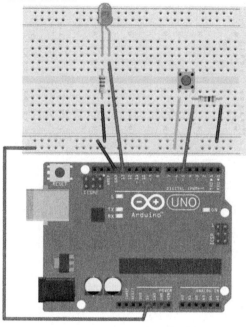

Schematic:

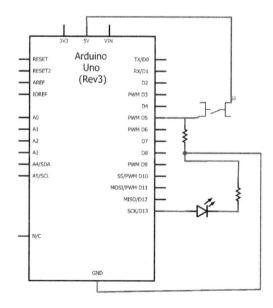

Step 2: Program: Open /Copy the code from the "CODE" Folder

```
/*********************************************************
Push button - LED Blinking
*********************************************************/
int ledpin=13;// definition digital interface
int inpin=5;//Define the number 5 Interface
int val;//Define the variable val
void setup() {
pinMode(ledpin,OUTPUT);//Define led as Output
pinMode(inpin,INPUT);//Button interface is defined as input
}
void loop() {
val=digitalRead(inpin);//Read digitalpin 5 level value assigned to val
if(val==HIGH)//Test button is pressed
{
digitalWrite(ledpin,LOW);
}
else {
digitalWrite(ledpin,HIGH);
}
}
```

Step 3: Now that the code has been compiled and uploaded to the Arduino UNO board, press the button, and you'll see that the LED will turn ON or OFF.

Push-buttons turn things on when pressed, completing a circuit. Release of the button will result in the circuit breaking and turn it off as soon as the connection is broken. As well as push-button switches, momentary and normally-open switches are found in computer keyboards, for instance. The push-button has four pins, but you generally only connect two at a time, unlike a toggle switch, which stays in one position until you toggle it to the other. Despite the two unused pins at the bottom of the board being able to do the same thing, you will be using the top connections on this project.

Project 4: RGB Blinking LED (Common Anode)

Overview:

With the Arduino, we will learn how to make the LEDs emit several colors of light, and we will program the Arduino to control RGB LEDs.

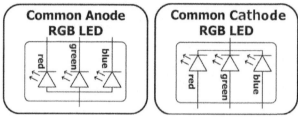

Components:

- 1 X Arduino UNO
- 1 X USB Cable
- 1 X RGB LED
- 3 X 220Ω Resistor
- 1 X Breadboard
- Several jumpers wire

Principle:

Red, green and blue LEDs make up RGB LEDs. Any colour can be produced by using these three LEDs. Three-color LEDs that consist of anode, cathode and red emitters.

A common anode LED RGB is used in this experiment. The longest pin of the three LEDs is called the common anode. With a current limiting resistor back-to-back, pins D8, D9, and D10 are connected to pin +5V and the 12 pins are connected to pins D8, D9, and D10.

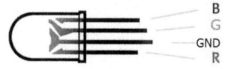

With this approach, RGB LEDs can be controlled by 3-channel PWM signals

Schematic:

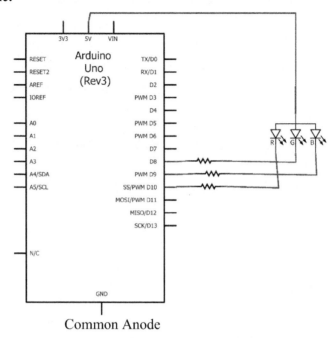

Common Anode

Procedure:

Step 1: Build the circuit

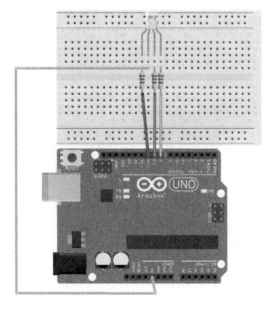

Step 2: Program code

```
/*********************************************************
 RGB LED Blinks, (Common Anode)
*********************************************************/
void setup() {
pinMode (8,OUTPUT);
pinMode (9,OUTPUT);
pinMode (10,OUTPUT);
}
Void loop() {
digitalWrite (8,HIGH);
digitalWrite (10,LOW);
delay(1000);
digitalWrite (9,HIGH);
digitalWrite (8,LOW);
delay(1000);
digitalWrite (10,HIGH);
digitalWrite (9,LOW);
delay(1000);
}
```

Step 3: It is important to compile and upload the program to the Arduino UNO. Now, you can see the RGB LED flash blue, yellow, white, green, and purple, then go out. The LED changes hues repeatedly in the same sequence for 1s each time.

Application:

An LED circuit that dances can be used to indicate highway signs as well as advertising hoardings, Using LED blinking circuits for signaling (to signal for help if you are in danger) can be useful.

Using an LED blinking circuit as a flashing beacon is possible. When a vehicle breaks down, a blinking LED circuit can serve as an indicator. Operation theaters and office spaces can use it to indicate work is in progress.

Project 5: Interfacing with Keypad Module

Overview:

With the Arduino UNO R3 board, we will be able to read the keys pressed by a user so that the board can communicate with that keyboard.
Components:

- 1 x Arduino Uno
- 1 x USB cable
- 1 x Membrane switch module
- 1 x Breadboard
- Jumper wires

Principle

The keypad is present in everything from cell phones to microwaves to door locks. There are practically thousands of them. Users can feed them into tons of electronic devices.

Making very different types of commercial products requires the knowledge of how to connect a keypad to microcontrollers like the Arduino UNO.

Eventually, when all has been properly connected and programmed, the signal will appear in your computer's Serial Monitor when you press a key. The Serial Monitor shows every key press on the computer. Further down the line, in another project, the circuit will be connected to an LCD, from where results will be observed on the screen. Let's start with just showing the key pressed on the pc right now for simplicity's sake.

A matrix keypad will be the most appropriate type of keypad for this project. There are far fewer output pins on this keypad than there are keys, allowing it to have much less encoding. There are 16 keys on the matrix keyboard we are utilizing, but only 8 output pins on the circuit. If you were to build a linear keyboard, you would have to put 17 output pins on the board (one for each key and a ground pin). Matrix encoding saves a lot of connections for the keyboard since smaller pins need to be utilized to have the keypad work. Because they require less wiring, they are less inefficient than linear keypads.

Schematic:

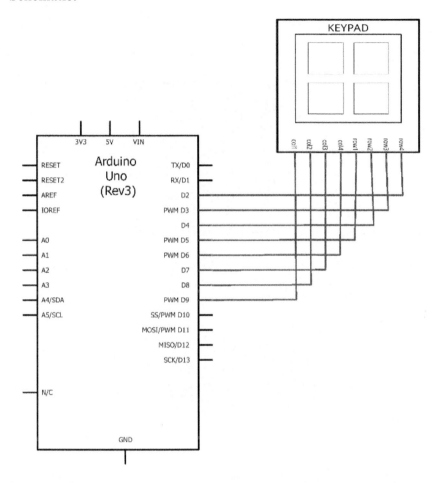

The Arduino UNO board uses the digital output pins, D9-D2, when the pins are connected to the pins. The first pin of the keypad is connected to D9, next to D8, then to D7, fourth pin to D6, then to D5, next to D4, next to D2, and the eighth pin to D2. These are the connections in a table.

There is also a code and wiring diagram for a 3X4 matrix keypad. For the purpose of this article, I'll be utilizing a matrix membrane keypad. It's easy to stick membrane style keypads to flat surfaces because they have an adhesive backing. For people who like the telephone style keypad style, there are thicker buttons as well. Using an Arduino, even an old telephone keypad can be converted to work with the device.

Procedure:

Step 1: Build the circuit

Step 2: Program

```
/*******************************************************
Project 05 - Interfacing with Keypad Module
*******************************************************/
#include <Keypad.h>
const byte ROWS = 4;   //four rows
const byte COLS = 4;      //four columns
char hexaKeys[ROWS][COLS] = {
{'1','2','3','A'},
{'4','5','6','B'},
{'7','8','9','C'},
{'*','0','#','D'}
};
byte rowPins[ROWS] = {9, 8, 7, 6};  //connect to the Rows of the keypad
```

```
pin 8, 7, 6, 5 respectively
byte colPins[COLS] = {5, 4, 3, 2};   //connect to the Columns of the
keypad pin 4, 3, 2, 1 respectively
Keypad customKeypad = Keypad( makeKeymap(hexaKeys), rowPins,
colPins, ROWS, COLS);
void setup() {
Serial.begin(9600);
}
void loop(){
char customKey = customKeypad.getKey();
if (customKey){
Serial.println(customKey); // Send the pressed key value to the arduino
serial monitor
}
}
```

Step 3: Compile the program and upload to Arduino UNO board.

Summary

I know this is a very simple example, but I think you can see how easy it is to input keypad data into an Arduino program. These inputs can be used for a variety of different projects, such as:

- Door lock
- Input PWM
- Alarm clock
- Security lock

Well, that pretty much sums it up. Setting up a keypad isn't hard at all. By modifying the code above a little and trying it out, you should be able to get the keypad to work with most of the projects you'd want to use it for.

Project 6: Control LED Blink Rate with Potentiometer

Overview:

A variable resistor (a potentiometer) is utilized to change the blink rate of an LED using the three digital inputs on the Arduino board. As the analog inputs work using voltages, the resistor's value is read in this manner.

Components

- 1 x Arduino UNO
- 1 x USB Cable
- 1 x Breadboard
- 1 x 5mm RED LED
- 1 x 220Ω Resistor
- 1 x 10kΩ Potentiometer
- Jumper wires

Principle

Your pot should be linked to a 5V supply, the center pin to analogue pin A2, and the remaining pin to ground. An LED is then connected to digital pin 13 with a 220-ohm resistor connected in series. LEDs should be connected to the resistance through the anode (the positive leg) and the cathode (the negative leg) to ground with the positive leg connected to negative ground

This type of function is mostly seen in light strings. In order to control the blinking delay time, we replace the potentiometer reading variable with the delay time value. The **analogRead** function on Arduino is used to read Analog values. Potentiometers are used to adjust voltage.

Schematic

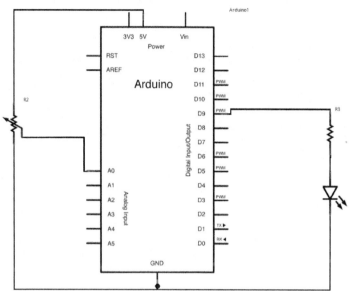

Procedure:

Step 1: Build the circuit

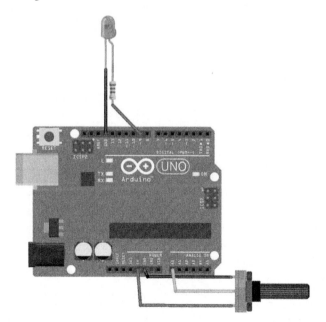

Step 2: Program

```
/*****************************************************
Project 06: Control LED Blink Rate with Potentiometer
*****************************************************/
int potPin = A0; // select the input pin for the potentiometer
int ledPin = 9; // select the pin for the LED
int val = 0; // variable to store the value coming from the sensor
void setup() {
pinMode(ledPin, OUTPUT); // declare the ledPin as an OUTPUT
}
void loop() {
val = analogRead(potPin); // read the value from the sensor
digitalWrite(ledPin, HIGH); // turn the ledPin on
delay(val); // stop the program for some time
digitalWrite(ledPin, LOW); // turn the ledPin off
delay(val); // stop the program for some time
}
```

Step 3: Compile the program and upload to Arduino UNO board.

This code can be modified according to your needs. A microcontroller/Arduino that controls LED brightness is flexible. In either direction, you can fade the lead as voltage increases or decreases. Depending on your preferences, you can program the controller. When you insert other hardware like the motor controller circuit, you can control the fan speed and the direction the motor rotates. A microcontroller in the intelligent unit is the only thing that makes it all possible.

If we rotate the potentiometer contact, the serial monitor will display values between 0 and 1023. Accordingly, whenever the potentiometer output voltage is high, the Flashing rate is slower because the delay and flashing rate are both high. As the output value is decreased, the delay will be less, the LED will blink faster, and every value will be displayed as an output on the #Serial Monitor

Project 7: Multiple tones with one Piezo Buzzer

Overview:

The purpose of this lesson is to teach you how to use a buzzer.

COMPONENTS

- 1 x Arduino UNO
- 1 x USB Cable
- 1 x Buzzer
- 1 x Breadboard
- 2 x Jumper Wires

Principles

To generate air vibrations, buzzers use PWM (pulse width modulation) to generate audio. Changed appropriately, the vibration can produce different sounds as long as the frequency is appropriate. The pulse of 523 Hz, for instance, can be sent to produce Alto Do, the pulse of 587Hz can be used to produce midrange Re, and the pulse of 659Hz can be used to produce mi. Play a song with a buzzer.

The pulse output of analog Write () on the UNO R3 board is fixed (500 Hz), so we should be careful not to use it to generate a pulse to the buzzer.

To use the **tone()** command, take over one of the Atmega's internal timers, set the frequency to what you want, and then pulse one of the output pins with the timer. It only allows you to play one note at a time since it only uses a single timer. Sequentially playing notes on different pins is possible, however. This can be accomplished by turning off the timer for one pin before proceeding to the next.

Are you planning on making some noise with Arduino? We all have our teen years, but maybe make the Super Mario Brothers soundtrack play to occupy your minds (it's OK -- we've all been there).

No matter what your audible need, using the **tone()** function and piezo speaker with your Arduino will likely be the easiest, quickest, and cheapest way to make some noise.

Schematic:

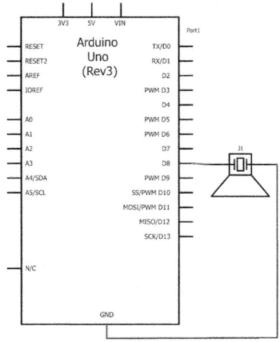

Procedure:

Step 1: Build the circuit

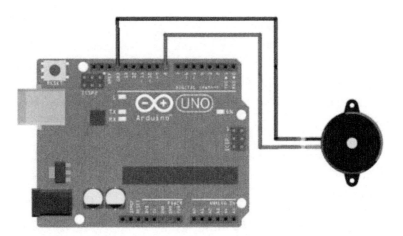

Step 2: Program: Open /Copy the code from the "CODE" Folder

```
/*********************************************************
File Name: Multiple Tones with One Piezo Buzzer
*********************************************************/
const int buzzer= 8;
void setup() {
pinMode (buzzer,OUTPUT);
}
void loop() {
tone(buzzer,1000);
delay(1000);
noTone(buzzer);
delay(1000);
}
```

Step 3: Compile the program and upload to Arduino UNO board.

TONE () FUNCTION HAS LIMITS YOU SHOULD KNOW

Tones () have some limitations, like everything else in life. You should be aware of them. Here are some of the points we need to discuss:

When using pins 3 or 11, you can't simultaneously use tone() and analogWrite(). Trying to use either of these in the same way results in wacky results. Since the tone() function for pins 3 and 11 uses the same timer that analogWrite() does, it's because it uses the same built-in timer. Just for the sake of hearing the weird noises, it's well worth the effort.

Tones lower than 31 Hz cannot be generated. Tones with values 31 and below can be passed to the tone() function, however, it does not necessarily mean you will get a good representation of them.

Tone() cannot be used by two different pins simultaneously. Suppose you have two piezo speakers connected to different pins. Playing both of them simultaneously isn't possible. You have to turn one on, after which you have to turn the other one on. Additionally, for the other pin to utilize the tone() function, the previous pin's tone must be turned off by calling the noTone() function.

Project 8: Seeing the light using Photo resistor with an Arduino

Overview:

Let's see how photo resistors are used to measure light intensity in this lesson.

Components

- 1 x Arduino UNO
- 1 x USB cable
- 1 x 10kΩ Resistor
- 1 x 220Ω Resistor
- 1 x LED
- 1 x Photo Resistor
- 1 x Breadboard
- Jumper wires

Principle:

Essentially, a photoresist or is a variable resistor that is sensitive to light. Photo resistors exhibit photoconductivity, implying that their resistance decreases with increased intensity of incident light. A photo resistor can be applied in light-sensitive detector circuits.

High resistance semiconductors are used to make photo resistors. At low levels of illumination, however, a photo-resistor can perform with a few hundred ohms as opposed to a few megohms in the dark. The semiconductor gives electrons bound to the semiconductor the energy necessary to jump into the conduction band when they are exposed to light above a certain frequency. The free electrons create resistance by conducting electricity (along with their partners). Photo resistors can have a wide resistance range as well as considerably different sensitivities between dissimilar devices. In addition, photo resistors following certain wavelength bands will react very differently.

Schematic:

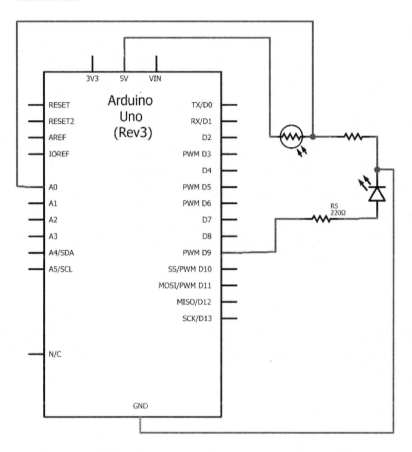

In order to make this circuit work, we installed a photo resistor in analog pin 0 (any analog pin would work) and an auxiliary 5V supply on the right side of the breadboard. An unsealed 1K ohm resistor is used as a grounding element. An LED (of any color) was attached to pin 13 of the breadboard (a digital pin would also work) and it was powered by a 220-ohm resistor (one hundred ohms would also work). Next, there is a wired LED of a different color connected to a different digital pin, just as the first LED was.

Procedure:

Step 1: Build the circuit

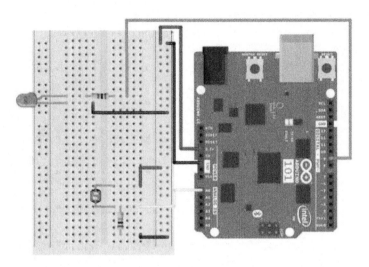

Step 2: Program

```
/*****************************************************
Project 8 Seeing the light using photo resistor with an Arduino
*****************************************************/
const int sensorPin = 0;
const int ledPin = 9;
int lightCal;
int lightVal;
void setup() {
pinMode(ledPin, OUTPUT);
lightCal = analogRead(sensorPin);
}
void loop() {
lightVal = analogRead(sensorPin);
if (lightVal < lightCal - 50) {
digitalWrite(9, HIGH);
} else {
digitalWrite(9, LOW);
}
}
```

Step 3: Compile the program and upload to Arduino UNO board.

Project 9: Arduino Flame Sensor

Overview:

We will be studying a flame sensor built with an Arduino board in this project.

Components:

- 1 x Arduino UNO
- 1 x USB Cable
- 1 x Flame Sensor
- 1 x Breadboard
- Jumper wire

Principle:

The flame detector module on the KY-026 is interacting with a lighter or a candle through its digital and analog interfaces. When the fire sensor detects fire, a HIGH signal is sent to the Arduino (pin A0), lighting up the LED. The detection threshold may be increased by turning the potentiometer clockwise, or decreased by turning it counterclockwise.

Industrial buildings and commercial buildings are very commonly equipped with fire alarm systems. Sensors are usually contained in these devices, and they continuously monitor for flames, gas, and fires in the building and trigger an alarm if they are detected. IR flame sensors contain an IR photodiode which is sensitive to IR light and is therefore one of the simplest ways of detecting fire. In a fire, fire does not only produce heat and light, but also emits infrared rays, yes, every burning flame emits some degree of infrared light. Flame sensors detect this light, which cannot be seen by human eyes, and inform microcontrollers such as Arduino that a fire has been detected.

A photodiode detects light, and an op-amp determines the sensitivity of the flame sensor. It detects fire and sends a HIGH signal as soon as it is detected. The Arduino reacts to the signals and activates the LED and buzzer to provide alert.

Schematic:

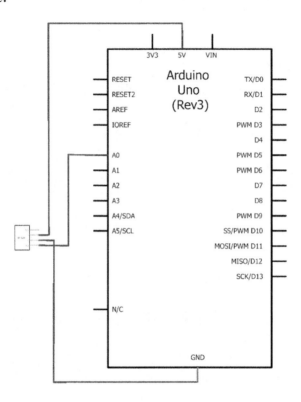

Procedure:

Step 1: Build the circuit

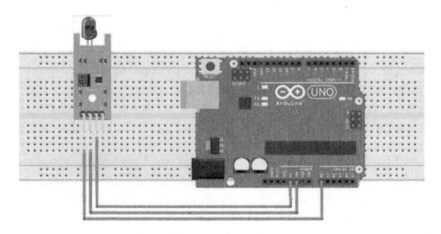

Step 2: Program

```
/*********************************************************
Project 9 Arduino Flame Sensor.ino Description:
Let, fire is detected by the sensor turning on the LED
*********************************************************/
const int sensorMin = 0; // sensor minimum
const int sensorMax = 1024; // sensor maximum
void setup() {
Serial.begin(9600);
}
void loop() {
int sensorReading = analogRead(A0);
int range = map(sensorReading, sensorMin, sensorMax, 0, 3);
switch (range) {
case 0: // A fire closer than 1.5 feet away.
Serial.println("** Close Fire **");
break;
case 1: // A fire between 1-3 feet away.
Serial.println("** Distant Fire **");
break;
case 2: // No fire detected.
Serial.println("No Fire");
break;
}
delay(1); // delay between reads
}
```

Step 3: Compile the program and upload to Arduino UNO board.

Applications of flame sensors

- Detecting fire in Hydrogen stations
- Monitors for burner combustion
- Petroleum and natural gas pipelines
- Production facilities for the automotive industry
- Facilities related to nuclear energy
- Keeping aircraft in hangars
- Enclosures for turbines

Project 10: LED Matrix display 8 x 8 dots (MAX7219)

Overview:

Here we will learn about Arduino Microcontroller connections with 8x8 LED matrix displays (MAX7219).

Components:

- 1 x Arduino UNO
- 1 x USB Cable
- 1 x Dot Matrix (MAX7219)
- 1 x Breadboard
- Jumper wires

Principle:

Essentially a programmable LED display at a lower cost than conventional LCD displays, these MAX7219/MAX7221 displays can be driven by either a microcontroller or a microprocessor. The MAX7219 microprocessor is equipped with a code-B decoder included in the circuit, MPC scan circuitry, 88-bit static RAM, a segment and digit driver, and a segment decoder (used for identifying letters and numbers). All segment currents of LEDs can be set with only one external resistor. A number of interfaces are supported, including SPI, QSPI, and MICROWIRE, and the MAX7221 has slew-rate-limited section drivers to minimize EMI. It is possible to address and update specific numbers in the connected LED display without addressing and altering the whole display. Attempting to encode each digit in the MAX7219/MAX7221 can be achieved through code-B decoding the digits or by leaving they unencoded.

Applications:

MAX7219 utilized in Bar-Graph Displays, 7-Segment Displays, Industrial Controllers, Electronic Panel Meters, LED Matrix Displays, PIXEL gaming, Character design, measuring instruments, Hobby projects, Display of symbols, simple graphics and texts.

Features:

- A Breadboard can be easily installed
- The LED lights are bright
- Designed compactly.
- The LED is 3mm in diameter

Schematic:

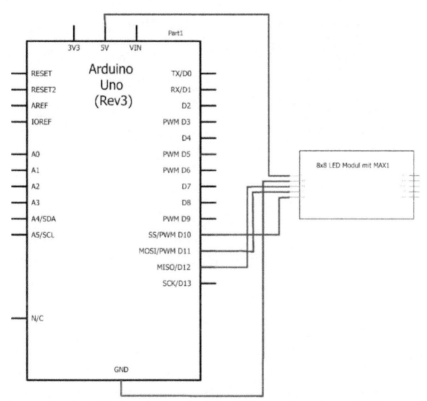

Two methods can be used to control the LED matrix. It is possible to send parallel (parallel data for each row or column) or serial (serial data is sent in serial format and a conversion IC is used to turn it into parallel data). MAX 7219 Driver supports serial and parallel outputs on common cathode displays. Microprocessors and microcontrollers can be interfaced with 64 LEDs (8 x 8 LED matrix has 64 LEDs, for example), seven segment displays up to 8 digits, or bar graph displays.

Procedure:

Step 1: Build the circuit

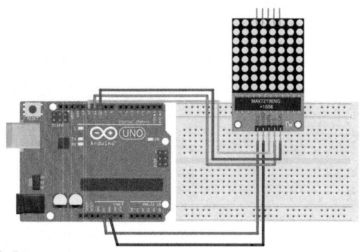

Step 2: Program

```
/***********************************************************
File Name: 10- LED Matrix display 8 x 8 dots (MAX7219).ino
Description:
Let, LED Matrix Displays 8×8 dots (MAX7219) Interface with Arduino.
***************************************************/
#include <LedControl.h>
int DIN = 12;
int CS = 11;
int CLK = 10;
byte e[8]= {0x7C,0x7C,0x60,0x7C,0x7C,0x60,0x7C,0x7C};
byte d[8]= {0x78,0x7C,0x66,0x66,0x66,0x66,0x7C,0x78};
byte u[8]= {0x66,0x66,0x66,0x66,0x66,0x66,0x7E,0x7E};
byte c[8]= {0x7E,0x7E,0x60,0x60,0x60,0x60,0x7E,0x7E};
byte eight[8]= {0x7E,0x7E,0x66,0x7E,0x7E,0x66,0x7E,0x7E};
byte s[8]= {0x7E,0x7C,0x60,0x7C,0x3E,0x06,0x3E,0x7E};
byte dot[8]= {0x00,0x00,0x00,0x00,0x00,0x00,0x18,0x18};
byte o[8]= {0x7E,0x7E,0x66,0x66,0x66,0x66,0x7E,0x7E};
byte m[8]= {0xE7,0xFF,0xFF,0xDB,0xDB,0xDB,0xC3,0xC3};
LedControl lc=LedControl(DIN,CLK,CS,0);
void setup() {
lc.shutdown(0,false); //The MAX72XX is in power-saving mode on
startup
```

```
lc.setIntensity(0,15); // Set the brightness to maximum value
lc.clearDisplay(0); // and clear the display
}
void loop() {
byte smile[8]= {0x3C,0x42,0xA5,0x81,0xA5,0x99,0x42,0x3C};
byte neutral[8]= {0x3C,0x42,0xA5,0x81,0xBD,0x81,0x42,0x3C};
byte frown[8]= {0x3C,0x42,0xA5,0x81,0x99,0xA5,0x42,0x3C};
printByte(smile);
delay(1000);
printByte(neutral);
delay(1000);
printByte(frown);
delay(1000);
printEduc8s();
lc.clearDisplay(0);
delay(1000);
}
void printEduc8s() {
printByte(e);
delay(1000);
printByte(d);
delay(1000);
printByte(u);
delay(1000);
printByte(c);
delay(1000);
printByte(eight);
delay(1000);
printByte(s);
delay(1000);
printByte(dot);
delay(1000);
printByte(c);
delay(1000);
printByte(o);
delay(1000);
printByte(m);
delay(1000);
}
void printByte(byte character []) {
int i = 0;
for(i=0;i<8;i++)
```

```
{
lc.setRow(0,i,character[i]);
}
}
```

Step 3: Compile the program and upload to Arduino UNO board.

Internal structure of an 8*8 LED matrix

First, you must understand a simple LED to understand the LED matrix. LEDs are powered by DC power with two pins that give out a light. There are 8 numbers of rows and 8 numbers of columns in the matrix. Since LED positive pins share common ground with those of adjacent LEDs in rows, and LED negative pins share common ground with those of adjacent LEDs in columns. One LED will be turned on when the power is turned on and single rows and columns are selected. A row 3 or column 3 led will come on if current is applied to those two rows or columns.

The 8x8 LED matrix has the following features

- LED matrix can be operated from any device with LOW voltage.
- Drawing text or images on the matrix is possible.
- Only 1.5-2V are required to drive the matrix in the forward bias.
- There is no special requirement for the LED matrix since it can be designed with simple LEDs.
- It may be difficult for some developers to understand the programming. So, there is a driver that helps simplify the programming process as well.
- It is possible to perform various patterns on the matrix, such as scrolling and blinking.

Applications for LED matrix

- Text signs are the most common application for LED matrix.
- It is used most often by developers to create snake games.
- In addition to the matrix clock, there are companies that use it
- A matrix can also be found on most watches to make it look even more attractive and unique.

Project 11: Interfacing with LCD 1602 Display

Overview:

This lesson shows you how to use an LCD1602 character display system on the Arduino environment. Let's display "Hello World!" on the LCD1602 first.

Components

- 1 x Arduino UNO
- 1 x USB Cable
- 1 x potentiometer
- 1 x LCD (16 x 2) Display
- 1 x Breadboard
- Jumper Wires

Principle

Displays like LCD1602 show characters. Microcontrollers have a parallel interface, which means that they have to manipulate several interface pins simultaneously to control the display. Three pins are present on the interface: pins:

There is a register select RS pin on the LCD that governs where in the ram you need to write data. The LCD's controller may look for instructions in either the data register or an instruction register - what goes on the screen has to be in the data register.

Read/Write pins are used to switch between reading mode and writing mode. Write access to the register is enabled by an Enable pin. This card contains 8 data pins (D0-D7). When the pins are high or low, the data that is being written to a register (or read), is represented by bits.

Additionally, there are three display pins (Vo, Bklt+ and Bklt-) as well as power supply and LED backlight pins to power the LCD and control the display contrast, respectively.

Display control involves putting data read from the data registers into the display's instruction register, and then writing commands into the information registers.

168

So that you don't have to know these low-level instructions, the Liquid Crystal Library simplifies these tasks for you. Two modes of control are available for the Hitachi LCDs: 4-bit and 8-bit. For text displays on the screen, you can do most anything in 4-bit mode. The 8-bit mode requires 11 I/O pins. Potentiometers have two contacts and at least three terminals each, making it possible to adjust the voltage divider. If only one terminal and the wiper are used, the resistor behaves like a variable resistor.

Schematic:

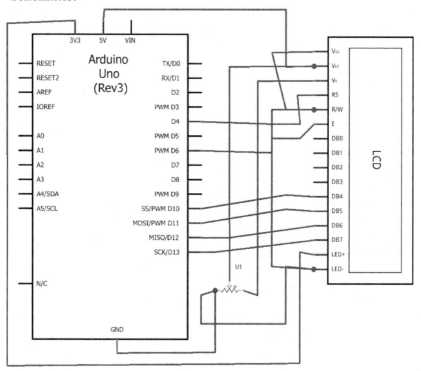

Connection to 16x2 Character LCD with Arduino Uno

Now that we've got the LCD hooked up to the Arduino, let's get started uploading code and sending data.

We'll show you how to wire up the LCD's 16 pins (total total of 16 pins). It is good to know that we do not need to connect all of these pins to the Arduino.

We know that the display contains 8 data lines carrying raw data. HD44780 LCDs are designed such that 4 data pins (4-bit mode) can be used to communicate with them instead of 8 data pins (8-bit mode). We will save four pins this way!

Therefore, we will be interacting with the LCD using 4-bit mode and only need six pins to interface with it: **RS, EN, D7, D6, D5**, and **D4.**

The LCD Display now needs to be connected to the Arduino. The LCD will be connected to Arduino's digital pins #4-7 via four data pins (D4-D7). A pin on the LCD will be connected to Enable on Arduino #2 and a pin on the LCD will be connected to RS on Arduino #1.

You can see how everything is wired in the following diagram.

Once that's done, all you need to do is upload some code and the display will start printing.

Procedure:

Step 1: Build the circuit as below

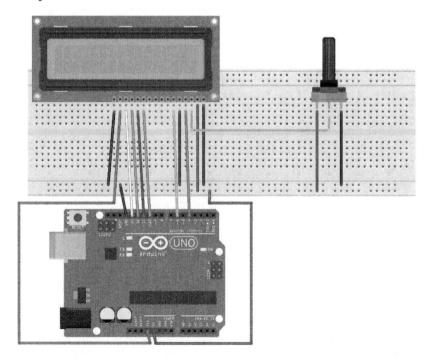

Step 2: Program: Open /Copy the code from the "CODE" Folder

```
/*****************************************************
File name: 11 Interfacing with LCD 1602 Display.ino Description:
Let, LCD display print HELLO WORLD.
*****************************************************/
#include <LiquidCrystal.h>
// initialize the library with the numbers of the interface pins
LiquidCrystal lcd(13, 12, 11, 10, 6, 4);
void setup() {
// set up the LCD's number of columns and rows:
lcd.begin(16, 2);
// Print a message to the LCD.
lcd.print("hello, world!");
}
void loop() {
// set the cursor to column 0, line 1
// (note: line 1 is the second row, since counting begins with 0):
lcd.setCursor(0, 1);
// print the number of seconds since reset:
lcd.print(millis()/1000);
}
```

Step 3: Compile the program and upload to Arduino UNO board.

The LCD16x2 has the following features

- The LCD is mainly equipped with the following features.
- Its operating voltage ranges from 4.7V to 5.3V
- You can create 16 characters from each row in two rows.
- There is no backlight and the consumption of current is 1mA
- A 5 by 8-pixel box can be used to create any character
- Alphabets and numbers are displayed on the alphanumeric LCDs
- There are two modes for the display: 8-bit and 4-bit

You can choose between a blue or green backlight, several characters are generated specifically for it

Project 12: HC-SR04 Ultrasonic Distance Sensor with Arduino

Overview:

This lesson explains the use of an ultrasonic distance sensor to measure distance.

Component:

- 1 x Arduino UNO
- 1 x USB Cable
- 1 x Ultrasonic sensor
- 1 x Breadboard
- Jumper wire

Principle:

It has the same functions as the GP2D12 module except it uses sound instead of light. When an object passes in front of the sensor the HC-SR04 sends a ping and measures the period between transmitting a signal and receiving a response.

Our measurement techniques use sound to reach a maximum distance of 4 meters. There is a connector with four pins on the module, larger than 45x20x15mm. The module should be powered with five volts by two pins. 15 mA is the working current. Several pins serve different functions. The first one is for triggering the measurements while the last one reads the result of that measurement, the echo pin. HC-SR04's measurement angle is 15 degrees. There should be about one meter of beam at 4 meters distance. Using 1m as the measuring point, this is 26cm, so remember this when utilizing this information.

You must set the trigger pin to the high state for 10 seconds in order to create an ultrasound. It is at the speed of sound that these pulses will travel to the Echo Pin and be received there. Using this tool, you can display the time in microseconds in which the sound wave traveled. In the case of an object 20 cm from the sensor and sound speed of 340 m/s, the sound wave will travel approximately 588 microseconds. Due to the fact that a sound wave travels forward and then bounces back, you will get twice the amount of echo from an Echo pin.

As a result, the distance measured in cm is calculated by multiplying the received travel time value by 0.034 and dividing it by 2 and converting it to centimetres.

Schematic:

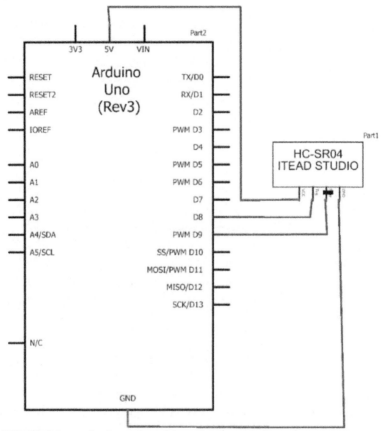

The HC-SR04 can be interfaced in a 3-wire mode

Three-wire mode requires only one connection to a single digital I/O pin on the Arduino instead of two. The exceptional parallax ping))) sensor is one of the many ultrasonic sensors that only work in 3-Wire Mode.

One I/O pin is used in both input and output modes in 3-Wire mode. Due to the fact that inputs and outputs are never used simultaneously, this is possible. Then we can use the Arduino connection for something else by eliminating one of the I/O pin requirements. This feature is also useful when dealing with chips such as the ATtiny85 which have limited I/O pins.

This is how you can connect the HC-SR04 sensor to the Arduino using 3-Wire mode.

Clearly, you simply need to connect pin 9 of the Arduino to both the trigger and echo. There is only one difference you need to make in the sketch: you must define both the Trigger and Echo pin values on pin 9. Everything else in the sketch is the same.

Procedure:

Step 1: Build the circuit

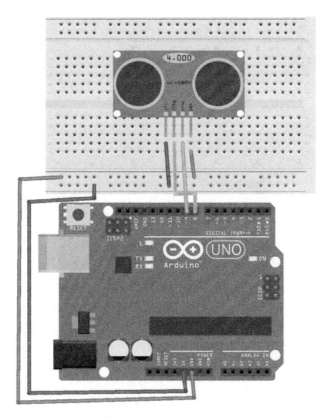

Step 2: Program

```
/***********************************************************
File name: 12 – HC-SR04 Project .ino Description:
```

```
Let, Distance measure with ultrasonic
sensor.***********************/
#include <HCSR04.h>
const int TriggerPin = 8; //Trig pin
const int EchoPin = 9; //Echo pin
long Duration = 0;
void setup() {
pinMode(TriggerPin,OUTPUT); // Trigger is an output pin
pinMode(EchoPin,INPUT); // Echo is an input pin
Serial.begin(9600); // Serial Output
}
void loop() {
digitalWrite(TriggerPin, LOW);
delayMicroseconds(2);
digitalWrite(TriggerPin, HIGH); // Trigger pin to HIGH
delayMicroseconds(10); // 10us high
digitalWrite(TriggerPin, LOW); // Trigger pin to HIGH
Duration = pulseIn(EchoPin,HIGH); // Waits for the echo pin to get high
long Distance_mm = Distance(Duration); // Use function to calculate the
distance
Serial.print("Distance = "); // Output to serial
Serial.print(Distance_mm);
Serial.println(" mm");
delay(1000); // Wait to do next measurement
}
long Distance(long time)
{
long DistanceCalc; // Calculation variable
DistanceCalc = ((time /2.9) / 2); // Actual calculation in mm
//DistanceCalc = time / 74 / 2; // Actual calculation in inches
return DistanceCalc; // return calculated value
}
```

Step 3: Compile the program and upload to Arduino UNO board.

Project 13: Touch Sensor Arduino Interface

Overview:

Here we made a touch sensor based on Arduino using a coin.

Components:

- 1 x Arduino UNO
- 1 x USB Cable
- 1 x Touch Sensor
- 1 x Breadboard
- Jumper Wires

Principle

This device connects to your body through its own electrodes. Capacitances of the circuit are changed when you touch the sensing pad. The output changes states as a result of the capacitance change.

The first time I got this device, I thought it would frequently produce unexpected results despite being functional.

It's possible I was wrong. The game seems to do whatever I expect it to do after playing for a few hours. The following might do the trick if you are looking for strong client input.

How to interface a touch sensor with an Arduino:

Our next step will be to interface the touch sensor with the Arduino. An Arduino board will be required to control the onboard LED via a touch sensor. In addition, three jumper wires are needed male to female. A breadboard and three male-to-male jumper wires can also be used if you do not have these jumper wires.

First you need to connect the jumper wires to the touch sensor PCB of the touch sensor to begin. In fact, the touch sensor is a resistor. If you press on the PCB, it will increase its resistance. The PCB detects this and sends a HIGH signal to the Arduino when you touch the sensor. Our touch sensor can now be plugged into the Arduino. Connecting red and black wires to 5V, ground and pin 8, green wires to digital pin 8 constitutes the five-volt supply. Now that our circuit is complete, we can move forward.

Schematic:

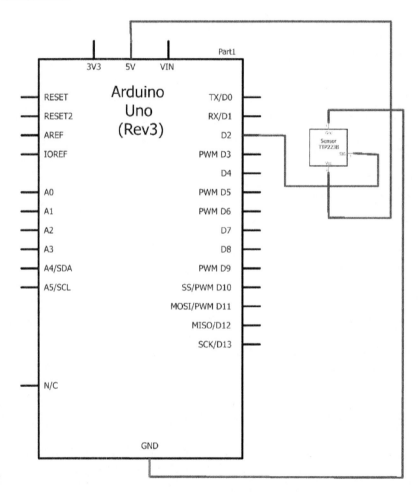

Procedure:

Step 1: Build the circuit

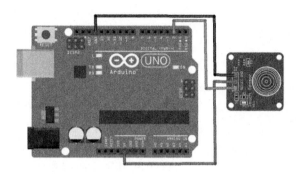

Step 2: Program: Open /Copy the code from the "CODE" Folder

```
/*******************************************************
Project 13: Touch Sensor Arduino Interface .ino
Description: Let, Touch sensor using.
*******************************************************/
#define sensorPin 2 // capactitive touch sensor - Arduino Digital pin D2
int ledPin = 13; // Output display LED (on board LED) - Arduino Digital
pin D13
void setup() {
Serial.begin(9600);
pinMode(ledPin, OUTPUT);
pinMode(sensorPin, INPUT);
}
void loop() {
int senseValue = digitalRead(sensorPin);
if (senseValue == HIGH){
digitalWrite(ledPin, HIGH);
Serial.println("TOUCHED");
}
else{
digitalWrite(ledPin,LOW);
Serial.println("not touched");
}
delay(500);
}
```

Step 3: Compile the program and upload to Arduino UNO board.

Project 14: Relay Module interface with an Arduino

Overview:

We will take a look at relay modules using this lesson.

Components

- 1 x Arduino UNO
- 1 x USB Cable
- 1 x Breadboard
- 1 x Relay Module
- Jumper wire

Principle

Relays are electrically operated switches. Other operating principles are also used in solid-state relays, as well as electromagnets used in many relays. Controlling a circuit with a relay is best suited where a low-power signal is needed (with complete electrical isolation between one circuit and its control, and one signal must control various circuits).

A relay was the first device used in wide-area telegraphy circuits as an amplifier. This signal was repeated on another circuit after it came from one circuit. Early computers performed logical operations with relays widely used in telephone exchanges.

Often referred to as a contractor, these relays are capable of handling high-powered loads such as electric motors. Instead of using moving parts, semiconductors are used to switch power circuits on solid-state relays. Electrical circuits are shielded from overload or defects by utilizing relays with calibrated operating characteristics and sometimes multiple coils. Digital instruments known as protective relays perform these functions in modern electric power systems.

LEDs will be powered by a 3v battery. To connect the positive and negative sides of the battery, we have connected the positive side to the com of each relay, and the negative side to the NO of each led. By giving a voltage range of 5 to 24V DC, you can also power the four relay modules externally.

Schematic

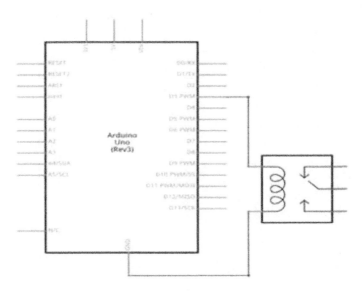

Procedure:

Step 1: Build the circuit

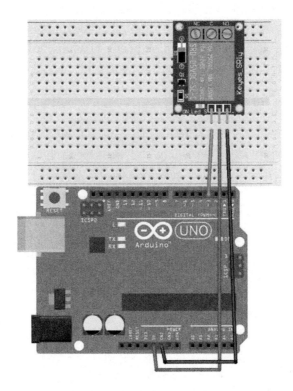

Step 2: Program

```
/*****************************************************
Project 14: Relay Module with Arduino
*****************************************************/
int relayPin = 3;
void setup() {
pinMode(relayPin, OUTPUT);
}
void loop() {
digitalWrite(relayPin, LOW); // turn the relay on (Active LOW operation)
delay(2000); // wait for a second
digitalWrite(relayPin, HIGH); // turn the relay off by making the voltage
HIGH
delay(2000); // wait for a second
}
```

Step 3: Compile the program and upload to Arduino UNO board.

Relays are used primarily in places where only low-power signals are suitable for controlling circuits. With the advent of computers, they were also used for Boolean operations and other logic operations. In order to drive electric motors and other high power relay applications, high power is required. Relays of this type are known as contactors.

Applications for relays

- Logical functions are accomplished by relay circuits. The logic they provide is extremely important for safety.
- As a time-delay function, relays are utilized. Their purpose is to time the delay open and delay close of contacts.
- The use of relays for controlling high voltage circuits is based on signals delivered at low voltages. Similar to this, they are used in high current circuits by using signals with low current.
- They can be used as protective relays as well. This function allows all faults to be detected and isolated during transmissions and receptions.
-

Project 15: Control Servo Motor with Arduino

Overview:

There is only one way to rotate a servo motor, which is in turn a type of geared motor. The Arduino UNO R3 board sends electric pulses to control it. The servo is instructed to move to that position by these pulses. The three conductors of the servo include the brown wire which is GND, the red one which is VCC and the orange cable which is the signal wire.

About Servo Motor

- There is a servo motor, which operates at angles between 0 and 180 degrees.
- Microcontrollers control servo motors, which are only powered from a microprocessor like the following: The Arduino/Genuino, The Raspberry Pi, Micro:Bit
- It has a DC motor that only consumes 35 milliamps. A potentiometer allows it to determine which angle it is in as well as some gears.

Electrical pulses are sent through the control wires of servos in the form of pulse width modulations (PWMs). Minimum pulse, maximum pulse, and repetition rate are all specified. In general, servo motors have a maximum turning circle of 180° in either direction. Neutral position refers to the servo having equal rotational potential clockwise or counterclockwise. As the motor receives a pulse via the control wire, it determines the position of the shaft, and the rotor turns to that position based on the duration of the pulse, a servo motor turns according to the length of the pulse it receives every 20 milliseconds (ms).

The motor will turn to the 90° position with a 1.5ms pulse. If the servo is moved faster than 1.5ms, it moves in the counterclockwise direction toward 0o, and if the servo is moved faster than 1.5ms, it turns in the clockwise direction toward 180o.

COMPONENTS:

- 1 x Arduino UNO
- 1 x USB Cable
- 1 x Servo Motor
- 1 x Breadboard
- 2 x Jumper Wires

Schematic

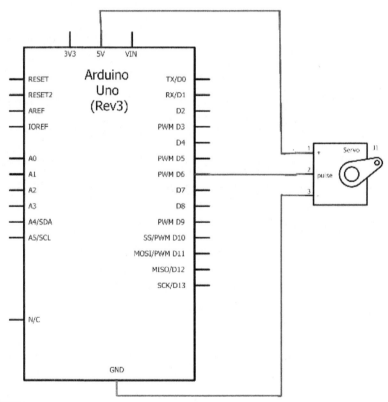

Procedure:

Step 1: Build the circuit

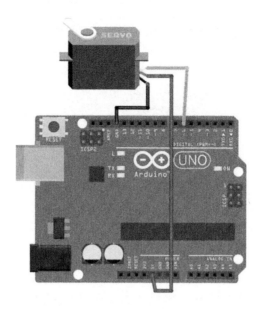

Step 2: Program: Open /Copy the code from the "CODE" Folder

```
/********************************************************
File name: 15 Control Servo Motor .ino Description:
Let, servo motor rotate
*********************************************************/
# include <Servo.h>
Servo myservo;
int pos = 0;
void setup() {
myservo.attach(6);
}
void loop() {
for (pos = 0; pos <= 180; pos += 5) {
myservo.write(pos);
delay(15);
}
for (pos = 180; pos >= 0; pos -= 5) {
myservo.write(pos);
delay(15);
}
}
```

Step 3: Compile the program and upload to Arduino UNO board.

Project 16: Stepper Motor Control with Arduino

Overview:

In this lesson we will learn how to control a stepper motor, a stepper motor is controlled by a stepper motor's rotational speed through an analog input, analog input 0. Various control pins are available for unipolar or bipolar motors including pins 2, 3, 4, and 5.

Components:

- 1 x Arduino UNO
- 1 x USB Cable
- 1 x Stepper Motor
- 1 x Motor Driver Module
- 1 x Battery
- Jumper wires

Principle

Motors that are operated by a stepper controller require the use of a driver module. In our case, the motor will not be able to run since the controller module (Arduino) is not capable of providing enough current through its I/O pins. A module such as ULN2003 will be utilized.

There are many different types of driver modules that are used as stepper motors. The rating of each driver module depends on the type of motor used.

Here is a circuit diagram showing how an Arduino stepper motor controller is implemented. In our setup, we used a Stepper motor 28BYJ-48 as well as the ULN2003 Driver module. A digital pin 8,9,10 and 11 is used to engage the four coils on the stepper motor. Powered by the Arduino's 5V pin, the driver module powers the Arduino Board.

When you connect the steppe motor to a load with an external power supply, the driver should be powered. The +5V rail of the Arduino Board was used because it is just being used as a demonstration. Keep in mind that you should always link the ground of the Arduino to the ground of the Diver module.

Pin definition

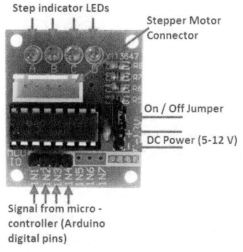

Connecting 28BYJ-48 Stepper Motor and ULN2003 Driver to Arduino

> The motor is now ready to be hooked up to our Arduino! We can begin connecting it to our Arduino now!
> The ULN2003 driver needs to be connected to the power supply.
> A stepper motor can be powered directly from the Arduino. As the motor might induce electrical noise onto the Arduino's power supply lines, this is not recommended since it could cause damage to the board.
> You should therefore use a separate 5V power source for your

stepper motor.

> Lastly, connect the ground of the power supply to the ground of the Arduino. It is very important to establish a voltage reference that is the same between the two.

> Assemble the driver board by connecting pins IN1, IN2, IN3, and IN4 to the Arduino digital pins 8, 9, and 10.

> The motor cable from the stepper motor should then be connected to the driver board.

> Upon completion, the illustration below should look like what you have done.

Procedure:

Step 1: Build the circuit

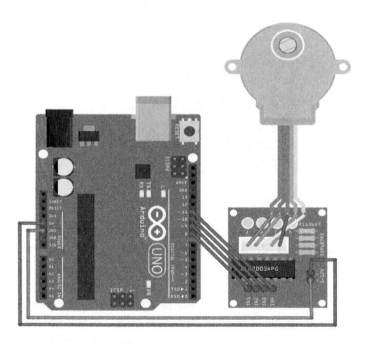

Step 2: Program: Open /Copy the code from the "CODE" Folder

```
/*********************************************************
File name: 16 stepper Motor Control .ino Description:
Let, Control stepper motor.
*********************************************************/
```

```
#include <Stepper.h>
#define STEPS 64
Stepper stepper(STEPS, 8, 9, 10, 11);
int previous = 0;
void setup() {
stepper.setSpeed(30);
}
void loop() {
int val = analogRead(0);
stepper.step(val - previous);
previous = val;
}
```

Step 3: The motor will rotate clockwise once the program is uploaded to the Arduino UNO board. Motor speed is increased by increasing the potentiometer value. You may notice the motor, which is subject to a time delay, is insensitive to changes in the sensor value when it is running at low speeds since setSpeed() extends the length of the delay between steps.

The applications of stepper motors

- Used in 3D printing equipment, Textile machines.
- Various printing presses are used, utilized in the gaming machines.
- Machines used in medical imaging, and a small robotics system.
- Machines for CNC milling, Typically, welding equipment is used.

There are some benefits associated with stepper motors.

- A motion sensor is not required for stepper motors because of their internal structure. A motor's position can be determined by simply counting the steps it takes to move.
- As well, stepper motors are pretty easy to control. Although the motor requires a driver, it does not require complex calculations or tuning. Most motors require less control effort than others. It is possible to achieve high position precision with micro stepping, up to approximately 0.007 degrees.
- A stepping motor offers good torque, holds positions well, and has a long lifespan.

Project 17: Interfacing Soil Moisture Sensor with an Arduino

Overview:

We will be studying soil moisture sensors in this project which have been specially developed to identify how much moisture or water a soil includes.

Components:

- 1 x Arduino UNO
- 1 x USB Cable
- 1 x Soil Moisture Sensor
- Jumper Wires

Principle

Soil Moisture sensors are utilized to precisely measure how much moisture the soil includes. Dielectric constants are measured using capacitance in soil. As the soil transmits electricity, the dielectric constant can be thought of as the ability to conduct electricity.

Increased water content of the soil increases the soil's water content. Because of its higher dielectric constant than any other portion of soil, water is used to measure moisture in soil sensors. The sensor detects the moisture content in the soil by generating a voltage proportional to its dielectric permittivity, which consequently determines how much water is available.

The most important thing for us to take care of plants and turf is to take care of them regularly when we have a home garden or a backyard with turf. Watering your lawn and plants with sprinklers is one of the more popular options, but for the best results, go for manual watering.

You must consider the amount of soil moisture when designing an Automatic Plant Watering System, in which the water supply is either sprinklers or drip irrigations.

A Microcontroller and a Water Pump can be used to precisely control the amount of water supplied to the garden by measuring the soil moisture. By integrating Soil Moisture with Arduino, I will demonstrate how to monitor the soil moisture of a small pot.

Schematic:

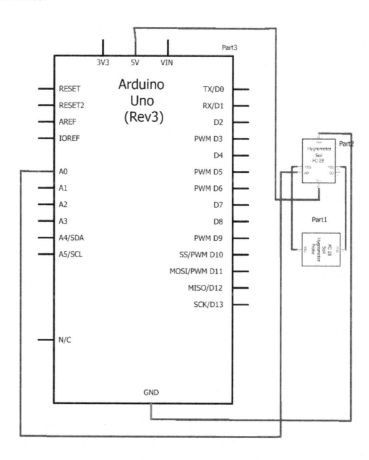

Procedure:

Step 1: Build the circuit

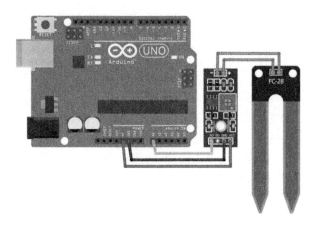

Step 2: Program: Open /Copy the code from the "CODE"

```
/********************************************************
Project: 17. Soil Moisture Sensor .ino Description:
Let, Detect the amount of moisture or water soil contains.
********************************************************/
const int hygrometer = A0;   // Soil moisture sensor analog pin output at
pin A0 of Arduino
int value;
void setup() {
Serial.begin(9600);
}
void loop() {
value = analogRead(hygrometer);      // Read analog value
value = constrain(value,400,1023);   // Keep the ranges!
value = map(value,400,1023,100,0);    // Map value : 400 will be 100
and 1023 will be 0
Serial.print("Soil humidity: ");
Serial.print(value);
Serial.println("%");
delay(1000); // Read every 1 sec
}
```

Step 3: Compile the program and upload to Arduino UNO board.

Project 18: Water Level Monitoring Experiments

Overview

The water level is being measured, and it is easily achieved since only the analog port value (A0) needs to be read, then it is converted to a percentage.

Specification

- Operating voltage: DC3-5V
- Operating current: less than 20mA
- Sensor Type: Analog
- Production process: FR4 double-sided HASL Humidity: 10% - 90% non-condensing
- Detection Area: 40mmx16mm

Circuit Diagram

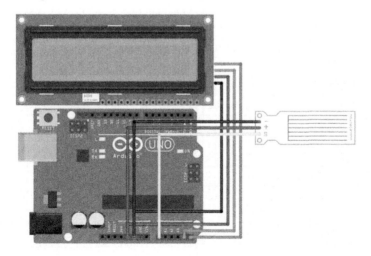

Hardware Required

Material diagram	Material name	Number
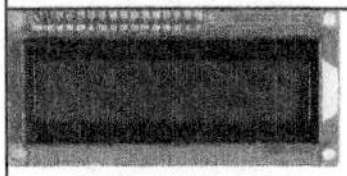	LCD1602	1
	Water Lever Sensor	1
	220/330Ω resistor	1
	10KΩ Potentiometer	1
	USB Cable	1
	UNO R3	1
	Breadboard	1
	Jumper wires	Several

PIN Configuration

UNO R3		Water sensor
GND	->	-
5V	->	+
A0	->	S

UNO R3		LCD1602_IIC
GND	->	GND
+5V	->	VCC
SDA	->	A4
SCL	->	A5

Program

```
// include the library code:
#include <LiquidCrystal.h>
//initialise the library with the numbers of the interface pins
LiquidCrystal lcd(12, 11, 5, 4, 3, 2);

int resval = 0; // holds the value
int respin = A5; // sensor pin used

void setup() {

  // set up the LCD's number of columns and rows:
  lcd.begin(16, 2);

  // Print a message to the LCD.
  lcd.print("WATER LEVEL: ");
}

void loop() {
  // set the cursor to column 0, line 1
  lcd.setCursor(0, 1);

  resval = analogRead(respin); //Read data from analog pin and store it
to resval variable

  if (resval<=100){ lcd.println("Empty "); } else if (resval>100 &&
resval<=300){ lcd.println("Low "); } else if (resval>300 && resval<=330){
lcd.println("Medium "); } else if (resval>330){
    lcd.println("High          ");
  }
  delay(1000);
}
```

Compile and Upload

The LiquidCrystal_I2C library file must be added to Arduino's library list,
otherwise the compiler may not pass. See Chapter 2 for information on
'adding library files. If the LCD doesn't display or if the brightness isn't
enough, you can alter the potentiometer.

Project 19: Vibration Sensor Module

Overview:

Here we will use an Arduino board with an LCD and a vibration sensor.

Components:

- 1 x Arduino UNO
- 1 x USB Cable
- 1 x Vibration Sensor Module
- 1 x LED
- 1 x BreadBoard
- Jumper Wires

Principle

Trouble might be coming if there are vibrations. There's nothing more dangerous than a machine gone haywire or a gear missing a tooth on a robot, or even worse, a looming earthquake! We will see how to use specially designed sensors to sense vibrations and an Arduino microcontroller for the purpose in this vibration sensor tutorial. SW-420 and an 801S vibration sensor are widely available on the market.

Arduino UNO requires only the input pin to be monitored in order to use a vibration sensor, so programming it isn't too difficult. In the beginning, only the headers are included. Because this tutorial was created using Eclipse IDE and its Arduino extension, the Arduino header file is included. When this sketch is used with Arduino IDE, no need for the Arduino IDE header file, since this sketch works with Arduino IDE as well.

There is no need for an additional breadboard for this circuit. A test can be done using the Arduino UNO Board. This led is monitored when the vibratory sensor is hit or when its state changes. A led connected to Pin 13 on Arduino UNO will blink when there is some vibration. The vibration sensor will not work if the power is disconnected or if the connection is poor. Connect the microcontroller and sensor without causing any loose connections.

Schematic:

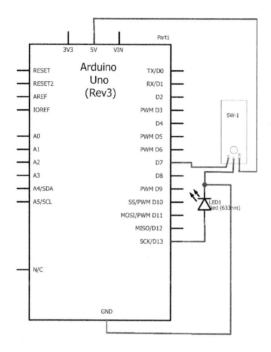

Procedure:

Step 1: Build the circuit

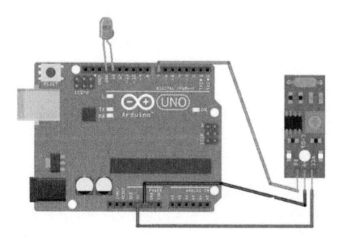

Step 2: Program: Open /Copy the code from the "CODE" Folder

```
/*********************************************************
File name: 18 - Vibration Sensor Module .ino Description:
Let, Vibration Sensor.
*********************************************************/
int vib_pin=7;
int led_pin=13;
void setup() {
pinMode(vib_pin,INPUT);
pinMode(led_pin,OUTPUT);
}
void loop() {
int val;
val=digitalRead(vib_pin);
if(val==1)
{
digitalWrite(led_pin,HIGH);
delay(1000);
digitalWrite(led_pin,LOW);
delay(1000);
}
else
digitalWrite(led_pin,LOW);
}
```

Step 3: Compile the program and upload to Arduino UNO board.

Applications of the SW-420 Vibration Sensor

- Geophysical earthquake detection
- The alarm system
- The Object Detection System
- Automobiles with artificial intelligence

Analyzing the circuit

Upload the code. The module can either be tapped or moved and evaluated by making some vibrations on the table. As long as it does not detect anything, it will keep blinking.

Project: 20: Infrared Sensor Receiver Module with an Arduino

Overview:

In this tutorial we are using Receiver modules KY-022.

Components:

- 1 x Arduino Uno
- 1 x USB Cable
- 1 x Infrared Receiver module
- 1 x Infrared remote control
- 1 x Breadboard
- Jumper wires

Principle:

Now we are going to introduce an infrared transmitter and receiver module, which, recently, has become increasingly common in daily life. Many household appliances include them, including air conditioners, televisions, DVDs, etc., It can be controlled by wireless remote control, and it uses wireless sensing for its functionality.

Let's see how we can use IR emission LEDs to make a TV remote by using this module.

Schematic:

- Arduino GND --> Module pin GND
- Arduino +5V --> Module PLUS (middle pin)
- Arduino Digital pin 11 --> Module S

A command will execute once the signal has been demodulated. Modules that receive IR signals are known as IR receivers. 3 and 8 KHz frequency are used for these modules. The Vout output is equal to VS (power supply) in the absence of any light at the sensor's working frequency. An infrared light with frequency 38 kHz will result in no output.

Procedure:

Step 1: Build the circuit

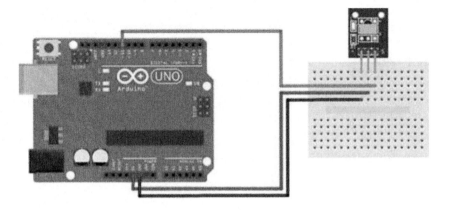

Step 2: Program: Open /Copy the code from the "CODE" Folder

```
/****************************************************
File name: 19 – Infrared sensor Receiver module KY-022
Let, Only Receiver modules.
****************************************************/
#include <IRremote.h>
int RECV_PIN = 11;
IRrecv irrecv(RECV_PIN);
decode_results results;
void setup() {
Serial.begin(9600);
irrecv.enableIRIn(); // Start the receiver
}
void loop() {
if (irrecv.decode(&results)) {
Serial.println(results.value, HEX);
irrecv.resume(); // Receive the next value
}
}
```

Step 3: Compile the program and upload to Arduino UNO board.

Project 21: IR Remote Control Experiment with Arduino

Overview

It is a study of the infrared transmission of data. Only the introduction of the use of methods involves the use of the infrared decoder, so the experiment utilizes the content of complex. There are lots of Arduino projects that utilize IR communication. Simple IR transmitter and receivers can be used to control robots, distance sensors, heart rate monitors, remote controls for DSLR cameras, and TV remote controls, among many other things.

Pin definition

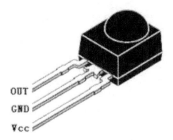 

The infrared remote can be used to control the Arduino easily. This particular remote control is available from many sources and is surprisingly affordable. There are many similarities between them, including how they look and operate.

A single Arduino is required for this project. The Arduino UNO that I used should work just about with any Arduino. Connect your infrared receiver to the kit's power supply. The wiring consists of three wires, PWR, GND, and SIG. Port 11 was used for SIG. Important! It has been reported that some readers have different wiring on their sensors. You should check it twice.

Hardware required

Material diagram	Material Name	Number
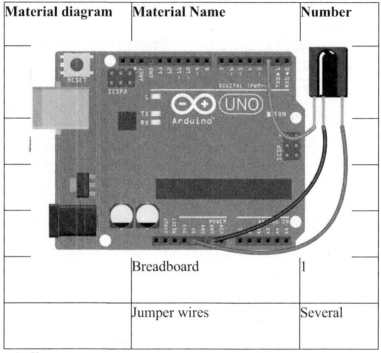		
	Breadboard	1
	Jumper wires	Several

Circuit diagram

UNO R3		IR Receiver
D2	->	OUT
GND	->	GND
+5V	->	VCC

Program

To find the key codes for your remote control, upload this code to your Arduino and open the serial monitor:

```
#include <IRremote.h>

const int RECV_PIN = 7;
IRrecv irrecv(RECV_PIN);
decode_results results;

void setup(){
  Serial.begin(9600);
  irrecv.enableIRIn();
  irrecv.blink13(true);
}

void loop(){
  if (irrecv.decode(&results)){
      Serial.println(results.value, HEX);
      irrecv.resume();
  }
}
```

Your computer must be connected to the USB port of the Arduino in order to upload the sketch. Open up the Serial Monitor, grab the remote, and start pressing the buttons. On the Serial Monitor, there should be some hex codes.

You can find the remote-control codes here. The FFFFFF command repeats, so if you keep pressing a button, a stream of them will appear. Now press each key on your remote and record the hexadecimal code printed for each key press.

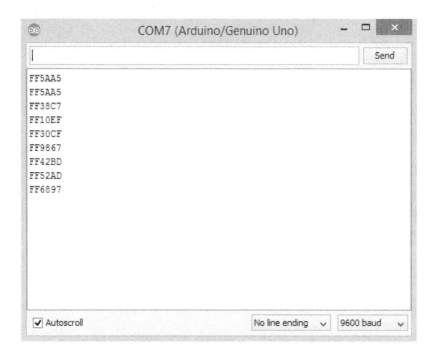

From the remote that came with my HX1838 IR receiver and remote set, using the program above I derived a table of keys and their corresponding codes. A 0XFFFFFFFF code will be displayed if you keep pressing the key continuously.

Hexadecimal code

Key	Code
CH-	0xFFA25D
CH	0xFF629D
CH+	0xFFE21D
<<	0xFF22DD

>>	0xFF02FD
>||	0xFFC23D
—	0xFFE01F
+	0xFFA857
EQ	0xFF906F
100+	0xFF9867
200+	0xFFB04F
0	0XFF6897
1	0xFF30CF
2	0xFF18E7
3	0xFF7A85
4	0xFF10EF
5	0xFF38C7
6	0xFF5AA5
7	0xFF42BD

8	0xFF4AB5
9	0xFF52AD

Compile and upload

Other than that, you need to contain the IR-remote library file directory to the Arduino library. Otherwise, it won't compile. Please see Chapter 2 for a description on adding library files.

Summary

There are several manufacturers of IR receivers available on the market. In Europe, Siemens, Vishay, and Telefunken are the main suppliers. A Siemens SFH506-xx series is available, where xx indicates that the modulation frequency is 30, 33, 36, 38, 40 or 56kHz. TFMS5xx0 and TK18xx0 are Telefunken's modulation frequency oscillators, where xx indicates the modulation frequency the device operates at. Apparently, these parts have now become obsolete. The product series has been replaced by Vishay's TSOP12xx, TSOP48xx, and TSOP62xx.

Three Asian IR receiver companies include Sharp, Xiamen Hualian, and Japanese Electric. The Sharp GP1UD26xK, GP1UD27xK and GP1UD28xK devices have very cryptic ID names, where x represents the modulation frequency. There is the Hualian HRMx00 series, like the HRM3700 and HRM3800. A series of devices from Japanese Electric do not indicate their modulation frequency in their part IDs. IC-12042LM and IC-12043LM are tuned to 36.7 kHz and 37.9 kHz, respectively.

IR Sensors Intended for consumer electronics, this theory describes the operation of IR remote control systems. The issue of security is not addressed here. As long as I'm controlling my VCR or TV, the security aspect is not important. But turning the key to open a car or door becomes literally a 'key' feature.

Project 22: Interfacing Sound Sensor Module with Arduino

Overview:

With this experiment, we will understand how to use a Sound Sensor module with an Arduino.

Components:

- 1 x Arduino Uno
- 1 x USB Cable
- 1 x Sound sensor module
- 1 x Breadboard
- Jumper wires

Principle:

There are two outputs that come from the Sound Sensor: AO, analog output, and DO, real-time digital output, the threshold-sensitivity of the noise to be achieved by potentiometer adjustment will be achieved when a certain threshold is reached for the intensity of the sound.

PIN Configuration

KY-037	Arduino
A0	-
+	5v
G	GND
D0	Pin 2

This type of sound sensor is inexpensive, easy to interface with, and detects sounds like **voices, claps, or doorbells.** These sensors can be used for a variety of purposes, such as making your lights clap-activated or tracking your **pets** when you're away.

Procedure:

Step 1: Build the circuit

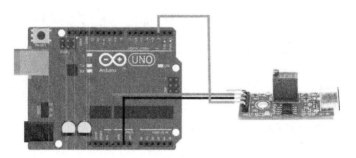

Step 2: Program: Open /Copy the code from the "CODE" Folder

```
/***************************************************
File name: 20 –Sound sensor module
***************************************************/
const int ledPin = 13; //pin 13 built-in led
const int soundPin = 2; //sound sensor attach to A0
int threshold = 600; //Set minimum threshold for LED lit
void setup() {
pinMode(ledPin,OUTPUT);//set pin13 as OUTPUT
Serial.begin(9600); //initialize serial
}
void loop() {
int value = digitalRead(soundPin);//read the value of A0
Serial.println(value);//print the value
if(value > threshold) //if the value is greater than 600
{
digitalWrite(ledPin,HIGH);//turn on the led
delay(200);//delay 200ms
}
else
{
digitalWrite(ledPin,LOW);//turn off the led
}
delay(1000);
}
```

Step 3: Compile the program and upload to Arduino UNO board.

Project 23: Analog Joystick Module with Arduino

Overview:

This tutorial will demonstrate how to use an analog joystick module. Adding some control to your projects is straightforward with analog joysticks.

Components:

- 1 x Arduino Uno
- 1 x USB cable
- 1 x Joystick Module
- 1 x Breadboard
- Jumper wires

Principle

Joystick

This module has 5 prongs: Vcc, Ground, X, Y, Key. Its labels may differ from yours. The module will depend on where you receive it from. With the thumb stick, you can pull the left side of the control stick to push down, and the right side of the control stick to push down. Furthermore, you can activate a „press to select" button by pressing the joystick down (which is quite hard on mine).

The data from the X/Y pins will be read using the Analog Arduino pins, and the button will be read with a digital pin. If the joystick is pushed, it connects to the ground, but it floats otherwise. Key and Select pins must be connected via a pull-up resistor to Vcc in order to yield stable readings. Digital pins on Arduino are equipped with built in resistors. The following schematic will guide you through activating pull-up resistors on Arduino pins that are designed as inputs.

In terms of analog joysticks, they are similar to two potentiometers connected together, one for the vertical movement (Y-axis), and another for the horizontal movement (X-axis). In addition to the joystick, it also has a Select button. A controller like this can be very handy for retro gaming, robotic control, and RC cars.

Schematic

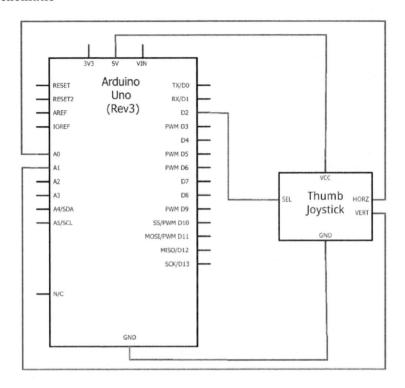

Procedure:

Step 1: Build the circuit

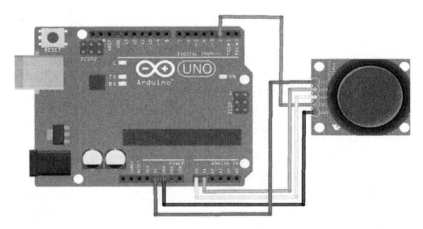

Step 2: Program

```
/*****************************************************
File name: 21 - Analog Joystick Module. No
Description: Let, Analog Joystick Module
*****************************************************/
const int SW_pin = 2; // digital pin connected to switch output
const int X_pin = A0; // analog pin connected to X output
const int Y_pin = A1; // analog pin connected to Y output
void setup() {
pinMode(SW_pin, INPUT);
digitalWrite(SW_pin, HIGH);
Serial.begin(9600);
}
void loop() {
Serial.print("Switch: ");
Serial.print(digitalRead(SW_pin));
Serial.print("\n");
Serial.print("X-axis: ");
Serial.print(analogRead(X_pin));
Serial.print("\n");
Serial.print("Y-axis: ");
Serial.println(analogRead(Y_pin));
Serial.print("\n\n");
delay(500);
}
```

Step 3: Compile the program and upload to Arduino UNO board.

Application

- A camera's pan/tilt can be controlled
- Controls and input for the game, Robotics control
- Input of Analog Parameters, and Often used in DIY projects

Game controllers come to mind when we hear the word "Joystick". There are many applications of the joystick in electronics. They are commonly used in DIY robotics projects and Arduino-based projects. Having an analog output, we can use this module to feed in an analog input based on movement or direction. Alternatively, it can be controlled with a movable camera.

Project 24: Interfacing DHT11 Sensor with Arduino

Overview:

This project will answer all your questions on how to receive humidity and temperature data using the DHT11 sensor and then send it to Arduino Ultra.

Components

- 1 x Arduino UNO
- 1 x USB Cable
- 1 x DTH11 Temperature Sensor
- 1 x BreadBoard
- Jumper Wires

Schematic:

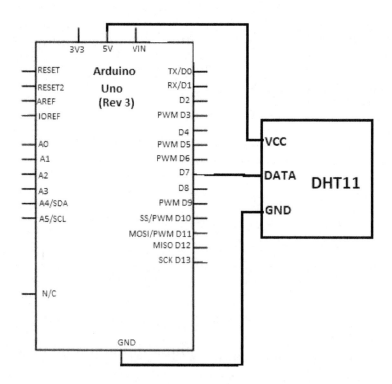

Procedure:

Step 1: Build the circuit

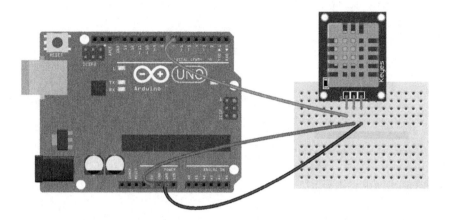

This is the time when the Arduino IDE software should be running. Next, you have to install the DHT Sensor library. This can be done via the Arduino Library Manager:

Sketch→Include Library→Manage Libraries...

Look for the "DHT sensor **library** by **Adafruit**" within the "**dht**" search field. Click "Install" or "Update" if you have an older version installed.

IMPORTANT: As of version 1.3.0 of the **DHT** library, the Adafruit_Sensor library is also required. This is available under the Arduino Library Manager.

Step 2: Program: Open /Copy the code from the "CODE" Folder

```
/*********************************************************
File name: 22 Interfacing DHT11 Sensor with Arduino .ino Description:
Let, Showing the temperature using DHT.
*********************************************************/
#include <SimpleDHT.h>
int pinDHT11 = 7;
SimpleDHT11 dht11;
void setup() {
Serial.begin(9600);
```

```
}
void loop() {
Serial.println("===================================");
Serial.println("Sample DHT11...");
byte temperature = 0;
byte humidity = 0;
byte data[40] = {0};
if (dht11.read(pinDHT11, &temperature, &humidity, data)) {
Serial.print("Read DHT11 failed");
return;
}
Serial.print("Sample RAW Bits: ");
for (int i = 0; i < 40; i++) {
Serial.print((int)data[i]);
if (i > 0 && ((i + 1) % 4) == 0) {
Serial.print(' ');
}
}
Serial.println("");
Serial.print ("Sample OK: ");
Serial.print((int)temperature); Serial.print(" *C, ");
Serial.print((int)humidity); Serial.println(" %");
delay(1000);
}
```

Step 3: Compile the program and upload to Arduino UNO board.

Applications

The sensor is used for a wide range of applications, including the measurement of humidity and temperature in HVAC systems. They can also be used to predict weather conditions in weather stations. In homes where humidity affects people, the humidity sensor provides a preventive measure. The sensor is used for measuring humidity values in offices, cars, museums, greenhouses, and industries as a safety measure.

This sensor gained popularity among hobbyists because of its small size and high sampling rate. Besides the DHT11 sensor, there are some other sensors that can be used instead, such as DHT22, AM2302, SHT71.

Project 25: Temperature and Humidity Monitoring Experiment

Overview

It consists of more complex experimentation, monitoring temperature and humidity of the indoor air, and the LCD display of the value.

Working of the Project

With an Arduino UNO multi-tasking device and a DHT11 Humidity and Temperature Sensor, a simple project built with Humidity and Temperature sensors is able to determine Humidity and Temperature from the surrounding.

When we connect, the program already takes care of everything, so we do not need to do anything else. The DHT11 module comes with a special library called "DHT", but we did not use it. This library must be downloaded separately by Arduino users, and it must be added to the Arduino libraries. Data timing diagrams in the datasheet were used in writing the program. By logging the data from the sensor and displaying it on the LCD Display, the program will automatically read the data from the Arduino.

DHT11 Temperature and Humidity Sensor

DHT sensors come in different types, such as the DHT11, DHT21, DHT22, DHT33, and DHT44. The difference is mostly in the accuracy and sampling rate, which they all measure temperature and humidity. A side-by-side comparison of DHT11 and DHT22, the two most popular sensors, is shown in the table below. In terms of accuracy and range, the DHT22 is better, but it has a slower sampling rate, is larger in size, and costs twice as much as the DHT11.

Hardware required

Material diagram	Material name	Number
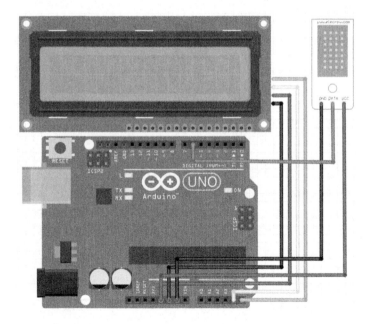	LCD1602_IIC	1
	DHT11	1
	USB Cable	1
	UNO R3	1
	Breadboard	1
	Jumper wires	Several

Connection diagram

PIN Configure

UNO R3		DHT11
GND	->	GND/'-'
D6	->	DATA/'out'
+5V	->	VCC/'+'

UNO R3		LCD1602_IIC
GND	->	GND
+5V	->	VCC
SDA	->	A4
SCL	->	A5

Program

```
#include <LiquidCrystal.h>
LiquidCrystal lcd(4, 5, 0, 1, 2, 3);
byte degree_symbol[8] =
        {
        0b00111,
        0b00101,
        0b00111,
        0b00000,
        0b00000,
        0b00000,
        0b00000,
        0b00000
        };
int gate=11;
volatile unsigned long duration=0;
unsigned char i[5];
unsigned int j[40];
unsigned char value=0;
unsigned answer=0;
int z=0;
```

```
int b=1;
void setup()
{

lcd.begin(16, 2);
 lcd.print("Temp = ");
 lcd.setCursor(0,1);
 lcd.print("Humidity = ");
 lcd.createChar(1, degree_symbol);
 lcd.setCursor(9,0);
 lcd.write(1);
 lcd.print("C");
 lcd.setCursor(13,1);
 lcd.print("%");
}

void loop()
{

 delay(1000);
 while(1)
 {
  delay(1000);
  pinMode(gate,OUTPUT);
  digitalWrite(gate,LOW);
  delay(20);
  digitalWrite(gate,HIGH);
  pinMode(gate,INPUT_PULLUP);//by default it will become high due to
internal pull up
 // delayMicroseconds(40);

  duration=pulseIn(gate, LOW);
  if(duration <= 84 && duration >= 72)
  {
    while(1)
    {
     duration=pulseIn(gate, HIGH);

     if(duration <= 26 && duration >= 20){
     value=0;}
```

```
    else if(duration <= 74 && duration >= 65){
    value=1;}

    else if(z==40){
    break;}

    i[z/8]|=value<<(7- (z%8));
    j[z]=value;
    z++;
    }
  }
answer=i[0]+i[1]+i[2]+i[3];

if(answer==i[4] && answer!=0)
{
lcd.setCursor(7,0);
lcd.print(i[2]);
lcd.setCursor(11,1);
lcd.print(i[0]);
}

z=0;
i[0]=i[1]=i[2]=i[3]=i[4]=0;
  }
}
```

Compile and Upload

To add these libraries to the **Arduino library** directory and pass the compiler, follow the instructions in 'How to add libraries in Chapter 2'. In order to make the LCD display or provide sufficient brightness, please adjust the potentiometer as below.

As a first step, the Arduino transmits a high to low start signal to DHT11 after a 18s delay to ensure that this device is detected. Once the data line is up and running, Arduino waits for the data from DHT to come in for a period of 20-40 seconds. With a time, delay of about 80s, DHT sends low voltage level response signals to Arduino once it detects the start signal. A DHT controller pulls up the data line and holds it for 80s for the purpose of arranging the data transmission.

A low voltage level on the data bus indicates that the DHT11 is transmitting a response. After this is complete, DHT performs data line pull-up for 80s again to prepare data transmission.

Every bit of data is sent by DHT by 50s of low voltage level and length of high voltage level signal determining if it is "0" or "1".

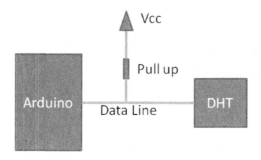

A key requirement is to make sure the pull up resistor is rated at 5K if DHT sensor is placed at 20 meters distance. Pull up resistors of appropriate value should be used when installing DHT at distances exceeding 20 meters.

Applications

- Various applications for the DHT11 Humidity and Temperature Sensor include:
- The HVAC system consists of ventilation, heating, and air conditioning (HVAC).
- Utilized in Weather Stations
- Medicinal equipment that measures humidity
- Automation Systems for the Home
- Weather control applications in automotive and other industries

Project 26: One digit 7 Segment Displays with an Arduino

Overview

In this project, the control of the LEDs is the same as the LED experiment, however, the experiment can record time.

Pin definition

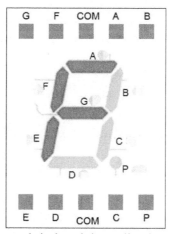

Embedded systems and industrial applications using one-digit seven segment displays commonly known beforehand the range of outputs that will be displayed. 0-9 numbers, and a few characters, can be displayed on this 7-segment display. The types of 7 segment displays differ, for example the number of characters and digits they can display varies. Basic 7 segment displays can display only one character or one digit, and they are essentially single units. In multiplexed 7 segment displays, 2 digits, 3 digits, or 4 digits are shown through the multiplexing of single unit displays. You can connect your Arduino to a 7-segment display very easily! We'll begin the tutorial now.

In regards to the number of characters the 7-segment display can display, it has many limitations. On the market are displays that are much more advanced than seven segment displays; they are capable of displaying nearly every alphabetical character. Suppose, for example, that you have a 16*2 LCD – which can display almost any ASCII character. It makes you wonder why there are still 7 segment displays available on the market today. There is no doubt that 7 segment displays represent the most affordable option among display devices available. A 7 segment display capable of displaying one digit or one character is available for one tenth the price of a LCD module.

The rectangular plastic package contains one of the LEDs' connection pins which led out from its positional segment. The LED pins are labelled "a" through "g", with each LED representing one of the individual LEDs. Each LED pin is connected to another LED pin, forming a common pin. When Forward Biased in a specific order, some LED segments will brighten but others will remain dim, thus showing the corresponding character on the display.

Displays are generally classified according to their common pins. Pin connections consist of two types: one pin with cathodes connected and another with anodes connected, indicating Common Cathode (CC) and Common Anode (CA). CA displays have all the anodes connected to the cathodes, while CC displays have all the cathodes connected to the anodes.

Hardware required

Material Diagram	Material	Number
	1 digit LED Segment Displays	1
	220/330Ω resistor	1
	USB Cable	1
	UNO R3	1
	Breadboard	1
	Jumper wires	few

Connection diagram

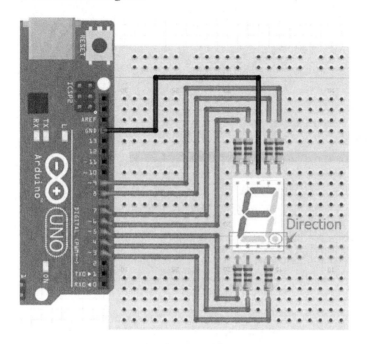

Note: Pay attention to the direction of digital tube Connection:

UNO R3		SEG
D3	->	C
D4	->	D
D5	->	E
D6	->	G
D7	->	F
D8	->	A
D9	->	B
GND	->	COM

Program

```
// declaring an array of integers
int numbers[] = { 90, 150, 30 };
int a, b;

void setup() {
  a = numbers[0] + numbers[1]; // Sets variable a to 240
  b = numbers[1] + numbers[2]; // Sets variable b to 180
}

// different ways of declaring arrays of chars
char string1[15];
char string2[7] = {'h', 'e', 'l', 'l', 'o', '!'};
char string3[7] = {'h', 'e', 'l', 'l', 'o', '!', ''};
char string4[] = "hello there!";

int a = 10;

// allocates an array for holding 10 characters
// (last position is for holding the '' or NULL string terminator
char *string5 = new char[a+1];
...
// releases the memory space allocated for string5
delete [] string5;
```

Compile and upload

After uploading code, you can see the number on the digital tube increased from 0 to 9. As you can see from the code given above, the Arduino code is extremely simple and follows the beginners' approach. An array or other advanced programming element can allow a program to be written in a smaller number of lines. As you can see in the following lines, the pin names for the segments have been assigned. Additionally, we have configured all the outputs that we will be using. Counting 0-9 is accomplished with a for loop, and switching between the relevant statements is achieved using a switch statement.

Project 27: Four Digit 7 Segment Display Module (TM1637)

Overview:

A four-digit, seven-segment display (TM1637) will be used in this lesson.

Components:

- 1 x Arduino UNO
- 1 x USB Cable
- 1 x 4 Digit 7-segment Display
- 1 x Breadboard
- Several Jumpers wire

Principle

The yellow pin of the 7-segment display is connected to the power source when the 7-segment display is common anode; and the red pin is connected to the GND when the 7-segment display is common cathode. Anodes or cathodes control the digits in a four-digit 7-segment display by the common electrode. The principle of Persistence of Vision allows you to recognize all numbers displayed even though only one digit is working since the scanning speed is so fast that you barely notice the intervals between the numbers.

A TM1637 LED driver from Titan Micro Electronics is at the heart of the module, In addition to being able to control LED brightness and ON/OFF state, the TM1637 can access those segments individually. Additionally, the LEDs can be made brighter by adjusting their brightness in software. Furthermore, once the microcontroller updates the display, the TM1637 then takes care of all the work of refreshing the display. The microcontroller can then concentrate on other important tasks, since the overhead has been removed.

Pin definition

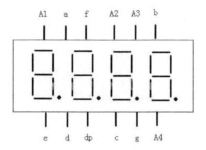

Schematic

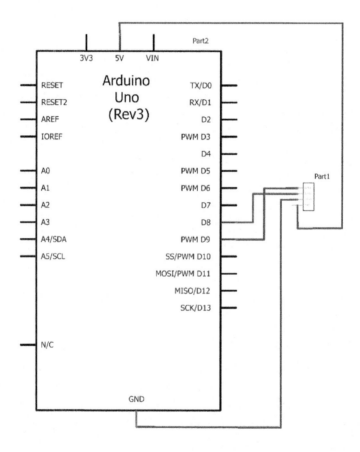

Procedure:

Step 1: Build the circuit

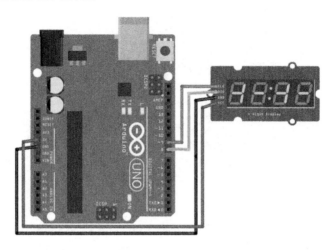

Step 2: Program code

```
/*********************************************************
File name: 23_ Four Digital Seven Segment Display(TM1637) .ino
Description:
Let, four digital segment display.
*********************************************************/
#include <TM1637Display.h>
const int CLK = 9; //Set the CLK pin connection to the display
const int DIO = 8; //Set the DIO pin connection to the display
int NumStep = 0; //Variable to interate
TM1637Display display(CLK, DIO); //set up the 4-Digit Display.
void setup() {
display.setBrightness(0x0a); //set the diplay to maximum brightness
}
void loop() {
for(NumStep = 0; NumStep < 9999; NumStep++) //Interrate NumStep
{
display.showNumberDec(NumStep); //Display the Variable value;
delay(500); //A half second delay between steps.
}
}
```
Step 3: Compile the program and upload to Arduino UNO board.

Project 28: Heart-shaped display experiment with Arduino

Overview

Here you will learn about using an 8x8 dot matrix to make an animated beating heart.

Pin definition

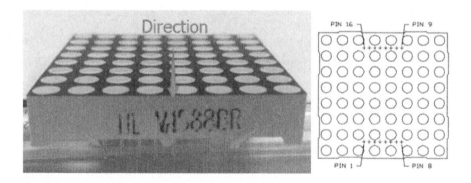

In this project, we will demonstrate the use of a MAX7219 8x8 LED matrix with Arduino. We will do this by connecting an 8*8 LED matrix module to an Arduino Uno board with a MAX7129 LED driver. 64 LEDs (Light Emitting Diodes) make up an 8*8 LED matrix, which has eight rows and eight columns. It is therefore known as a LED matrix.

Utilizing different Arduino codes, we will design and generate different LED patterns; the patterns will be displayed on an LED matrix.

Hardware required

Material diagram	Material name	Number
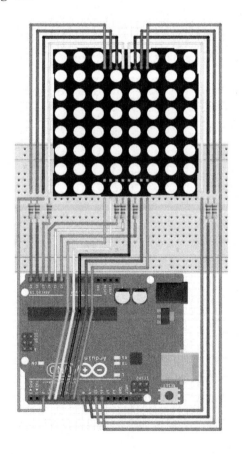	8*8 Dot-matrix Display	1
	220/330Ω resistor	8
	USB Cable	1
	UNO R3	1
	Breadboard	1
	Jumper wires	Several

Connection diagram

Pin Configuration:

```
pin1 ->D3
pin2 ->D4
pin3 ->A2    Need connection resistance.
pin4 ->A1    Need connection resistance.
pin5 ->D5
pin6 ->A0    Need connection resistance.
pin7 ->D6
pin8 ->D7
pin9 ->D11
pin10->D10   Need connection resistance.
pin11- >D9   Need connection resistance.
pin12 ->D8
pin13 ->A3   Need connection resistance
pin14 ->D2
pin15 ->A4   Need connection resistance.
pin16 ->A5   Need connection resistance.
```

Note : Some pin ports need connection resistance

Program

```
// Name: #define
// replaces COUNT with number 1000
// doesn't allocate ram for a variable
#define COUNT 1000

int i = 0;

void setup()
{
  Serial.begin(9600);
}

void loop()
{
  if (i < COUNT) {
    Serial.print("i = ");
    Serial.println(i);
```

```
}
 i = i+1;
 // i will overflow to -32768 eventually
 // printing again
}


// replaces MYLED with number 8
// doesn't allocate ram for a variable
#define MYLED 8

void setup()
{
  pinMode(MYLED, OUTPUT);
}

void loop()
{
  digitalWrite(MYLED, HIGH);
  delay(100);
  digitalWrite(MYLED, LOW);
  delay(100);
}
```

// Name: unsigned char
```
unsigned char m; // Declare variable "m" of type char
m = 'A';      // Assign "m" the value "A"
m = 200;      // Assign "m" the value 200
```

Compile and upload

Tips: By changing the "unsigned char table1 [8][8] = {}" or "unsigned char table2[8][8] = {}" function, you can show various animations.

Result

You will see the heart beating animation after ensuring that the connection is correct and uploading the code.

Project 29: Interfacing tilt sensor with Arduino

Overview:

The purpose of this lesson is to demonstrate the function of the tilt sensor module, which is equipped with a tilt sensor and a potentiometer.

Components

- 1 x Arduino UNO
- 1 x USB Cable
- 1 x Tilt Switch Module
- 1 x Breadboard
- Several jumpers wire

Principle

These days, security alarms are built with tilt sensors. Individual tilt sensors sense movement or angle of tilt. There are numerous mounting methods such as threading, magnets, and adhesives for tilt sensors; the method it is used for mounting may differ based on the type of surface being used.

PIN Configuration

Tilt Sensor Module	Arduino
D0	2
G	GND
+	5v

For the Arduino to operate, the tilt sensor must be connected to 5v DC. Arduino UNO is used to supply the 5V, and Pin 4 of the Arduino is used to receive the tilt sensor's output. In order to limit the current to a safe level, the LED is connected to PIN 2 of the Arduino UNO through a 220-ohm resistor. In addition, the buzzer interacts directly with Arduino UNO Pin 3.

Procedure: Step 1: Build the circuit

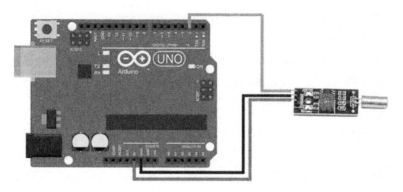

Step 2: Program

```
/********************************************************
File name: 24 Interfacing tilt sensor with arduino. ino
********************************************************/
const int sigPin = 2; // the number of the tilt switch pin
const int ledPin = 13; // the number of the LED pin
// variables will change:
boolean sigState = 0; // variable for reading the tilt switch status
void setup() {
// initialize the LED pin as an output:
pinMode(ledPin, OUTPUT);
// initialize the tilt switch pin as an input:
pinMode(sigPin, INPUT);
}
void loop() {
// read the state of the tilt switch value:
sigState = digitalRead(sigPin);
if (sigState == HIGH) {
// turn LED on:
digitalWrite(ledPin, LOW);
}
else {
// turn LED off:
digitalWrite(ledPin, HIGH);
}
}
```

Step 3: Compile the program and upload to Arduino UNO board.

Project 30: Interfacing RC522 RFID Module with Arduino

Overview:

The RC522 RFID Reader Module will be applied in this project to UNO R3. These modules communicate with controllers like Arduino, Raspberry Pi, beagle board, etc. through the Serial Peripheral Interface (SPI) bus.

Components:

- 1 x Arduino Uno
- 1 x USB cable
- 1 x Rc522 module
- 1 x Breadboard
- Jumper wires

Principle:

With the MFRC522 reader you will have the ability to communicate with contactless technology at 13.56 MHz while providing support for ISO 14443A / MIFARE® compatibility

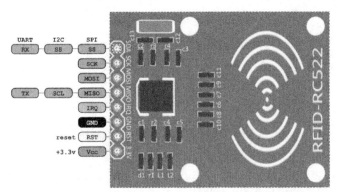

It can drive the reader or writer antenna of the MFRC522's inner transmitter part with no extra active circuitry. Receivers are provided with demodulation and decoding circuits that are robust enough to process signals from ISO/IEC 14443A/MIFARE® compatible cards and transponders. ISO/IEC 14443A (Parity & CRC) specifies requirements for framing and error detection. In addition to MIFARE Classic products, the MFRC522 supports devices utilizing MIFARE® Standard. MIFARE®

higher-speed wireless technology supported by the MFRC522 enables faster communication with higher transfer speeds of about 848 Kbit/s in both directions.

RFID WORKING

An RFID reader generates a high-frequency electromagnetic field, which induces a voltage in the tag's antenna coil when it is in close proximity to it. Consequently, the tag receives its power from this voltage. A reader reads the signal from the tag, which then converts it to power

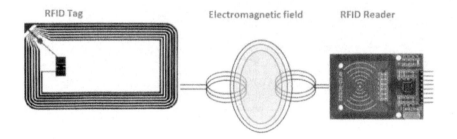

Schematic:

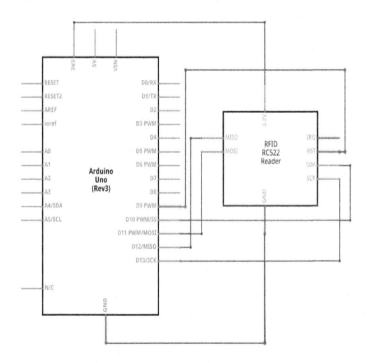

Procedure:

Step 1: Build the circuit

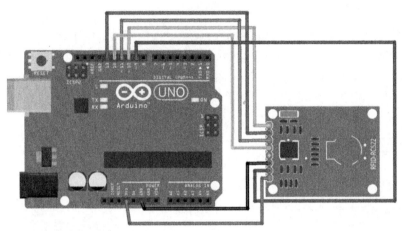

Step 2: Program

```
/*************************************************
File name: 25- Interfacing RC522 RFID Module with Arduino.ino
Description:
Let, RFID module. *******************************/
#include <SPI.h>
#include <MFRC522.h>
#define RST_PIN 9 // Configurable, see typical pin layout above
#define SS_PIN 10 // Configurable, see typical pin layout above
MFRC522 mfrc522(SS_PIN, RST_PIN); // Create MFRC522 instance
#define NEW_UID {0xDE, 0xAD, 0xBE, 0xEF}
MFRC522::MIFARE_Key key;
void setup() {
Serial.begin(9600); // Initialize serial communications with the PC
while (!Serial); // Do nothing if no serial port is opened (added for
Arduinos based on ATMEGA32U4)
SPI.begin(); // Init SPI bus
mfrc522.PCD_Init(); // Init MFRC522 card
Serial.println(F("Warning: this example overwrites the UID of your UID
changeable card, use with care!"));
for (byte i = 0; i < 6; i++) {
key.keyByte[i] = 0xFF;
```

```
}
}
void loop() {
if ( ! mfrc522.PICC_IsNewCardPresent() || !
mfrc522.PICC_ReadCardSerial() ) {
delay(50);
return;
}
Serial.print(F("Card UID:"));
for (byte i = 0; i < mfrc522.uid.size; i++) {
Serial.print (mfrc522.uid.uidByte[i] < 0x10 ? " 0" : " ");
Serial.print(mfrc522.uid.uidByte[i], HEX);
}
Serial.println();
byte newUid[] = NEW_UID;
if ( mfrc522.MIFARE_SetUid(newUid, (byte)4, true) ) {
Serial.println (F ("Wrote new UID to card."));
}
mfrc522.PICC_HaltA();
if ( ! mfrc522.PICC_IsNewCardPresent() || !
mfrc522.PICC_ReadCardSerial() ) {
return;
}
Serial.println(F("New UID and contents:"));
mfrc522.PICC_DumpToSerial(&(mfrc522.uid));
delay(2000);
}
```

Step 3: Compile the program and upload to Arduino UNO board.

In this 13.56MHz RFID Card Reader Module based on MFRC522, there is a low-cost RFID Reader Module that can be used for a wide range of applications at a low price. An integrated reader/writer IC with a frequency of 13.56 MHz, the MFRC522 is suitable for contactless communication.

In the development of portable hand-held devices and smart meters, the NXP RC522, a highly integrated RFID card reader working on non-contact 13.56mhz communication, is the best choice since it is low power, low cost and compact in size.

Project 31: Interfacing Bluetooth module HC-05 with Arduino

Overview:

This project will help you understand the Arduino using the HC-05 Bluetooth module.

Components:

- 1 x Arduino Uno
- 1 x USB Cable
- 1 x Bluetooth Module HC-05
- 1 x Breadboard
- Jumper wires

Principle:

Bluetooth modules such as HC-05 (master/slave) allow Arduino to communicate with other devices. Using it, the Arduino can connect to smartphones, computers or other microcontrollers and exchange information with them. With Bluetooth communication, you can control robots remotely, view and store data remotely on your PC or smartphone inside your home, for example.

PIN Configuration:

- Key – Arduino Pin 9
- Vcc – Arduino 5v
- GND – Arduino GND
- TXD – Arduino Pin 10
- RXD – Arduino Pin 11

A Brief Introduction to Bluetooth Protocols and Communication

There are several wireless communication methods, such as NRF, ZigBee, Wi-Fi, and Bluetooth. PAN communication with Bluetooth protocol; a wireless communication method with a maximum data rate of 1 Mb/S, working on 2.4 G frequency, at a distance of up to 100 meters is a prevalent method of wireless communication.

The HC05 Bluetooth module, usually used in electronics projects, is a serial communications Bluetooth module. The following are important specifications for the Bluetooth module HC05: An internal antenna is included with the device. Automatic connection to the last device is available.

Bluetooth data transmission to Arduino

You can connect the HC05 module to a 5V voltage because it has an internal 3.3v regulator. The serial communication pins of the HC05 module operate at 3.3V, so we strongly recommend 3.3V voltage from the power supply.

Modules that receive 5V voltage may be damaged. A resistance division circuit (5v to 3.3v) should be used between the Arduino TX and module RX pins to prevent damage to the module. A blue and red LED on each board blinks every 2 seconds when the master and slave are connected. When they are not connected, only the blue light blinks every 2 seconds.

Procedure:

Step 1: Build the circuit

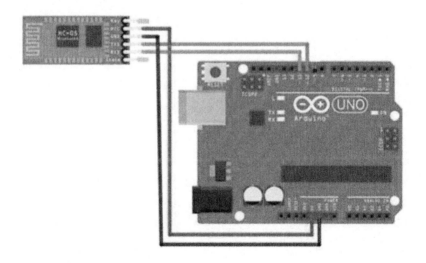

Step 2: Program: Open /Copy the code from the "CODE" Folder

```
/*****************************************************
File name: 26 – Interfacing Bluetooth module HC-05 with Arduino Let,
Bluetooth module HC 05.
*****************************************************/
// This program shown how to control arduino from PC Via Bluetooth
// Connect ... // arduino>>bluetooth
// D11 >>> Rx // D10 >>> Tx
//Written By Mohannad Rawashdeh
//for http://www.genotronex.com/
// you will need arduino 1.0.1 or higher to run this sketch

#include <SoftwareSerial.h>// import the serial library
SoftwareSerial Genotronex(10, 11); // RX, TX
int ledpin=13; // led on D13 will show blink on / off
int BluetoothData; // the data given from Computer

void setup()
{
// put your setup code here, to run once:
Genotronex.begin(9600);
Genotronex.println("Bluetooth On please press 1 or 0 blink LED ..");
pinMode(ledpin,OUTPUT);
}
void loop() {
// put your main code here, to run repeatedly:
if (Genotronex.available()) {
 BluetoothData=Genotronex.read();
if(BluetoothData=='1') { // if number 1 pressed ....
digitalWrite(ledpin,1);
Genotronex.println("LED On D13 ON ! ");
 }
if (BluetoothData=='0')
{ // if number 0 pressed ....
digitalWrite(ledpin,0);
Genotronex.println("LED On D13 Off ! ");
 } }
delay(100); // prepare for next data ...
}
```

Step 3: Compile the program and upload to Arduino UNO board.

AT Commands

In general, typing the command AT+<command>? will prompt the saved parameter (ex: AT+PSWD? will display the module PIN code). If you enter AT+<command>=<Param>, you can set the parameter value(ex: AT+PWSD=0000 to modify the PIN code to 0000).

Following is a list of AT commands:

- If everything is setup correctly, enter AT in the serial monitor on the Arduino IDE. If the communication was successful, it should show OK.
- To change the component name, enter AT+NAME=<Param>. The component should answer OK (Defaut HC-05, Ex: To modification the name to BTM1 enter AT+NAME=BTM1).
- To modify the PIN code, enter AT+PSWD=<Param> . The module should answer OK(Default 1234 Ex: To change the PIN to 0000 enter AT+PSWD=0000).
- AT+ROLE=<Param> to midy the role of the module as slave or master (Default 0, Ex: to change the role as master enter AT+ROLE=1, as slave enter AT+ROLE=0).
- To modify the baudrate, enter AT+UART=<Param1>,<Param2>,<Param3> with Param1, 2 and 3 serial communication parameters: baudrate, stop bit and parity bit respectively (By default,set to 9600,0,0. Ex: to modify the baudrate to 115200 enter AT+UART=115200, 0, 0).

There are multiple **AT commands available** for the HC-05 Bluetooth module on the Internet.
https://cdn.instructables.com/ORIG/FOR/4FP2/HKZAVRT6/FOR4FP2H KZAVRT6.pdf

Slave Configuration

To set the module as a slave, you can change the name as AT+NAME=HC05-Slave and choose the communication parameters and the PIN code that you want. You'll need to make sure that master and slave as the same communication parameters.

- AT returns OK
- AT+NAME=HC05-Slave
- AT+UART=9600,0,0
- AT+ROLE=0

Enter AT+ADDR to obtain the module address (ex: +ADDR:98d3:32:21450e)

Master Configuration

The slave module needs to be made master by changing the module's role and setting the same communication parameters as the master module.

- AT returns OK
- AT+NAME=HC05-Master
- AT+UART=9600,0,0
- AT+ROLE=1

The slave module address must be entered in the master module to allows it to appair: AT+BIND=98d3,32,21450e (replace dots ":" by coma ",")

How do these AT commands work?

Hayes developed a simple command language from 1981 until 1984 to control his smart modem, eventually combining a series of short text strings into instructions for tasks strings which can be combined to produce commands for operations such as dialing, hanging up, and changing the parameters of the connection. It is from this point that the idea of enhancing the Hayes set or the AT commands set and interacting with more devices with a prefix character is born.

You can interface the Bluetooth modules with AT commands in order to set their parameters like the other devices. For this reason, before we can use AT commands on a Bluetooth module, it must first be switched to AT mode. This tutorial will use the HC-05 and HC-06 Bluetooth modules, which are the most common Bluetooth modules. If you use a breakout board, you can tell the difference between these two Bluetooth from the pins

Project 32: Interfacing Thermistor Module with Arduino - To measure Temperature

Overview:

In this project, we will look at an implementation of the Thermistor Sensor Module that takes temperature information and converts it into output signals.

Components:

- 1 x Arduino Uno
- 1 x USB Cable
- 1 x Thermal sensor
- 1 x Breadboard
- Jumper wires

Principle:

Temperature is sensed using Thermistor Sensor Module that gives off output signals. There are two different pins associated with it, each labelled as AO or DO on the board. Semiconductor materials are used in Thermistor Sensor Module. NTC thermistors generally have a negative resistance when subjected to a temperature increase, i.e., they will have negative electrical resistance if their body temperature increases. An adjustment potentiometer has been involved in this module to modify the thermistor's sensitivity towards temperature.

Configure:

Thermistor	Arduino
A0	A5
D0	-
G	GND
+	5v

Procedure:

Step 1: Build the circuit

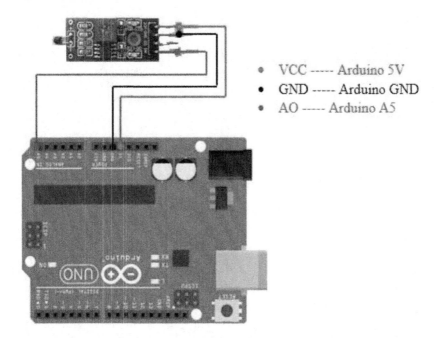

- VCC ------ Arduino 5V
- GND ------ Arduino GND
- AO ------ Arduino A5

Step 2: Program: Open /Copy the code from the "CODE" Folder

```
/**********************************************************
File name: 27 – Interfacing Thermistor Module with Arduino:
To measure Temperature Let, Thermistor sensor module
**********************************************************/
void setup(){
Serial.begin(9600);
}
void loop() {
unsigned int AnalogValue;
AnalogValue = analogRead(A5);
Serial.println(AnalogValue);
delay(1000);
}
```

Step 3: Compile the program and upload to Arduino UNO board.

Project: 33: DC Motor Direction Control

Overview:

With these projects we have examined how DC Motors can be controlled to drive forward or to reverse through the use of RGB LEDs.

Components

- 1 x Arduino UNO
- 1 X USB Cable
- 1 x Breadboard
- 1 x RGB LED
- 1 x Push Button
- 1 x Dc Motor
- 1 x 10kΩ Resistor
- Jumper wires

Principle:

Make the RGB LED into the motion indicator and control the rotation of the DC Motor either clockwise or counter clockwise. There are DC Motors in everything, from electronic equipment to toys, fans, tools, discs, and pumps. A DC motor is an actuator that converts DC energy into rotational motion. It is possible to get a DC motor in different designs: Brushed DC motor, Brushless DC motor, Geared DC motor, Servo motor, Stepper motor and DC Linear Actuator.

In different applications such as robotics, precision positioning, and industrial automation, different types of motors are used.

Motor Driver ICs are used to supply the necessary current to run any DC motor in a microcontroller-based system. The IC is what drives the DC motor. They can also control the speed of the motor. Using Arduino as the motor driver IC, the project aims to control the speed and direction of a DC motor without the use of an IC.

It is not possible to connect a DC Motor to a Microcontroller since the output current of the Microcontroller is very small and can't drive the motor.

Applications

- A single DC motor can be driven with this circuit without Motor Driver IC.
- It is possible to implement dual H-bridges and connect two motors in the circuit.
- Control of speed and direction of single motors can be achieved by using this device in simple robotics applications.

Schematic:

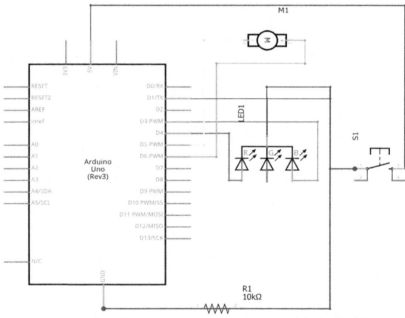

The main processing unit of the project is the Arduino. A0 is the Analog Pin of the Arduino connected to the wiper terminal of the POT. The other terminals of the POT are connected to Vcc and GND. On the circuit diagram you can see four transistors connected together.

They connect together as an H - bridge when the load, i.e. DC motor, is in the middle. In a backward direction, transistor Q1 is the dominant component, while transistor Q3 is dominant.

Inputs to the transistors are provided by the Arduino. The Arduino pins 3 and 2 are connected to Q4's base and Q1/Q4's base, respectively. A pin 5 is connected to the base of Q2, and a pin 4 is connected to the base of Q3. A total of four 1K resistors are used to connect each pin.

We can generate back EMF from DC motors when we change their direction, as they are inductive loads. The two collectors and emitters of each transistor are connected together through four diodes in order to eliminate any back EMF.

Procedure:

Step 1: Build the circuit

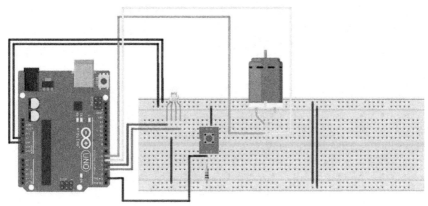

Step 2: Write a Program

```
/*********************************************************
File name: 28 DC Motor Direction Control.ino Description:
Let, DC motor control by RGB LED.
*********************************************************/
const int inputPin=1;
const int blue=3;
const int red=4;
const int motorPin1=5, motorPin2=6;
int dir = LOW;
int prevState=0, currentState=0;
void setup() {
pinMode(inputPin, INPUT);
```

246

```
pinMode(motorPin1, OUTPUT);
pinMode(motorPin2, OUTPUT);
pinMode(blue, OUTPUT);
pinMode(red, OUTPUT);
}
void loop () {
currentState=digitalRead(inputPin);
if (currentState!= prevState)
{
if (currentState == HIGH)
{
}
}
prevState = currentState;
if (dir==HIGH)
{
digitalWrite(motorPin1,HIGH);
digitalWrite(motorPin2,LOW);
digitalWrite(blue,HIGH);
digitalWrite(red,LOW);
}
else {
digitalWrite(motorPin1,LOW);
digitalWrite(motorPin2,HIGH);
digitalWrite(blue,LOW);
digitalWrite(red,HIGH);
}
}
```

Step 3: Compile the program and upload to Arduino UNO board.

Summary

This chapter has covered a lot of Arduino projects with the hope that you have completed many of them. There will be 100 Arduino project ideas in the next chapter. Using them will help you to come up with ideas that will help you to visualize your dream project.

CHAPTER 5

TOP 100 ARDUINO PROJECTS IDEAS

1. Arduino Based Autonomous Fire Fighting Robot

Firefighters can independently detect fires with this sophisticated firefighting robotic system. Fire fighters face an increasing risk of death as technology leads to an automated system and self-traveling vehicles. If a fire is not controlled, it will spread rapidly. Even an explosion is possible in the event of a gas leak. The system delivers by overcoming this issue, safeguarding the lives of our heroes. An Arduino Uno is used to power this firefighting robotic system which is comprised of an ultrasonic sensor positioned on a servo motor for obstacle detection and free route navigation. Despite its small size, it has the capability to detect and extinguish fires. It also has water tank and spray mechanism for extinguishing flames. Servo motor is used to cover maximum area with water spraying nozzle. The 12V pump uses an electric motor to pump water from the main tank to the water nozzle. Because of its constant current consumption, this pump needs driver circuit.

Hardware Specifications

- Arduino Uno
- Ultrasonic Sensor
- Fire Fighter Robot Body
- Fire Sensor
- Buzzer
- LCD Display
- Resistors
- Capacitors
- Transistors
- Cables and Connectors
- Diodes
- PCB and Breadboards
- LED
- Transformer/Adapter
- Push Buttons
- Switch
- IC
- IC Sockets

Firefighting robotic systems are designed with specific tasks in mind. The primary aspects of fire control and suppression are analyzing and locating fires as well as conducting search and rescue operations. Robotic systems

248

for controlling fire, such as automatically activating fire alarms and sprinklers, can quickly extinguish anything in a heavily populated or hazardous area. These systems are usually simpler and primarily rely on UV or infrared sensors. Since they are fixed, they don't typically change over time.

Software Specifications

1. Arduino Compiler
2. Programming Language: C

Block Diagram:

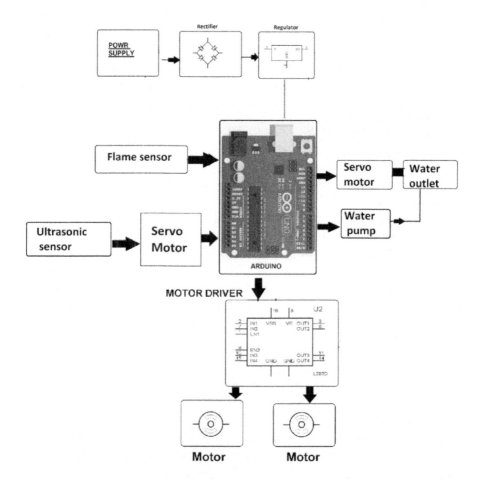

2 Robot Snake based on Arduino controlled by Android

Twelve servo motors drive the snake's segments, which are joined with metal brackets. A 7.4-volt battery pack powers the servos and controls them with an Arduino Mega. An android app can be used to control the snake using Bluetooth. In addition to autonomous movement, the snake is additionally capable of passive activity. Various different types of servos and brackets can be used to construct such a robot. There are 12 segments of the robot, each containing a servo motor, a C-bracket, a side bracket, a set of Lego wheels, and a wire clip. The Lego wheel axle must have two screw holes for the C-bracket to be attached to it.

In spite of the fact that nine segments are already connected, they need to be expanded with two tail segments in order to accommodate the Arduino and batteries. The side brackets and C-brackets are connected to the side brackets. A 5AA battery holder is used to power the Arduino and therefore the tail of the snake. A separate energy supply powers the servos. That is the 7.4-volt battery pack. The voltage pin is attached to a five-volt Arduino pin. On the receiver, the lower pin is attached to ground.

Block Diagram:

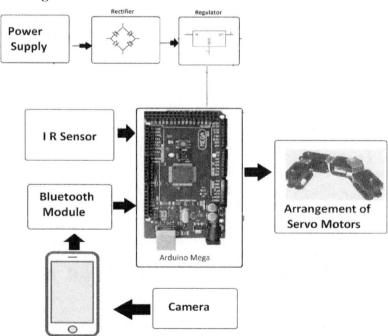

Hardware Specifications

- Arduino mega
- IR Sensor
- Servo Motors
- Bluetooth module
- Camera
- Cables and Connectors
- PCB and Breadboards
- Push Buttons
- Switch
- IC

Software Specifications

1. Arduino Compiler
2. Programming Language: C

3. Intelligent Gas Leakage Detector based on IoT

LPG leaks, which result in explosions, are common occurrences in day-to-day life. If leakage is not detected early, it can cause major damage. The MQ5 gas sensor can detect gas leakage but we were not able to use it before. In this IOT gas leak sensor, the machine will get attached to Wi-Fi, and the device will enable you to adjust parameters accordingly. Installed in gas storage areas, hotels, homes, and hotels, such IoT and Arduino systems detect leaks of LPG.

It uses a gas sensor called the MQ5 to detect the presence of LPG gas. LPG gas present in the air will be monitored continuously by this device. A green LED on the control circuit will light up if the value of LPG gas in the air is within the set limit, thereby giving a safe signal. In addition, if excessive gas levels are detected in excess of the predefined boundary, the RGB LED will turn red, and the solenoid will shut off and update the IoT value. Detecting gas leakage in the surrounding will be easy and effective with this Arduino and Internet of Things project.

The advantages and future development of LPG leakage detection system

- IOT and Arduino systems for the detection of LPG leaks can be installed in hotels, homes, and any area that maintains LPG cylinders. One of the major advantages of this project is that it can identify leaks, and send the data into a website, where it can then be monitored and corrective action taken.

- The IOT can save lives and property if appropriate measures are taken quickly after they are reported.
- The project can detect toxic gases by enhancing the gas leakage detection system. Furthermore, we can install detectors that detect fires as well.

Block Diagram:

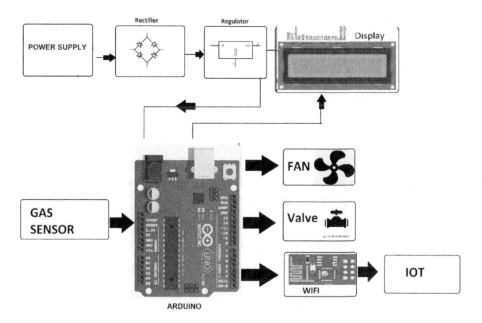

Hardware Specifications

- Arduino
- LCD
- Wi-Fi module
- Dc fan
- Gas sensor
- Buzzer
- Regulator
- Crystal Oscillator

- Resistors
- Capacitors
- Transistors
- Cables and Connectors
- Diodes
- PCB and Breadboards
- LED
- Transformer/Adapter
- Push Buttons
- Switch
- IC
- IC Sockets

Software Specifications

- Arduino Compiler
- Programming Language: C

4. Wireless Black Box for Cars

The project is about "Wireless recording systems for cars". This project has a primary objective of developing a vehicle black box system that would allow the installation of it into any vehicle all over the world. These paradigms are usually designed with a minimal range of circuits. Wi-Fi black boxes tell us about crashes and store information like the time, date, temperature, vibration, alcohol level, etc. in real-time every three seconds. The system built into the car will send a message to the registered telephone numbers, such as emergency numbers of the police station, hospitals, relatives, and vehicle owners, depending on their location.

Sensors including temperature and humidity sensors (DTH11) have been used. Vibration sensors from cars monitor vibrations during accidents. A steering wheel mounted alcohol sensor would tell if the driver was drunk. The tilt is detected by the gyroscopic sensor during an accident. Arduino mega2560 will receive a signal from all the sensors, which will then be sent to the microcontroller.

These projects used GSM, SD card, GPS, and the like. Their contributions were vital to the completion of the project. This project may be enhanced by adding video cameras, voice recorders, voice-controlled systems, and automatic warning systems in the future.

Hardware Specifications

- Arduino 2560
- GPS/Gsm module
- Temperature Scanner
- Alcohol Scanner
- Vibration sensor
- Gyroscope
- SD card module
- LCD
- L293D
- DC motor
- Power supply
- Buzzer
- LED
- Switch
- LCD
- Crystal
- Push Buttons
- Capacitors
- Resistors

Software Specifications:
1. Arduino ide
2. MC Programming Language: C

Project Implementation:

As a part of this project, there are specific sensors, like the temperature sensor (DTH11), which calculates temperature and humidity. Vibration sensors pick up sensations felt by drivers throughout an accident.

If a driver is drunk, indicators on the steering wheel will indicate this. A gyroscopic detector is used during a crash to show tilt. All parameters are measured and sent directly to the Arduino. By uploading all data to the fire department's server, the ESP8266 module collects data. This model utilizes the GSM module, the SD card module, and the GPS module to achieve the desired outcome.

Block Diagram:

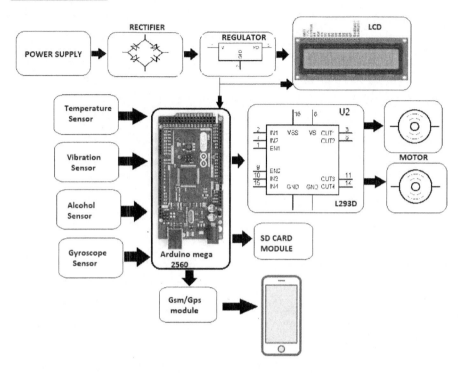

5. Smart Charger Monitoring System using Arduino

Batteries are charged or recharged by transferring energy into them via the use of a device called a battery charger or recharger. There are a variety of charging protocols available for batteries of different sizes and types. Smart battery chargers are primarily switch-mode power supplies that function in concert with battery handling and storage devices to control and monitor charging processes.

An Arduino is used to power this smart charger. This intelligent charging system charges three batteries with 12V power simultaneously. During full charge, a battery is automatically disconnected from the mains.

It has an automatic power cut-off system. A smart charger is mainly an inverter for switching on and off power supplies. It also communicates with the smart battery packs. Moreover, the LCD display module periodically displays the charge level for the battery.

Hardware Specifications

- Arduino Uno
- Relay
- Relay Drivers
- LCD Display
- Crystal Oscillator
- Resistors
- Capacitors
- Transistors
- Cables and Connectors
- Diodes
- PCB and Breadboards
- LED
- Transformer/Adapter
- Push Buttons
- Switch
- IC
- IC Sockets

Block Diagram:

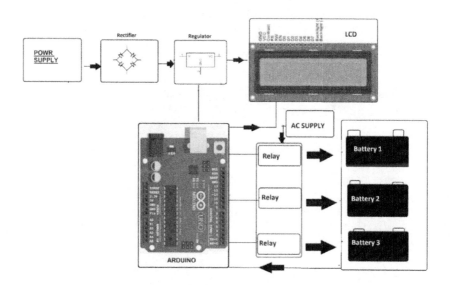

6. Arduino Based Autonomous Fire Fighting Robot

This sophisticated firefighting robotic system independently detects and extinguishes fire. Today, as the world slowly grows toward the automation of systems and self-driving cars, firefighters continue to run the risk of dying in the line of duty. When fire is not controlled it spreads rapidly. An explosion may occur in the case of a gas leak. Therefore, to meet the challenge of overcoming this issue and protecting our hero, the systems we have in place come to the rescue. An Arduino Uno development board is used to power the firefighting robotic system, which utilizes an ultrasonic sensor and servo motor for obstacles sensing and free route guidance. Fire flame sensors ensure that the sensor can detect and move in close proximity to the fire. Firefighters extinguish the fire with water tanks and spray mechanisms. Servo motors drive water spraying nozzles to cover maximum area. The primary water tank has a 12V pump which pumps water up to the water nozzle. As such a pump consumes much more current than a controller can handle it needs its own driver circuit.

Block Diagram:

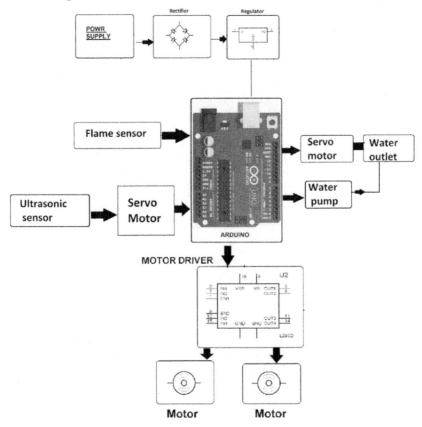

Hardware Specifications

- Arduino Uno
- Ultrasonic Sensor
- Fire Fighter Robot Body
- Fire Sensor
- Buzzer
- LCD Display
- Resistors
- Capacitors
- Transistors
- Cables and Connectors
- Diodes
- PCB and Breadboards
- LED
- Transformer/Adapter
- Push Buttons
- Switch
- IC
- IC Sockets

Software Specifications

1. Arduino Compiler
2. Programming Language: C

7. Automatic Sketching Machine Project

With the advent of machines, machines can now also draw perfect sketches. Using the process proposed here, a machine can sketch pictures accurately and fast just like a human. With an Arduino based circuit, which is attached to motors and belt-based machinery, the designed system will be able to draw a sketch with a pen.

In order to transmit movement commands according to the image fed into the Arduino based circuit, two stepper motors are interfaced with it. The sketching process is controlled then with a well-planned mechanism to achieve this task. The motor raises the pen above the page where it is not needed, so the pen touches the paper only where a dot has to be placed. A 2D sketching mechanism has been created using this mechanism in conjunction with the motion of the x and y axes.

Block Diagram:

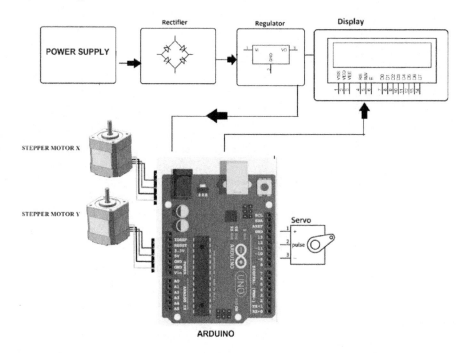

Hardware Specifications:

- Arduino UNO
- Stepper Motors
- Servo Motor
- LED's
- Resistors
- Capacitors
- Diodes
- Connectors & Cables
- Connecting Rods
- Pulley
- Rubber Belts
- Bed Frame
- Bearings
- Screws & Joints

Software Specifications:

- Arduino IDE
- MC Programming Language: C

7. Arduino based Sun Tracking Solar Panel

The future of mankind depends upon harnessing solar energy properly, in place of the traditional energy sources it has used for a long time. We branched out from the existing project to design this so solar energy can be harnessed even more efficiently.

This project is designed to be controlled by a solar panel using a controller board based on the Arduino controller board. Solar panels harness the power of the sun. The solar panel is attached to a motor so it can gather more solar energy since it is incident on the sun. Electrical connections are made between this motor and the controller board. Checking on the availability of solar energy constantly from one horizon to another, the system makes sure that this is happening. In the scan, the scanner determines which direction receives the greatest amount of solar energy and therefore captures the brightest incident sunlight. As a result, the system utilises the maximum amount of power it can generate with the Solar Panel.

Block Diagram:

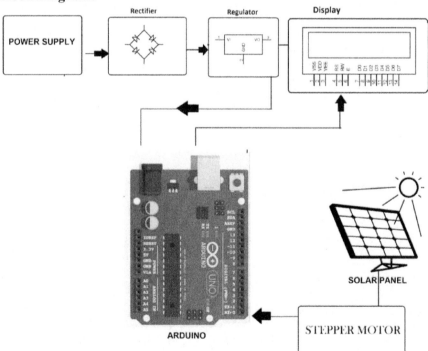

Hardware Specifications

- Arduino Uno R3
- Solar Panel
- Stepper Motor
- Crystal Oscillator
- Resistors
- Capacitors
- Transistors
- Cables & Connectors
- Diodes
- PCB
- LED's
- Transformer/Adapter
- Push Button

Software Specifications

- Arduino Compiler
- Programming Language: C

9. Fire Department Alerting System using Internet of Things and Arduino

Accidental deaths occurring due to fires are among the most common. Fire departments need to be alerted instantly in order to ensure immediate response. Every second can make all the difference in these situations. The system lets the fire department know about the situation at any time instantaneously and automatically, so instant activity may be taken. Fire sensors are used in conjunction with a PIR system to sense flames and alert fire departments through the Internet of Things. Arduinos are used to check if a sensor has been triggered. Then it uses temperature sensors to confirm that there is truly an outbreak of a fire. The system connects to an internet-connected server via Wi-Fi and transmits data about this incident over the Internet. IoT Gecko is the platform we here use to develop the IoT interface. It displays device id (named after area/flat id) data immediately upon receiving sensor data from IOT Gecko. In the 21st century, the fire department begins to receive alerts via the internet about fire incidents so it can act quickly.

Block Diagram:

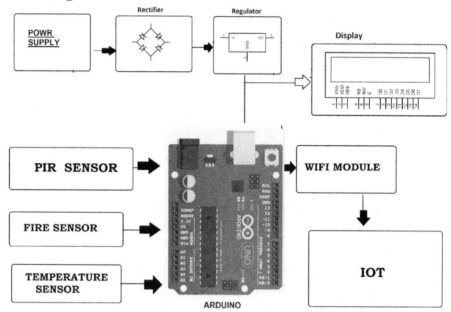

Hardware Specifications:
- Rectifier
- Regulator
- Power Supply
- LCD Display
- PIR Sensor
- Arduino Uno
- Wi-Fi Module

Software Specifications:
- Arduino Compiler
- MC Programming Language: C

10. Internet of Things based Irrigation Monitoring & Controller System using Arduino

A farmer is typically a person who works on a huge plot of land in order to grow several kinds of crops. Not all farmlands can be monitored by one person at any one time. There are times when a particular patch of land can get so much water that it becomes water-logged, or it might get so little water that it becomes dry. A farmer could suffer losses in either case if his crops are damaged, or if the crops are damaged by a storm. We propose an "Internet of Things Irrigation Monitoring and Control" project to solve this problem. One of the features of this project is that the utility company may monitor and regulate the supply of water from a faraway place. The Internet of Things concept is used in this system. As such, our system uses a wireless module to connect to the internet. A web server is connected to our desired website using an Arduino Uno board.

In these project, two concepts are shown; a) Motor status b) Moisture level a moisture sensor is equipped in the circuit, which keeps an eye on the soil moisture content. Users can then control the water supply remotely by checking the current moisture level on the website. Using the motor control switch, the water pump can be switched from 'ON-OFF' to 'OFF-ON'. Therefore, the issue of 'soil hydration' can be monitored and the 'supply of water' manipulated just by turning on or off the 'motor'. Thus, there is no need for the user to worry about his crops getting damaged because of 'waterlogging' or 'drought'. A person may not be able to constantly be present at their garden for people having small gardens. This project could be used to keep track of "soil-moisture" and supply water even from a distance.

Block Diagram:

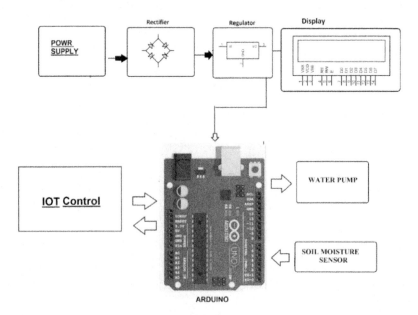

Hardware Specifications
- Rectifier
- Regulator
- LCD Display
- Power Supply
- Wi-Fi Modem
- Water Pump
- Soil Moisture Sensor
- Arduino Uno

Software Specifications
- Arduino Compiler
- MC Programming Language: C
- IOT Gecko

11. Internet of Things based Smart Agriculture Monitoring System Project

Since ancient times, agriculture has been practiced in every country. Science and art are both involved in cultivating plants. In human civilization's rise to sedentary civilization, agriculture was paramount. Farmers have been cultivating crops by hand for ages. Agriculture needs to adopt new technologies and implement implements to keep up with the trending of the world.

Agriculture is becoming smarter with the use of IoT. Technology such as IoT sensors has the potential to provide valuable information about agricultural fields. By automating IoT-connected smart agriculture systems, we propose a new model. In order to monitor agriculture using IoT, wireless sensor networks were deployed throughout the system and sent the collected data to remote nodes using a wireless protocol.

IoT technology used in this smart agriculture consists of an Arduino, a Temperature, and Water level, GPRS, and Moisture sensor. Monitoring the water level, moisture, and moisture content of the soil is part of the IoT-based agriculture monitoring system. Whenever there's a problem, it sends an alert to the user's phone. Water level sensors sense a fall and start the pump automatically if necessary. The fan starts when the temperature reaches that level. The LCD display module displays all of this. This is also seen in the Internet of Things, which provides information on Humidity, Moisture and water level by the minute based on the date and time.

Different crops demand different temperatures; they are cultivated at different altitudes and temperatures. If it is desired to forcefully stop the water flow using the IOT, a button is available from which it can be forcibly stopped.

Block Diagram:

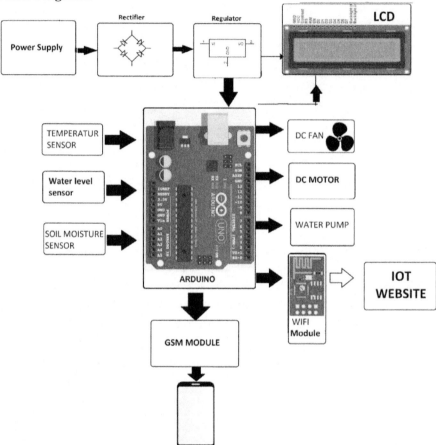

Hardware Specifications

- Arduino
- GSM Modem
- Wi-Fi Modem
- Temperature Sensor
- Humidity Sensor
- Water Sensor

- Mini Exhaust Fan
- Water Pump
- Crystal Oscillator
- Resistors
- Capacitors
- Transistors
- Cables and Connectors
- Diodes
- PCB and Breadboards
- LED
- Transformer/Adapter
- Push Buttons
- Switch
- IC
- IC Sockets

12. Arduino Ultrasonic Sonar/Radar Monitor Project

These advanced Arduino sonar technologies can be utilized to screen the patch area as well as detect suspicious objects. A car that has explosive material in it can be controlled remotely. We are able to prevent enemies from entering the public with this Arduino sonar radar, which in turn will save many lives.

The Sonar Arduino system continuously scans the surrounding area and produces a beep upon detecting a moving target that is within our range. Moreover, the radar measures the angle and distance of the target from our source. Our system enables us to track the exact position of the object in real time and traces its path.

Radar: How does it work?

Radio detection and range technology is used in RADAR systems. Microwaves are used by radar to determine the range, altitude, direction, and speed of objects within a radius of about 100 miles of their location. By using a radar antenna, radio wave/microwave signals are transmitted and bounced off various objects on their path. As a result, we can estimate the proximity of a certain object.

The operating principle is:

With the use of **electromagnetic sensors**, a radar can detect and locate objects. Radiation from a radar is in the form of microwave waves or radio waves. Reflections from objects around them can intercept the waves.

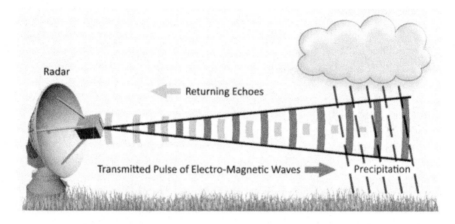

Radio waves intercepted by radar are reflected in many directions after they reach their target. The radar can direct these waves back to the receiver after receiving and amplifying them. Once again receiving these waves at their origin indicates that an object is in the propagation direction.

In addition to air traffic control and air defense, radar astronomy, antimissile systems, and outer space surveillance are some applications of modern radar systems.

Hardware Specifications
- Arduino Uno
- Ultrasonic Sensor
- Servo Motor
- LCD Display
- Resistors
- Capacitors
- Transistors
- Cables and Connectors
- Diodes
- PCB and Breadboards
- LED
- Transformer/Adapter

- Push Buttons
- Switch
- IC
- IC Sockets

Software Specifications

1. Arduino Compiler
2. Programming Language: C

Block Diagram:

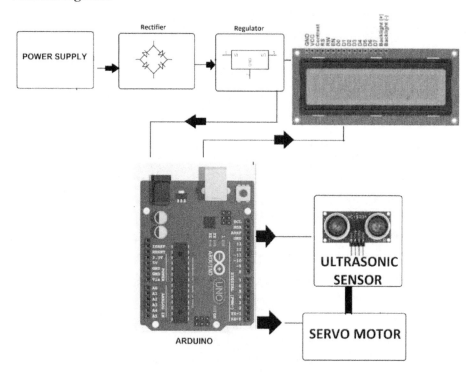

13. Smart Dustbin with IOT Notifications

Increasing populations result in an increase in trash in urban areas. With IoT and sensor-based circuitry, we present here an intelligent dustbin that can assist in solving this problem. In the normal dustbin, you must open it with your foot and throw garbage. Also, a person must remember to empty their trash cans when they are at capacity, so they do not overflow. In this paper we develop a smart dustbin which can do all of these tasks without any human involvement. Essentially, our system pairs a clap sensor with a foot switch. In response to the clap or foot tap, the door opens and closes automatically by itself.

Upon receiving the signal, the dustbin opens its hatch and closes it. Additionally, the dustbin has an ultrasonic level sensor that continuously looks for level changes and triggers an automatic alarm if garbage is expected to fill the bin. A smart circuitry inside the dustbin sends data to the garbage collector over the internet, so he can empty it, if necessary. Web development of the IoT system is carried out using IoT Gecko. In offices, homes and public places this bin is of great use for garbage disposal. Therefore, garbage can be automatically cleaned with the help of an automated smart dustbin.

Block Diagram

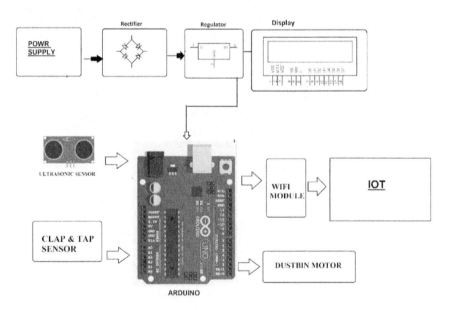

Hardware Specifications

- Arduino Uno
- Ultrasonic Sensor
- Mic Sensor
- Wi-Fi Module

- Resistors
- Capacitors
- Transistors
- Cables and Connectors
- Diodes
- PCB and Breadboards
- LED
- Transformer/Adapter
- Push Buttons
- Switch
- IC
- IC Sockets
- Bin Frame
- Mounts & Joints
- Supporting Frame

Software Specifications

- Arduino Compiler
- Programming Language: C
- IoT Gecko

14. IOT Solar Power Monitoring System

It is important that solar power plants are monitored for maximum voltage output. This monitoring system helps in recovering optimum power from plants by detecting problems like faulty solar panels, connections, dust accumulating on panels, and decreased production in addition to other such things. In response, we propose an IOT-based monitoring system for solar power that allows for the automated monitoring of solar power from any internet-connected device.

A 10Watt solar panel is monitored by an Arduino based system. The solar panel is continuously monitored by our system and the power output is transmitted to the IoT system via the internet. IOT Gecko is used here to send solar power parameters remotely to an IOT Gecko server. The new program also displays these parameters in a user-friendly interface so that you can alert the system manager when the output falls below certain limits. Solar plants can be monitored via the Internet from anywhere in the world, ensuring the best power output.

Block Diagram:

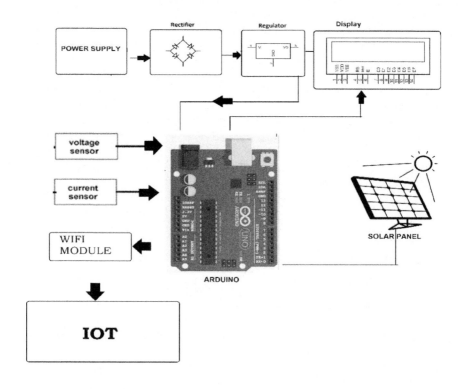

Hardware Specifications:
- Rectifier
- Regulator
- Power Supply
- LCD Display
- Voltage Sensor
- Current Sensor
- Wi-Fi Module
- Arduino Uno
- Solar Panel

Software Specifications:
- Arduino Compiler
- Programming Language: C

15. Arduino PID based DC Motor Position Control System

This motor placement control project involves the implementation of a PID Control System for an Arduino using the Derivative-Integral Formula. A PID controller with Arduino and a basic DC motor allows position control to be precise. With one shaft connected to the encoder and the other side connected to a pointer, a DC gear motor with two shafts can also be used as a power source. One encoder connected to Arduino interrupt pins points to the angle that is set on the protractor; one L293D motor IC is connected to our system, and an HC-05 module is used to connect it to an android device. The encoder sends a real-time input to Arduino in the meantime when sending a predefined angle set point from the robot device. If Arduino detects the encoder pulse matches a required position, it halts the DC motor at that position. A PID system controls the entire process for sleek, accurate motion.

Block Diagram

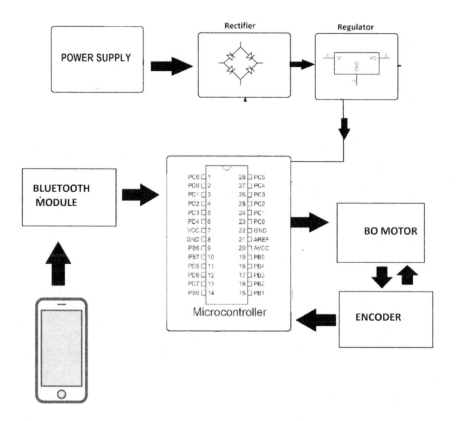

Hardware Specifications

- Arduino
- Dc motor

- Protractor
- L293d IC
- Optical encoder
- Crystal Oscillator
- Resistors
- Capacitors
- Transistors
- Cables and Connectors
- Diodes
- PCB and Breadboards
- LED
- Transformer/Adapter
- Push Buttons
- Switch
- IC
- IC Sockets

Software Specifications

- Arduino Compiler
- MC Programming Language: C

16. Open-Source COVID-19 Pulmonary Ventilator

The non-invasive, open-source ventilator is easy to build and is low-cost if there are no ventilators available and no patient is sedated or intubated while the patient needs to be ventilated. This project was inspired by a challenge I accepted from my former teacher and friend Serafim Pires. He presented a Spanish project to me and asked me to create a project to help fight the worldwide economic crisis. This functional prototype was built on the basis of two existing technologies, after conducting several researches and tests on the topic of non-invasive ventilation. All tests were successful and the functional test lasted in excess of 20 days without any interruption.

David Pascoal INOVT COVID-19 Pulmonary Ventilator project	Portugal 13-06-2020

Adaptation of the full face mask

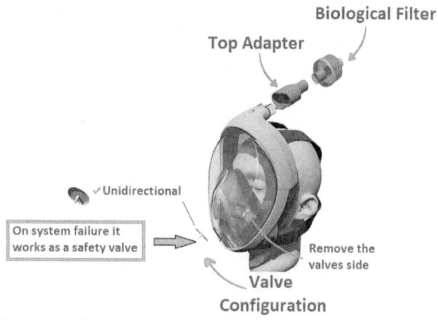

Biological Filter

Top Adapter

✓ Unidirectional

On system failure it works as a safety valve

Remove the valves side

Valve Configuration

Components Required

- Arduino UNO
- Arduino 4 Relay Shield
- Digital Servo MG995, LM2596S Module
- 10k linear Multi-turn Potentiometer
- Digilent 60W PCIe 12V 5A Power Supply
- 5mm LED Red, 5mm LED Green
- Alphanumeric LCD 20*4
- Switch button 220V
- Snorke Full Face, Solenoid Valve, 2 ways

Software Specifications

- Arduino Compiler
- MC Programming Language: C

274

Circuit Diagram of **COVID-19 Pulmonary Ventilator**

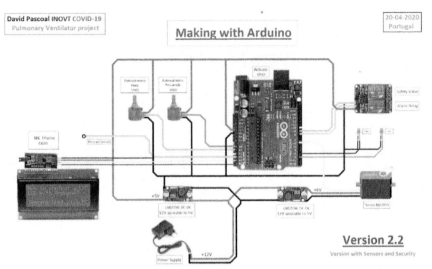

Through the use of nasal and face masks, non-invasive ventilation is made possible by delivering controlled amounts of compressed air into the lungs. This helps the body fight infection and recover when the lungs are failing from disease. During the height of the coronavirus outbreak, and based on research conducted in Italy, I turned a Decathlon snorkel mask into an emergency ventilator for patients suffering from COVID-19, in order to reduce the lack of ventilators. Because of their low cost and ease of adaptation, these masks are used throughout the world.

WARNING:

- This prototype does not have official validation, nor will I accept any responsibility with it.
- Furthermore, this equipment is intended to save lives in an extreme peak situation and will be used as a last resort by trained medical personnel.
- In Portugal, the Portuguese authorities may approve the duplication of the non-profit project in bulk.

17. Arduino based Snake Robot Controlled using Android

Twelve segments are driven by servo motors, all of which are joined together with metal brackets. An Arduino Mega controls the servos, which are powered by a 7.4-volt battery pack. A mobile device can control the snake via a Bluetooth app. The snake can also move autonomously. Servos and brackets can be used to make such a robot. One set of Lego wheels is built with each segment. Each segment includes a servo motor, a side bracket, a wire clip, and a C-bracket.

A Lego wheel axle had to be drilled with two screw holes so it can be connected to a C-bracket. It would be recommended to add rows and columns at the head and tail so that the Arduino and batteries can be accommodated. The brackets have two long C-braces that can connect on the side. A battery holder for 5AA batteries will power the Arduino, which is installed in the tail section of the snake. Battery packs with 7.4 volts powered the servos, which were mounted in the snake's head. An Arduino is connected to the receiver's ground on the bottom pin. A 5-volt pin from the Arduino is connected to the voltage pin.

Block Diagram:

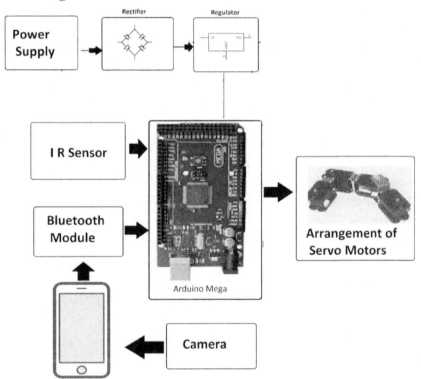

Hardware Specifications

- Arduino mega
- IR Sensor
- Servo Motors
- Bluetooth module

- Camera
- Cables and Connectors
- PCB and Breadboards
- Push Buttons
- Switch
- IC

Software Specifications

1. Arduino Compiler
2. Programming Language: C

18. Advanced Automatic Self-Car Parking using Arduino

Both developed and developing countries facing a major car parking issue in urban areas. Several cities lack car parking areas as a result of the rapid rise of car ownership. A significant part of this imbalance results from ineffective land use planning and a miscalculation of space requirements at the start of the planning process. There are several examples of problems that arise from parking throughout the day, such as lack of parking space, high parking rates, and the congestion of traffic caused by visitors in search of a parking spot. Parallel parking is generally the worst nightmare a driver has because not only is it difficult if you do it well, but it increases the risk of other drivers hitting your parked vehicle. We developed an automated parking system to solve the above parking problems, thus enabling cars to park themselves. A self-parking car project is a self-parking car which utilizes an Arduino board, obstacle sensor, ultrasonic range finder to identify the parking distance. This robot uses a small LCD module to display various program information, a DC motor and servo motor for steering, and several algorithms for path finding.

Hardware Specifications

- Robotic Chassis
- Arduino
- Ultrasonic
- Servo Motor
- Resistors, Capacitors, Transistors
- Cables and Connectors
- Diodes, PCB and Breadboards
- LED

- Transformer/Adapter
- Push Buttons, Switch
- IC
- IC Sockets

Block Diagram

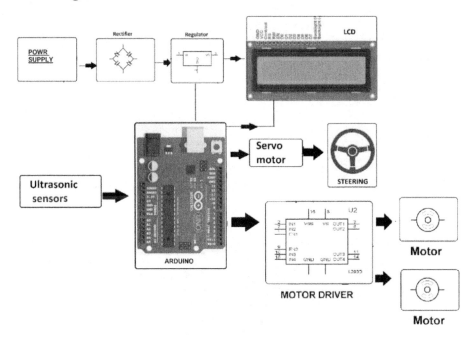

Software Specifications

Programming Language: C

19. IOT Industry Protection System Arduino

A Smart Industry Protection System, which is designed for industries to protect themselves from losses caused by incidents using the Internet of Things, protects them from unnecessary costs. Gas leaks can cause fires, which can cause massive industrial losses, as well as needing instant fire detection in case of blasts in furnaces, etc.

In addition, dim lighting may lead to improper lighting conditions in certain industries, which may result in increased accident risks. Arduino is used to make this system work. Temperature, light, and gas sensing make up the system, which works diligently to facilitate industrial accidents and loss prevention by detecting fire, gas leakage, and low lighting.

Sensors for light, gas, and temperature are interfaced to Arduino devices and an LCD screen to constitute the system, which has a display and a keyboard. Sensors continuously scan data for fire, gas leak or low light exposures, record values, and then submit this information online for transmission. The internet is achieved via the Wi-Fi module. Once this data is stored, it is displayed online using IOT gecko, and the desired output can be achieved.

Block Diagram:

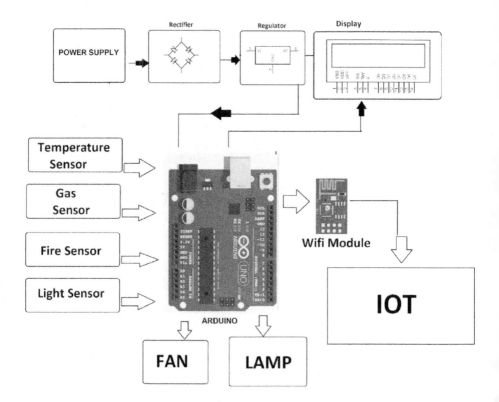

Hardware Specifications

- Arduino Uno
- LCD Display
- Wi-Fi Module

- LDR Sensor
- LPG CNG Gas Sensor
- Temperature Sensor
- Resistors
- Capacitors
- Transistors
- Cables and Connectors
- Diodes
- PCB and Breadboards
- LED
- Transformer/Adapter
- Push Buttons
- Switch
- IC
- IC Sockets

Software Specifications

- Arduino Compiler
- MC Programming Language: C
- IoT Gecko

20. Rotating Solar Panel Using Arduino

The energy demand in the commercial and residential markets is growing rapidly over the last few years. It leaves no other choice but to rely on renewable resources to generate usable energy as non-renewable resources are rapidly dwindling. Solar panels are another way to harness solar energy as it is the easiest and most abundant resource. Using this method, solar energy can be harnessed more efficiently.

It uses a Solar Panel attached to a rotating platform, which is powered by a motor, to charge a 12VDC Battery. An Atmega328 microcontroller attached to an Arduino Uno board, mounted on the PCB, is controlling this motor. In order to know the current position of the sun, the Rotating Solar Panel system scans from one horizon to another. This allows the greatest solar energy to be harnessed from that position. It is chosen to charge the Battery at the position that has the highest energy capacity. By aligning the Solar panel against the Sun, we can harness the most benefit from it.

Thus, harnessing solar energy under this project is more efficient and thus smarter.

Block Diagram:

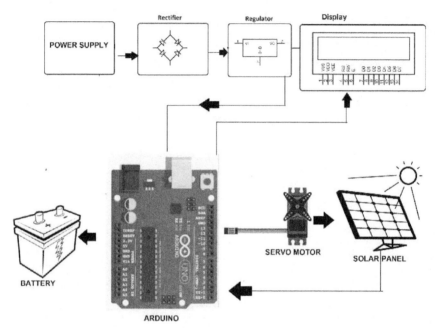

Hardware Specifications

- Arduino
- Servo Motor
- Solar Panel
- Solar Panel Mount
- Resistors
- Capacitors
- Diodes
- Screws

Software Specifications

- Arduino Compiler
- Programming Language: C

21. GPS Clock using Arduino

An exact time can be obtained from GPS synchronized clocks. Generally, clocks like this are used at railway stations, airports and other transport stands. In general, these are also used in military applications.

An Arduino Uno R3 with six simple pin inputs and 14 digital inputs and outputs (I/O) pins referred to as a GPS clock has been developed. Its flash memory is 32kB, its EEPROM memory is 2kB, and its ISP flash memory is 8kB.

Circuit diagram

A serial connection can be made between the board and the computer via UART, SPI, and I2C.

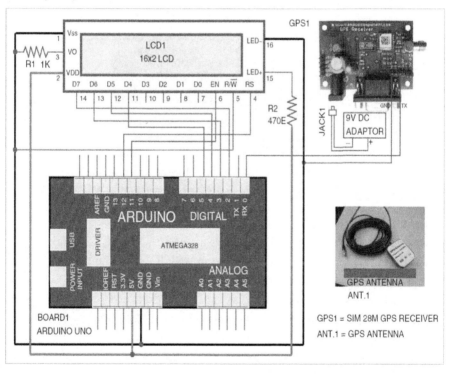

Block diagram of GPS clock using Arduino

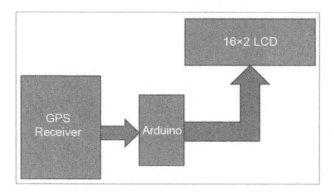

22. Touch Free Hand sanitizer dispenser using LDR

Touch-free hand sanitizer dispenser that automatically dispenses sanitizer utilizing LDR sensors and MOSFETs to switch the motor we designed this to be in accordance with COVID 19 coronavirus.

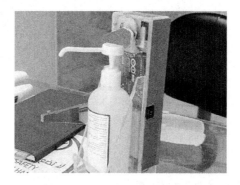

Coronavirus (COVID-19) is spreading across the world. Nearly every country is experiencing the devastating effects of the Coronavirus. A Pandemic disease has been declared by WHO and many cities are in lockdown situations. Many people's lifestyles have been changed drastically. Globally, the WHO is advising disease control officials to maintain Healthy Hand washing and Sanitation Habits, but our problem mainly involves our physical contact when we do this. The virus can be spread by touching infected bottles of alcohol or sanitizers with infected hands. We will make an automated hand sanitizer dispenser by using infrared sensors to detect a hand, and an automatic pump will pour the liquid on the hand.

Many Arduinos automated liquid dispensers are floating around the web. Nevertheless, my aim is to keep it straightforward and inexpensive, so anyone can produce it. A simple transistor or MOSFET with an IR proximity sensor would probably be the easiest solution for this purpose, and it would drastically reduce the costs as well. Because no microcontroller is present, spills are unlikely to be controlled, but the use of a smaller nozzle may reduce the flow of liquid.

Components Required

- Arduino UNO & Genuine UNO
- Fairchild semiconductor
- Power MOSFET N-Channel
- LDR, 5 Mohm
- Fairchild semiconductor 1n4004.
- 1N4007 – High Voltage, High Current Rated Diode
- Fairchild semiconductor 1n4004.
- 1N4007 - High Voltage, High Current Rated Diode
- 09590 01
- LED (generic)
- Resistor 220 ohm
- Keystone 233 image 75px
- 9V Battery Clip

Automatic Dispenser

A basic working principle of the automatic sanitizer dispenser is that when the distance sensor detects an obstruction within its line-of-sight, it will trigger the servo to turn on the sanitizer tap.

When the person's hand gets in the way of the sensor and obstructs the line of sight, the Arduino board detects the low distance and instructs the servo motor to activate the sanitizer.

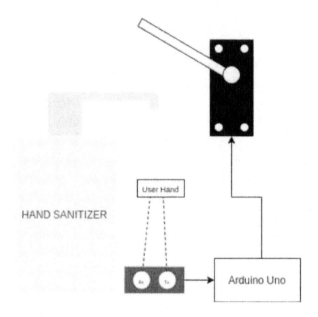

HAND SANITIZER

Circuit Diagram:

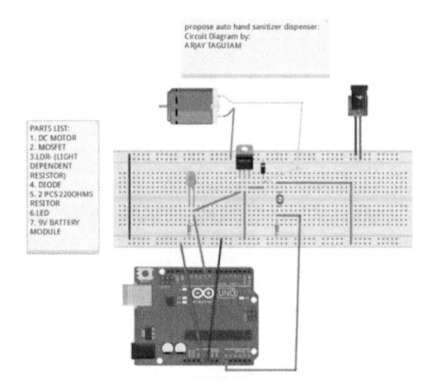

propose auto hand sanitizer dispenser:
Circuit Diagram by:
ARJAY TAGUIAM

PARTS LIST:
1. DC MOTOR
2. MOSFET
3.LDR- (LIGHT DEPENDENT RESISTOR)
4. DIODE
5. 2 PCS 220OHMS RESITOR
6.LED
7. 9V BATTERY MODULE

Here is the Circuit Diagram of a sanitizer or alcohol dispenser based on IR sensor. No microcontroller is required.

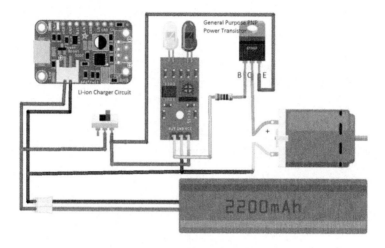

23. Line Follower Robot with Arduino

An object that is near can be detected by detecting its proximity without physical contact. Sensors that detect proximity usually emit electromagnetic fields (outside infrared light, for instance) in which changes in these fields or returns are monitored.

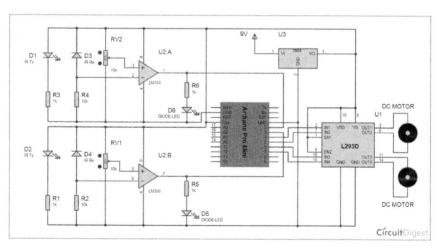

Concepts of Line Follower

Line following involves the use of light. This article discusses the behaviour of light at white and black surfaces. White surfaces reflect light almost completely while black surfaces absorb it entirely. An automated line follower robot is built using this behaviour of light.

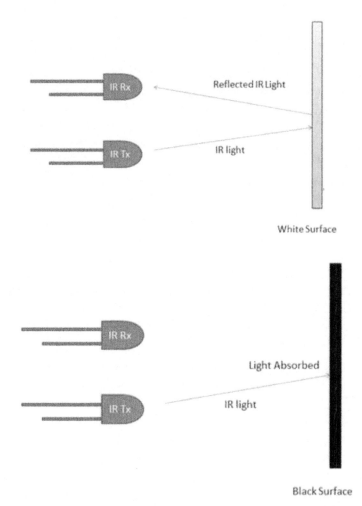

IR Transmitters are an essential part of this Arduino Line Follower Robot, also referred to as photodiodes. These devices are used to send and receive light. Infrared transmitters transmit infrared lights. Photodiodes generate voltage changes when infrared rays fall on white surfaces, and they reflect back. The photodiode does not receive any light or rays when infrared waves fall on a dark surface, since light is absorbed by the dark surface.

This Arduino line following robot receives 1 input as the sensor detects white surfaces while 0 input is received when it detects black surfaces.

There are three sections in the robot:

1. A **sensor** section,
2. **Control** section and
3. **A Driver** section.

Sensor section:

In this section, you will find IR diodes, potentiometers, comparators (Op-Amps) and LEDs. The comparator's two terminals receive their references through a potentiometer, while IR sensors provide the voltage change at the comparator's second terminal. Using the comparator, then, both voltage signals are compared, producing a digital signal. Using two comparators for two sensors we have implemented a line follower circuit here. A comparator is created using the LM 358, which has two ultra-low noise Op-amps inbuilt.

Working of Line Follower Robot using Arduino

It is very fascinating to operate as a line follower. It uses a sensor that senses a black line and then transmits the signal to an Arduino board, Afterwards, the motor is driven by Arduino based on the sensors' output

Basic Components
- Arduino UNO & Genuino UNO
- SparkFun Dual H-Bridge motor drivers L298
- Proximity Sensor

24. IoT Based Home Automation controlled by smartphone

Human life is increasingly driven by the use of automation, whether it's at home or at work. Automation in the manufacturing industry is a concept that is frequently used to automate large machines and/or robots to facilitate increased production, energy, and time efficiency.

In contrast, home automation affects the environment of the homeowners. The smartphone and the internet have allowed us to do this. There are two main ways of home automation. One type is controlled by just a smartphone, while the other type involves sensors and actuators to control lighting, temperature, door locks, electronic gadgets, and electrical appliances.

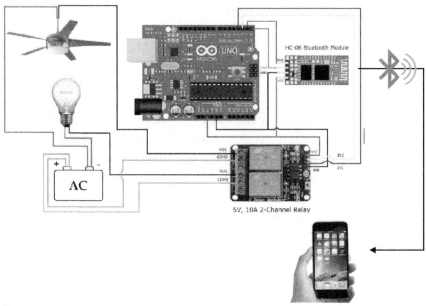

Essential Components

- Arduino UNO
- 12 V Relay X 4
- HC – 05 Bluetooth Module
- Prototyping board (Bread board)
- Connecting wires
- 12 V Power supply
- Smartphone or tablet (Bluetooth enabled)

Modern homes require sophisticated control in the electronic appliances they have in their homes. As a result of the integration of home appliances with smart phone and tablet connectivity, the home automation field has been transformed, enabling a greater level of affordability and simplicity. In addition to the features, they have already, smart phones can be made to communicate with any other device in an ad hoc network through connectivity options like Bluetooth. As mobile phones have become more prevalent, development of mobile applications has also increased. A mobile phone commonly found in a traditional household can be connected to the electronic equipment of a smart home in a temporary network using the opportunity of automating tasks for a smart home. The

Android mobile application platform is provided by Google Inc., which is used to develop applications for Android phones and tablets. Android-based home automation system will benefit the masses as it targets a large market who uses it for their mobile devices. Android maintained its leadership position in the Worldwide Quarterly Mobile Phone Tracker, published by International Data Corporation (IDC). Using Bluetooth for home appliances and mobile phones in an ad hoc network environment, such as in your home, is an excellent solution for short-range wireless communication. A wireless technology works over 2.4 GHz frequency range up to a distance of 100 m with 1 Megabit per second, making it a secure and efficient method for controlling home automation.

25. Covid-19 Patient Monitoring Device based on LoRa using The Things UNO

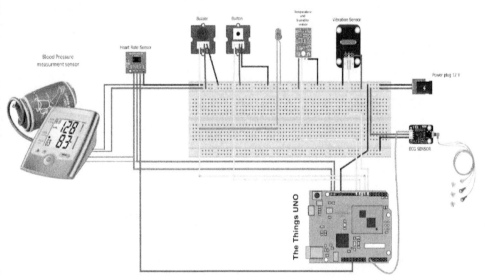

Lora network based covid-19 patient monitoring device.

Using sensors and connected networks, we have developed a patient monitoring system that can autonomously monitor patients' health conditions. The Covid-19 system was specially manufactured for patients with this condition. The biological behaviour of a patient can be gathered by several sensors. Information about biological processes then goes into the IoT cloud. By processing sensor data, the system is more intelligent, and can tell when a patient is in critical condition. Nurses and doctors receive instant alerts and hospital personnel receive push notifications.

Nurses and doctors' benefit from this system because they can observe the patients remotely without having to visit them personally. Relatives of patients can also gain access to the system with limited access.

Name of the components	Purpose
The Things UNO	The main controller board
Temperature and Humidity sensor	For body temperature and humidity measurement
Heart rate sensor (MAX30100)	Measure the pulse
ECG sensor	Measure the ECG data
Buzzer	Emergency Alarm
LED	Emergency indicator
Push button	call for assistance
Movement sensor	Detect the unexpected movement
Blood pressure sensor	Measure the blood pressure
360 Camera, Optional	Optionally streams the video
Others sensors	Air quality sensor and room temperature sensor are used for measuring room environment
12volt DC power supply	Power source

Sensor (notation)	Threshold	Threshold level [1]
Heart rate, h_r	$T_{heartrate}$	less than 50 and greater than 120
Temperature, $temp_{body}$	$T_{temperature}$	less than 35 and greater than 39 in Celsius
Humidity, $humidity_{body}$	$T_{humidity}$	less than 40% and greater than 55%
Movements, $move_{body}$	$T_{movements}$	Unexpected
SPO2, $spo2_{blood}$	T_{SPO2}	Under 90 %
Upper blood pressure, $upper_{blood}$	$T_{upperblood}$	less than 120 and greater than180
Lower blood pressure, $lower_{blood}$	$T_{lowerblood}$	less than 80 and greater than 110
Push button, $button_{call}$	T_{button}	On
ECG, ecg_{heart}	T_{ECG}	N/A

This monitoring system is controlled using the Things UNO, a Lora development board. This board collects information from various health sensors (described in the Hardware Components section) that provide information about patient health parameters. Data transmission from the Things UNO to the Lora Gateway (The Things Gateway) is also handled by the Things UNO. The Lora gateway provides a connection to the Amazon Web Services IoT cloud platform. This cloud is used for managing this system.

The data has been visualized using a Mobile application. For displaying real-time sensors data, such as the present health condition of a patient, various charts and gauges have been employed. Doctors and nurses can use this application remotely to monitor patients without visiting an ICU unit. A push notification is sent to appropriate doctors or nurses regarding the emergency situation of the patient due to the nature of intelligence, by processing the sensor data, Equation -I identifies the patient's emergency condition. During a 24-hour period, the hospital in charge personnel (ICU in charge person) continuously monitored multiple patients online via our cloud-based desktop application (shown in Figure), which makes the ICU process more efficient, Throughout the application's lifetime, all of the applications tapped into the Internet of Things and visualized the data in real-time, using visualizations such as gauges, Sparklines, and Text.

26. Open-Source Pulse Oximeter for COVID-19

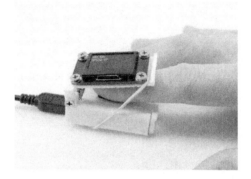

This is an easy-to-make, USB-powered pulse oximeter that can be built for around $20 and features an OLED display.

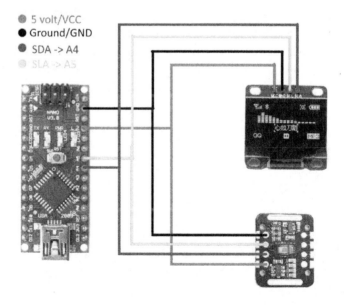

The SARS-CoV-2 virus is the virus responsible for causing COVID-19, a disease which mostly attacks the respiratory system. Fever, chills, and muscle aches and pains are some of the milder symptoms, but a severe case can lead to pneumonia. A person suffering from pneumonia or even slight shortness of breath might not recognize when to seek medical attention, especially when they begin to feel even worse. Hence, I am developing this open-source pulse oximeter so that the people can be better informed about their current condition and which can assist them in getting the help they need.

Disclaimer

Using this device for accurate medical diagnosis is not recommended!

27. Touch less doorbells can operate without touching the switch.

TOUCHLESS DOORBELL

One of the most effective ways to escape from COVID-19 is through social isolation. Staying at home is strongly recommended in the beginning days. However, we still have to make some emergency visits to certain homes. We first searched the doorbell button of a house when we arrived. Then press the doorbell button. However, in this specific situation, this doorbell button can cause the virus to spread. A virus is held on the button when someone who is not infected presses the button, and when a second person touches the button, the virus is spread. A touchless doorbell will help to eliminate this danger. Touchless doorbells are available to convert existing doorbells.

Working

Infrared LED transmitters transmit light within the range of the infrared spectrum. Wave length of IR waves is longer than wave length of visible light. This transmitted IR light will be picked up by the photodiode receiver. The photodiode will only conduct when it is illuminated. The semiconductor is reverse biased as well.

It can be shown that the current flow is directly proportional to the amount of light it receives. In this photo, we see the LM358 Operational amplifier in voltage comparator mode. Comparison is made between the voltage set by the variable resistor and the voltage set by the photodiode series resistor

- (PSR voltage). A ground connection is maintained between the "OUTPUT" pin and the OP-AMP output.
- The PSR Voltage has dropped below the Threshold Voltage - the output is HIGH
- Voltage drops on PSR < Threshold Voltage - Output is LOW
- By calibrating the variable resistor, the distance at which objects should be detected can be determined.

Key point

In case an object is presented in front of the sensor, the sensor output will be HIGH, but if not, the sensor output will be LOW

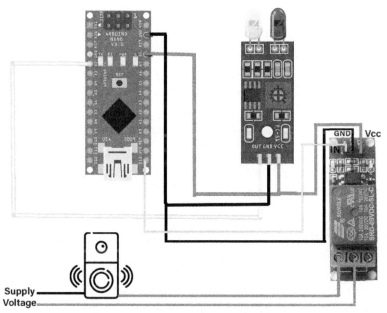

Essential Components

Arduino Nano R3, Relay, IR Sensor, Buzzer

A signal will be sent to the Arduino board when we show our hand to the

IR Sensor. And Arduino drives the relay. The relay is connected to the doorbell. The bell will ring the moment the relay is activated.

28. Social Distancing Device (Safety Card)

During this pandemic, we trust everyone is following social distancing and keeping safe, which is why we made an ultrasonic sensor device at my home to do social distancing. With this device, a buzzer sounds and vibration occurs when the distance between two people is less than one meter, signaling that the distance needs to be maintained.

Parts

Arduino UNO, Ultrasonic Sensors, Buzzer, LED

The device automatically turns off if the space is greater than 1 meter.

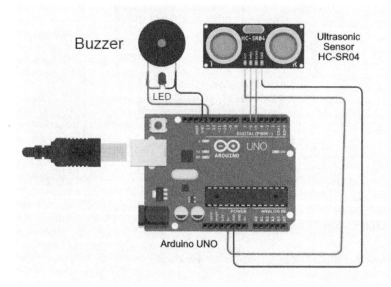

I think this is a very interesting and useful project that you can easily build at home. Wearable's can be manufactured by using an Arduino Nano or you can shrink their size by using an Arduino Micro. Put together the materials like Arduino Uno Arduino Nano, ultrasonic sensor, buzzer, vibrator motor, 9v battery, switch, card or cardboard box, Velcro strips, take the card and glue the face of the box with the electronics, proceed to upload the code, Once the code has been uploaded, place the Arduino

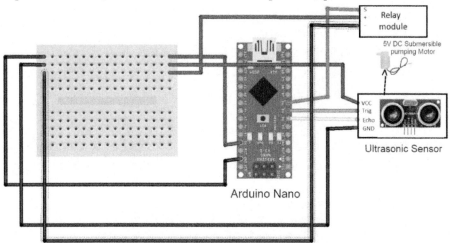

inside the box, along with the switch, nine-volt battery, and circuit symbols, and do circuit connections. Attach the front portion of the box and then check that everything functions well, now decorate the box and stick it with Velcro.

29. Automatic Faucet (Touchless) for COVID-19 Using Arduino

Wash your hands comfortably and avoid getting coronavirus disease. Don't touch the surface of the faucet after you wash them.

A disease caused by the severe acute respiratory syndrome coronavirus 2 is known as coronavirus disease (COVID-19), also known as the coronavirus severe acute respiratory syndrome (SARS-Cov-2). More than a million people worldwide have been affected by COVID-19 and hundreds of thousands of people have lost their lives as a result. People are affected by this disease in different ways. Many people develop mild to moderate illnesses that require no hospitalization or special treatment, while others develop severe illnesses that ultimately lead to death. A person infected with this virus can incubate for an average of 5-6 days, but it can also incubate for 2 weeks. It could be contagious during this period, even though the person may not be experiencing any symptoms. If the person doesn't take any precautions, he will be a virus carrier and will spread the illness easily.

Components Required

- Arduino Nano R3
- Solderless Breadboard Half Size
- Jumper wires (generic)
- Ultrasonic Sensor - HC-SR04 (Generic)
- Submersible water pump - 5V
- Relay Module (Generic)

Coronavirus has been spreading rapidly around the world and will continue to spread. The second wave of the coronavirus is still affecting some countries while others are still in lockdown and still aren't seeing any recovery.

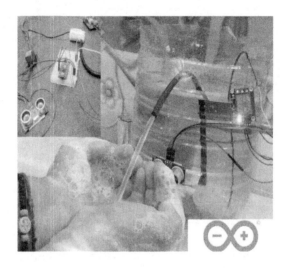

Program

```
#define trig 5
#define echo 4
const int Relay = 6;
long duration;
int distance;
```

```
void setup() {
pinMode(trig, OUTPUT);   // Set the trigger pin as OUTPUT
pinMode(echo, INPUT);    // Set the echo pin as INPUT

pinMode(Relay, OUTPUT); // Configure the pin of the relay module as
OUTPUT
Serial.begin(9600); // Set baud rate as 9600
}
void loop() {
digitalWrite(trig, LOW);
delayMicroseconds(5);
digitalWrite(trig, HIGH);
delayMicroseconds(10);
digitalWrite(trig, LOW);

duration = pulseIn(echo, HIGH); // Calculate time taken (in
microseconds) for the pulse emitted by the trigger pin to reach the echo
pin.

distance = (duration/2) * (331.3/10000); // Calculate the distance from
the sensor to the obstacle in cm, using the speed of sound in air(m/s) and
the time taken (stored in duration variable)

Serial.println(distance);
if(distance>1 && distance<10){
   digitalWrite(Relay, HIGH); //Turns on the submersible water pump or
solenoid water valve
   }
Else
{
   digitalWrite(Relay, LOW); //Turns off the submersible water pump or
solenoid water valve
   }
   delay(2000); // Set a delay period of 2 seconds to prevent the clicking of
the relay module
}
```

30. Automatic Hand Sensing Water and Soap Tank with Tap

This automatic tank for water and soap prevents the spread of coronaviruses in public places while, at the same time, prohibiting touch-ups of the faucet.

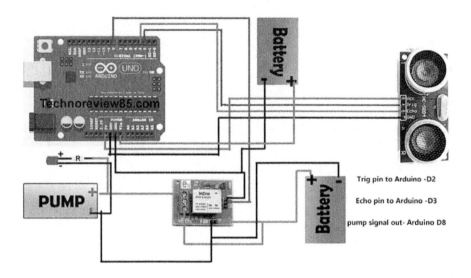

Trig pin to Arduino -D2

Echo pin to Arduino -D3

pump signal out- Arduino D8

Materials:

The major Materials used in this project are:

1. Transparent Pipes
2. Jumper Wire
3. 9 volts Battery
4. Ohms Resistor
5. Arduino Uno
6. Hc-sr04 Ultrasonic sensor
7. Relay Module
8. DC Powered Pump
9. Water Tank
10. Soap Container
11. Metal tank stand
12. Solar Power Source
13. Ceramic Zinc
14. Outlet Pipes

In March 2020, the World Health Organization (WHO) declared a global pandemic of a novel coronavirus outbreak that caused a respiratory illness that was first discovered in Wuhan, China. The World Health Organization estimates that the number of confirmed HIV cases and deaths is over 3 million by the end of April 2020.

People can contract the disease directly from an infected person or indirectly through touching surfaces contaminated with viral droplets. Since specific treatments for the outbreak or a vaccine are not yet available, it is crucial to prevent the outbreak from spreading from person to person and affecting people's lives, health, livelihoods, and the healthcare systems we are all relying on.

Infected people spread the COVID-19 virus mainly by sneezing or coughing droplets of saliva. It is important to properly wash your hands in order to prevent COVID-19.

By providing safe water, sanitation and basic hygiene measures during hand washing, as well as prohibiting retouching of the faucet to avoid decontaminating the water source or tap and posing further risks to another user, this can be achieved.

People who obtain automatic hand sensing water and soap dispensers will not only be able to wash their hands with ease, but will also be afforded proper hygiene facilities, however limiting the time in which people are in contact with the tap would prevent recontamination.

Statement of Problems.

In order to prevent the spread of this virus, the government of Nigeria has taken the necessary measures by ensuring a lockdown policy in states with high incidence of the coronavirus. The major contact point for people moving out of and into the city after lockdown when they're using the Motor Parks doesn't have running water. Spreading the virus in this manner would make one more vulnerable to infection by infecting one another. Recent data from UNICEF indicates that worldwide, only three out of five people have basic hand washing facilities.

People should thus be taught to keep proper hygiene, as well as wash their hands often in order to remain safe and alive in these parks. The most important thing is to reduce the spread of this virus and defeat coronavirus.

31. DIY GPS Speedometer using Arduino and OLED

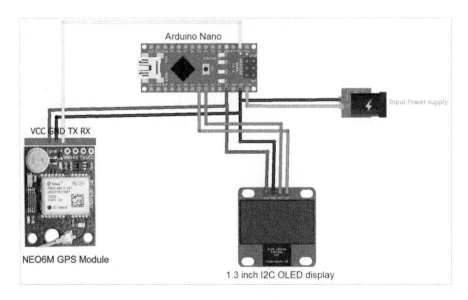

Speedometers are used to determine how fast a vehicle is traveling. We previously built Analog speedometer and digital speedometer using the IR and hall sensors respectively. The vehicle speed will be measured using a GPS today. It is more accurate to use a GPS speedometer than a conventional speedometer because it can constantly locate the vehicle and can calculate the speed. Smartphones and vehicles incorporate GPS technology to provide navigation and traffic alerts.

Materials Used

- Arduino Nano
- NEO6M GPS Module
- 1.3 inch I2C OLED display
- Breadboard
- Connecting Jumpers

32. Automatic Bottle Filling System using Arduino

The industry which uses automatic bottle filling machines the most is the beverage & soft drink industry. With a conveyor belt being used, these machines are an economical and efficient way to fill bottles. Automation of bottle filling machines is mostly done using PLCs, but an Arduino can also be put to work in this regard. IR or ultrasonic sensors can be programmed to automatically detect the bottle and stop the conveyor belt for a short period of time thereby permitting the bottler to fill the bottle. Continue to move the belt where you stopped when the next bottle was detected.

With an Arduino Uno, conveyor belt, solenoid valve, infrared sensor, and stepper motor, we are going to build a prototype for an Automatic Bottle Filling Machine. An electronic stepper motor controls the speed of the belt conveyor. Once the IR sensor is detecting the bottle, the stepper motor will continue driving the belt. As an external trigger, we used the IR sensor. A solid-state relay switches on the solenoid valve whenever the IR sensor goes high. For bottle filling, the code already describes a delay that is necessary. In that case the Arduino will continually power on the solenoid valve and turn off the stepper motor. A solenoid valve turns off the filling after a fixed amount of time, enabling the conveyor to move to the next bottle.

Previously, we used Arduino with an IR Sensor and Solenoid valve, so you can learn more about the basics of interfacing Arduino with these components by visiting the links.

Components Required

- Arduino Uno
- Stepper Motor (Nema17)
- Relay
- Solenoid Valve
- IR Sensor
- A4988 Motor Driver
- Battery

Circuit Diagram

Following is the circuit diagram for the Automated Bottle Filling System using Arduino.

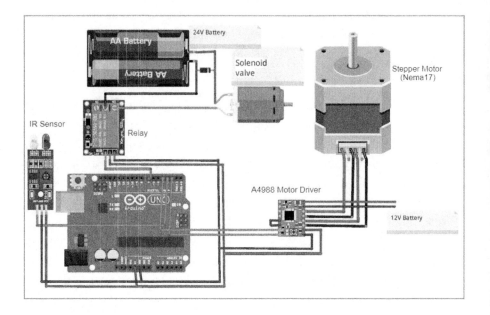

33. Control a Solenoid Valve with Arduino

In many process automation systems, solenoids play an important role in actuating the components. In addition to solenoid valves, there are solenoid plungers which produce linear motion and can be used to open and close water or gas pipelines. In most homes and offices, we are all familiar with ding-dong doorbells, which use solenoid technology. Upon being energized with AC power, a small rod will be moved up and down by the Doorbell's plunger-type solenoid coil. A rod attached to the solenoid will strike metal plates connected to each side, producing the soothing sound. It's also used as a starter for vehicles or in sprinkler systems and RO systems.

Circuit Diagram

The circuit diagram for controlling solenoid valve with Arduino is shown below:

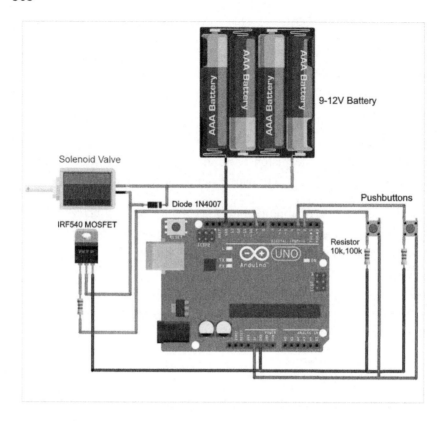

Components Required

- Arduino UNO
- Solenoid Valve
- IRF540 MOSFET
- Pushbutton - 2 nos.
- Resistor (10k, 100k)
- Diode - 1N4007
- Breadboard
- Connecting Wires

How Does a Solenoid Valve Work?

Solenoids are devices that convert electrical energy into mechanical energy. In this setup, there is a coil wrapped around conductive material, acting as an electromagnet. Electric magnets are better than natural magnets, because they can be switched on or off using a coil electrically charged. As a conductor is turned energized, a magnetic field is generated around it because the current-carrying conductor is a coil. Since a coil is a magnet, a strong magnetic field is created that magnetizes the material, thus creating linear movement.

A type of relay, it operates by means of a coil which when energized pulls a conductor (piston) inside it, which then lets liquid flow through it. The spring force pushes the piston back in the previous position when the electric motor is de-energized, which again blocks the liquid flow.

Therefore, it is not possible to control a Solenoid coil directly through a logic circuit during this process, as it draws large amounts of current and produces hysteresis problems. It is common to control flow of liquids with a 12V solenoid valve when building a pump. Because this particular solenoid valve draws up to 1.2A of peak or continuous current during energization, it has to be taken into consideration when designing the solenoid driver circuit.

34. An Arduino-based Gesture Controlled Air Mouse that uses Accelerometer

Did you ever wonder why we're moving toward an immersive reality? With the advent of virtual reality, mixed reality, augmented reality, etc., we are constantly finding new ways to interact with our surroundings. We are continually impressed by these fast-paced interactive technologies of new devices coming out every day.

They are used in a wide variety of applications, including gaming, entertainment and interactive activities. In this tutorial, you will learn about a new sort of user interface that will replace the traditional mouse with something more interesting. It is obvious to our game geeks that Nintendo was the company to devise a way to interact with video games with a 3D interactive motion console known as a Wii. Gestures for games are sent wirelessly through the accelerometer to the system using the accelerometer. Check out their patent EP1854518B1 to find out more information about this technology. This will give you a complete understanding of how it works.

Pre-requisites

- Arduino Nano (any model)
- Accelerometer ADXL335 Module
- Bluetooth HC-05 Module
- Push buttons
- Python Installed computer

Circuit Diagram

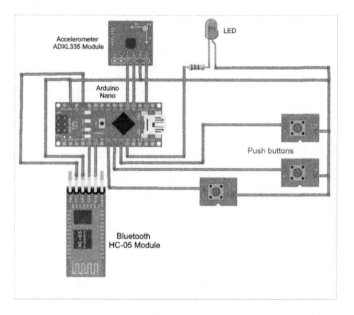

This idea inspired us to create an "Air mouse", which will make it possible to control a system just by waving it in the air, however, instead of using 3D coordinates, we will only be using 2D coordinates in order to make the computer mouse mimic actions since the mouse works in two dimensions X and Y.With the Wireless 3D Air Mouse, the technical concept is very simple, through the use of an accelerometer we will measure the speed of the actions and motions of the Air Mouse along the x and y axis, with the help of the Python software drivers running on the computer, we will control the mouse cursor and perform certain actions based on the values of the accelerometer.

Flow Chart

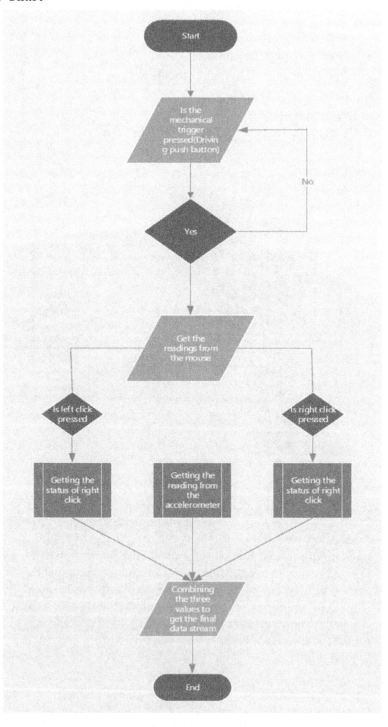

35. Arduino Whistle Detector Switch using Sound Sensor

In my childhood I was fascinated by a music car that got triggered when you clapped your hands, and as I grew up, I wondered if we can use the same thing to control lights and fans in a home. My fan and light switches could be operated with a simple handclap rather than walking up to them. As this circuit constantly responds to any loud noise, like a loud radio or my neighbour's lawn mower, it would often malfunction. However, clap switches can also be fun to build.

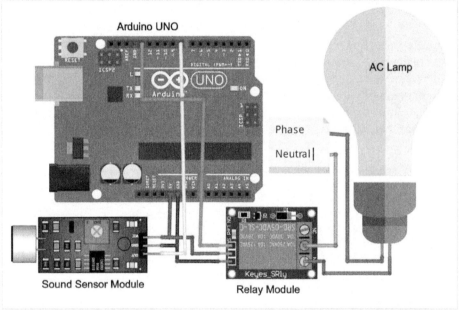

That is when I discovered this whistle detecting circuit, which detects a whistle. Like speech or music, a whistle has a specific frequency that is constant for a particular duration, thus can be distinguished from other sounds. We'll see how to identify whistles by using a Sound Sensor and an Arduino for this tutorial, and we will use an AC lamp and a relay to control it when a whistle is heard.

As we proceed, we will learn how sound signals are received by devices such as microphones and learn how to use Arduino to measure frequency. This sounds interesting, so let's get started with our home automation project using Arduino.

Materials Required

- Arduino UNO
- Sound Sensor Module
- Relay Module
- AC Lamp
- Connecting Wires
- Breadboard

Sound Sensor Working

As we know, the microphone is the part of the sound sensor that converts acoustical vibrations, called sound waves, into electrical energy. An electronic signal is created on an output pin when the microphone's diaphragm vibrates to sound waves in the environment. A microcontroller like Arduino cannot directly process these signals since they are very small in magnitude (mV). The output from the microphone is by default analog, so it is a sine wave of variable frequency, but electronic microcontroller are digital devices and hence can handle square waves better.

36. Obstacle Avoiding Robot using Arduino

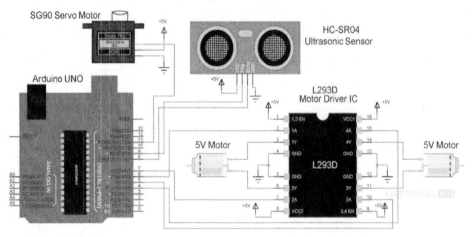

A simple Robot Obstacle avoidance project is designed here. The field of robotics is fast growing and has a lot to offer. Technology advances are increasing the applications of robotics since it is a branch of engineering. Mobile Robots are becoming more and more complex, and the number of mobile robots and their applications are increasing rapidly.

The navigation techniques used for mobile robots include path planning, self-localization and map interpretation. Robot-type vehicles known as Obstacle Avoiding Robots are designed to avoid collisions with unexpected obstacles. We have designed an obstacle avoidance robot in this project. Ultrasonic range finders are the key to avoid collisions with this Arduino-based robot.

Hardware Required

- Arduino Uno
- Ultrasonic Range Finder Sensor – HC – SR04
- Motor Driver IC – L293D
- Servo Motor (Tower Pro SG90)
- Geared Motors x 2
- Robot Chassis
- Power Supply
- Battery Connector
- Battery Holder

Ultrasonic Sensor

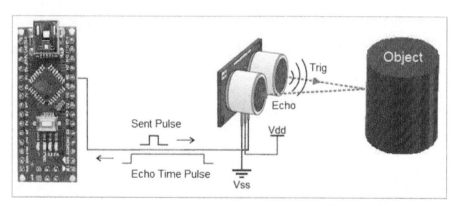

You need to know how the ultrasonic sensor works before tackling the project, read chapter 1 for more information on ultrasonic sensors. Ultrasonic Ranger - uses ultrasonic waves to measure distance between sensors and objects based on the time between generating the ultrasonic wave and receiving its echoes. There are four pins on the HC-SR04 Ultrasonic sensor: Vcc+, Trigger, Echo, and Ground.

37. Speed, Distance and Angle Measurement for Mobile Robots using Arduino and LM393 Sensor (H206)

Throughout human history, robots have gradually made our lives easier. Starship has already deployed six wheeled robotic food delivery vehicles on the UK's roads, smartly avoiding motorists to reach their destinations. All mobile robots that navigate within the environment need to be aware of their own position and orientation with regard to the environment. A variety of technologies can be used to accomplish this, including GPS, RF Triangulation, Accelerometers, and Gyroscopes. All of the techniques have their own advantages, so each is unique in its own way. Here we will be reading speed and distance from the Arduino microcontroller using the simple and readily-available LM393 speed sensor. By using these parameters, the robot will be able to gain an understanding of its current status in the real world and, as a result, navigate safely.

Required Components

- Arduino Nano
- 16x2 LCD module
- L298N H-Bridge Motor Driver
- Analog Joystick
- H206 Sensor
- LM393 Speed Sensor

Circuit Diagram

Here is the circuit diagram for this speed and distance sensing robot. A L298N H-Bridge Motor Driver module drives two DC motors powered by the Arduino Nano as the Robot's brain. Both the Joystick and the H206 speed sensors are used for controlling speed, direction, and angle of the bot, while the Joystick and second speed sensor are used to measure distance, speed, and angle of the bot respectively. Displayed in the LCD 16x2 module are the measured values. LCD contrast can be adjusted by the potentiometer connected to it, and the resistor is used to limit the current flowing through the LC's backlight.

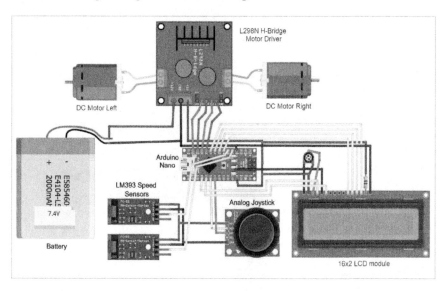

This 7.4V Lithium cell is used to power the whole circuit. Its 12.0V pin is connected to the Motor driver module. Once the motor driver module is connected to the Arduino, +5V is regulated by the voltage regulator, which powers the LCD, Sensors, and Joystick.

Using Ariana's digital pins 8,9,10, and 11, the Motor can be controlled. In order to control the motor's speed, PWM signals must be provided to the positive terminal of the motor. We have a PWM capable pin which corresponds with pin 9 and an analog pin A2, which is read from the Joystick.

When a gap in the grid plate is detected by the H206 sensor, it will generate a trigger. Both the triggers (output pins) from both boards are connected to External interrupt pins 2 and 3 of the Arduino board since they should not always be read accurately to calculate the correct speed and distance. I assembled my bot like the following, with the circuit board mounted on the chassis and the speed sensor installed as explained, after the connections were made, it looked like this.

38. Build a Smart Watch by Interfacing OLED Display with Android Phone using Arduino

A 162 Dot matrix LCD display is probably familiar to most of us, but we are also familiar with the 16x2 LCD display used as some kind of information display in our everyday lives. However, there are many limitations in what these LCD displays can do.

Fig.Smartwatch Project Picture

The basic information from the Android smartphone will be displayed using OLED in this tutorial like the time, date, network strength, and battery level. Here is a collection of simple tools and pictures that will allow you to build a simple but powerful Arduino based Smartwatch, which will also act as a watch for incoming calls and messages on your OLED display.

In this case, we are using an android phone application to fetch data from the OLED Display and then Bluetooth Module and Arduino Pro Mini are used to send this data to the OLED Display. Bluetooth modules with Arduino work well for sending data to Android smartphones. It is also possible to use the Bluetooth module HC-05 instead of HC-06.

The Arduino is connected to the mobile phone by means of a String, which fetches data from the mobile phone and is sent to the Arduino. When Arduino receives the string of bytes, it decodes it into a string of temporary variables that will be displayed on an OLED display. In OLED displays, some graphics have been created that help with displaying values

Hardware Required

- 128×64 OLED display Module (SSD1306)
- Arduino (we have used Arduino Pro Mini. But we can use any Arduino Board)
- Bluetooth HC05/HC06
- Connecting Wires
- 3.7v Li-On Battery
- Jumper

Circuit Diagram

Here is a simple circuit for using an SSD1306 OLED board with Arduino.

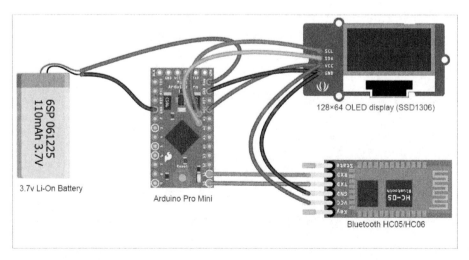

Our board for controlling all the operations is an Arduino Mini. One of the reasons why Arduino pro mini should be chosen is that it uses 3.3v power supply.

The HC-06 OLED can be operated at 3.3v as well. Therefore, all of these modules can be operated from a single 3.7v Li-on. Li-on batteries are the most compact and lightweight type of battery. Wearable devices benefit greatly from this technology. This project also includes a wearable smartwatch that connects to a smartphone.

Several questions arise regarding the power supply. All the modules are working on 3.3v but the 3.7V Li-ion battery is causing damage to the modules. The solution to this problem we used was to apply 3.7 volts of battery power to a raw pin of Arduino pro mini that could change that voltage into 3.3 volts.

39. Arduino Bluetooth with MATLAB for Wireless Communication

This protocol is the most popular solution for wireless communication in embedded systems due to its simplicity and ability to support short range communication. Besides being used to transfer data between two devices but also to control them wirelessly, Bluetooth is also used for controlling certain devices. Bluetooth is built into almost every electronic gadget nowadays, so securing Bluetooth control in your embedded app is a wise choice.

Using Bluetooth in MATLAB and wireless communication, we will learn how to accomplish this in this tutorial. On one side, we will use Bluetooth in MATLAB, and on the other, we will use HC-05 with Arduino. MATLAB and Arduino can communicate via Bluetooth in two ways, one via the command window and the other via MATLAB GUI. Both of these methods use the same Arduino code.

Components Required

- MATLAB installed Laptop (Preference: R2016a or above versions)
- Arduino UNO, Bluetooth Module (HC-05)
- LED (any color)
- Resistor (330 ohm), Jumper Wires

Circuit Diagram

The following schematics are needed to communicate between MATLAB and Arduino using Bluetooth.

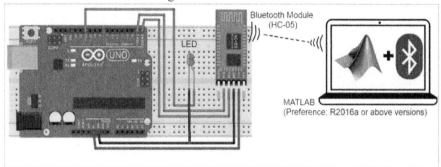

The Arduino UNO needs to be uploaded with the given code and then MATLAB Command Window should be used to start programming.

```
#include <SoftwareSerial.h>
int TxD;
int RxD;
int data;
SoftwareSerial bluetooth(TxD, RxD);
void setup() {
  Serial.begin(9600);
  bluetooth.begin(9600);
}
void loop()
{
if(bluetooth.available() > 0)
{
data = bluetooth.read();
Serial.print(data);
Serial.print("\n");
if(data == '1')
{
digitalWrite(11, HIGH);
}
else if(data == '0')
{
digitalWrite(11, LOW);
}}}
```

316

Then, copy and paste the below MATLAB code in the Command window for Bluetooth communication between MATLAB and Arduino.

```
instrhwinfo('Bluetooth','HC-05');
bt = Bluetooth('HC-05', 1);
fopen(bt);
```

```
Command Window
  >> instrhwinfo('Bluetooth','HC-05');
  bt = Bluetooth('HC-05', 1);
  fopen(bt);
fx >>
```

In the below code, command *fprintf(bt,'0')* is used to turn OFF the LED by sending '0' to the Arduino. Now, if you want to turn ON the LED just send '1' instead of '0' using the below command.

```
fprintf(bt,'1');
```

```
Command Window
  >> instrhwinfo('Bluetooth','HC-05');
  bt = Bluetooth('HC-05', 1);
  fopen(bt);
  >> fprintf(bt,'1');
  >> fprintf(bt,'0');
fx >>
```

To check the information about the available hardware, use below command

```
instrhwinfo('type','Name of device');
```

To open the bluetooth port, below command in used

```
fopen(bt);
```

Check the video below to understand the complete process of **Sending Data from MATLAB to Arduino using Bluetooth**.

Arduino can be programmed in MATLAB. For MATLAB to run on Arduino target hardware, you need to install a support package from add-ons. The Bluetooth modules HC-05 or HC-06 can be used.
For more information about Bluetooth communication through MATLAB, please refer to the below link
https://www.mathworks.com/help/instrument/reading-and-writing-data-over-the-bluetooth-interface.html

40. Smartphone Controlled Arduino Mood Light with Alarm

It's quite impressive how this LED strip works, I've recently purchased the NeoPixel LED strip. We control each LED individually on the board by using a driver IC which delivers a vibrant spectrum of colors. As an obsessive color freak, I was intrigued by the tiny LED's changing colors during night times, which is why I realized that I could build a similar project for myself.

This LED light should not only be able to change color, but should have a rational reasoning behind it as well. A professor of Color Science and Technology at University of Leeds by the name of Stephen Westland, I discovered that article. In response to colored light, humans exhibit a physical and psychological response based on the color. There have been many studies conducted on this process under the name of chronotherapy and the equipment used to accomplish this has been called a Mood Lamp.

Hence, I decided to venture deeper into chronotherapy and build a lamp with color changing capabilities that also can be controlled by a phone. Also, I enhanced the setting by adding a daytime dimming screen and an option to set a bright orange wake-up light (sunshine), This alarm allows you to sleep by putting the LEDs into sleep mode in a mild purple (night sky) color. Isn't that cool? Let's get building.

Materials Required

- Enough science we are supposed to be working with electronics, so let's gather the required components.
- NeoPixel LEDs
- Arduino, DS3231 RTC module
- HC-05 Bluetooth Module
- LDR, 100K resistor, 12V Power supply.
- Chronotherapy - Mood Lamp

Many of these DIY mood lamps offer nothing more than switch on and off at random, without any purpose behind it. A mood lamp should have a minimum brightness, be gradually colored, and have progressively varying intensities. After a bit of research, I discovered that such a lamp should have a minimum brightness. Below is a table which compares how each color affects mental and physical level.

Circuit Diagram

The complete circuit diagram for this Bluetooth Controlled Arduino Mood Lamp Project is given below.

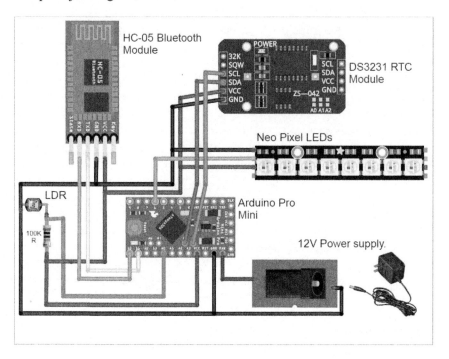

41. Interfacing nRF24L01 with Arduino: Controlling Servo Motor

Wireless communication is becoming increasingly ubiquitous, with more machines/devices communicating on cloud-based platforms such as Internet of things (IoT), Industry 4.0, Machine to Machine communication, etc. Bluetooth Low Energy (BLE 4.0), Zigbee, ESP43 Wi-Fi modules, 433MHz RF modules, Lora, nRF etc. are some of the wireless communication systems that engineers use, and their choice of medium is determined by the type of application.

Most popular among all is the nRF24L01, which is a radio frequency-based interconnect system. In addition, modules of this type operate on 2.4GHz bands with baud rates between 250Kbps and 2Mbps and have been legal throughout the world.

They claim that they can also transmit and receive 100-meter distances with proper antennas. So, what will this tutorial teach you? This tutorial will give you a deeper understanding of how to successfully interface this module with microcontroller platforms such as Arduino. This module also provides solutions to some of the problems that may occur when using it.

Getting to know the nRF24L01 RF Module

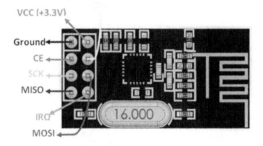

A transceiver, the nRF24L01 modules are capable of communicating in both directions but are half-duplex, which means they can only send or receive data at the same time. It uses the Nordic semiconductors nRF24L01 chip, which is responsible for transmit and receive functions. SPI is the protocol the IC uses, so it can communicate with any microcontroller. Because Arduino has libraries readily available, it gets a lot easier. Here is a list of pinouts of nRF24L01 modules.

Operating at voltage levels from 1.9V to 3.6V (typically 3.3V), the module consumes only 12mA during normal operation, making it battery efficient and therefore allowing the module to run on coin cells. The pins are tolerant of 5V despite the operating voltage of 3.3V, and so can be directly connected to 5V microcontrollers like Arduino.

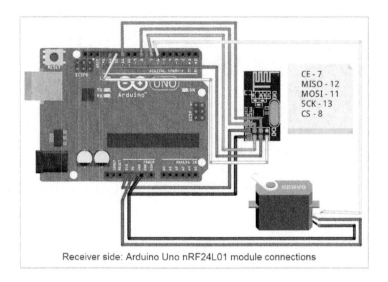

Receiver side: Arduino Uno nRF24L01 module connections

CE - 7
MISO - 12
MOSI - 11
SCK - 13
CS - 8

Using these modules has another advantage in that each one comes with 6 Pipelines. Specifically, each module can communicate with 6 other modules each time data is transmitted and received. As a result, the module can be used to create star networks and mesh networks in IoT applications. Their address range is wide as well, 125 unique identifiers are capable of being used in a closed area, so if you have 125 of them you can't interfere with each other.

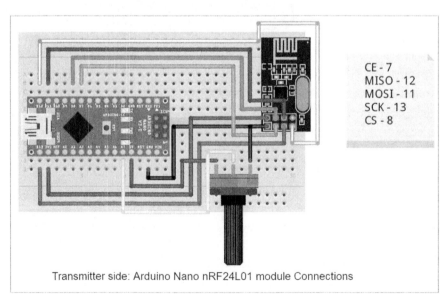

CE - 7
MISO - 12
MOSI - 11
SCK - 13
CS - 8

Transmitter side: Arduino Nano nRF24L01 module Connections

42. Build your own self-balancing robot with Arduino

After being inspired by and wanting to create something similar to the Segway self-balancing scooter models, I built the RYNO motor. I decided to build a self-balancing Arduino robot based on my thinking. Therefore, I can learn about the PID algorithms while understanding the underlying theory behind these scooters.

I realized that building this bot was quite difficult the first time I did it. With so many options to choose from, including motor selection and PID tuning, it is only natural to be confused. There are a number of variables to consider, including the CoG, the battery type, the battery location, wheel grips, motor drivers, etc.

However, let me reveal to you that once you learn how to do it, you will see for yourself that it's not as difficult as it sounds. In this tutorial we'll discuss the path I took in order to build the self-balancing robot. This may be the first time you are getting started with bots or maybe you have been frustrated for a long time and are now looking for help. Having arrived here, you will feel like you have arrived at your final destination.

Required Components

- Arduino UNO
- Geared DC motors (Yellow colored) – 2Nos
- L298N Motor Driver Module
- MPU6050
- A pair of wheels
- 7.4V Li-ion Battery
- Connecting wires
- 3D Printed Body

Circuit Diagram

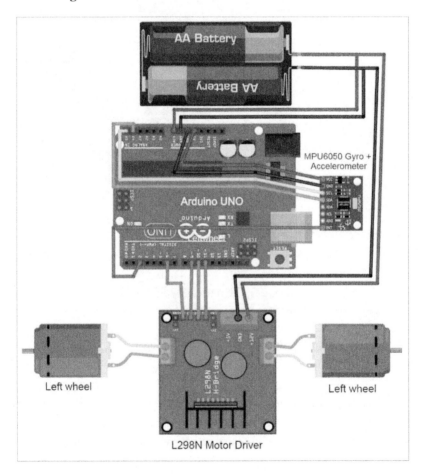

43. Automatic Water Dispenser using Arduino

Water covers about 71% of the earth, but sadly there is only drinking water in 2.5% of it. In 2025 we can expect perennial water shortages due to increased population, pollution, and climate change. We waste a lot of drinking water each year due to human negligence. On one hand, there are a number of minor disputes among nations and states regarding water sharing rivers, and on the other, there are national disputes among states regarding water sharing rivers.

One gallon of water is enough for an average human to live two days if your tap drips a drop of water every second. This might not seem like a big amount of water at first, but it would take you about five hours to waste one gallon of water. This problem can be solved through technology improvement. The answer always lies in technology development. The water consumption rate can be drastically decreased by replacing all manual taps with a smart faucet that automatically opens and closes without requiring us to touch the handle. Therefore, we will build a Solenoid Valves and Arduino based Automated Water Dispenser that can automatically dispense water to a glass when it is placed near it.

Materials Required

- Solenoid Valve, Arduino Uno (any version)
- HCSR04 – Ultrasonic Sensor
- IRF540 MOSFET, 1k and 10k Resistor
- Breadboard, Connecting Wires

Working Concept

The water dispenser works by dispensing water at the touch of a button. A HCSR04 Ultrasonic Sensor will be used to verify that no glass is placed in front of the dispenser. A solenoid valve will control the flow of water. Which generates electricity to operate when activated, and de-energizes when not in use. The solenoid will be turned on and will wait until the object is removed. We will write an Arduino program that checks if anything is placed near the tap, on the other hand if it is, the solenoid will be turned off, when you remove the object, the solenoid will turn off the water supply automatically.

Circuit Diagram

An electromechanical solenoid containing a 12-volt battery is used in this project. It has a continuous current capacity of 700mA. In other words, when the valve is on, it uses about 700mA to keep it on. Hence, a Solenoid driver circuit needs a switching driver to operate an Arduino board that operates with 5V and hence requires a 5V switching driver circuit.

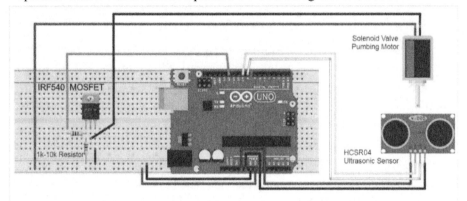

IRF540N is the MOSFET used in this project and its switching device is referred to as a N-Channel MOSFET with the Gate, Source and Drain pins originating from pin 1. According to the circuit diagram, the Arduino's Vin pin powers the solenoid's positive terminal.

As the Arduino will be powered by a 12V adapter and its Vin pin is 12V, the control of the solenoid can be performed. Several connections are made between the negative terminal and the ground via the MOSFET's Source and Drain pins. Only if the MOSFET is switched on will the solenoid be powered. Turning the MOSFET on or off is done with the gate pin. A gate pin grounded to ground will remain off while a gate voltage applied to it will turn it on. The gate pin of the MOSFET is pulled down to ground by a 10k resistor when no power is applied to it. A 1K resistor limits the current flowing to Arduino pin 12, which controls the MOSFET.

The Ultrasonic Sensor is powered by connecting a power supply to the Arduino's +5V and ground pins. To pins 8 and 9, respectively, are connected the trigger and echo pins. The Ultrasonic sensor can then be programmed to make use of the Arduino in order to detect objects and turn on the MOSFET if one is detected. My circuit was somewhat like this below after connecting all the wires. The whole circuit is simple and can be easily built on a breadboard.

44. Interfacing Flame Sensor with Arduino to Build a Fire Alarm System

Generally, a flame detector is a sensor that is designed to detect and respond if there is a fire present or if it is rapidly spreading. An alarm would sound, a fuel line would be deactivated, a fire suppression system would activate, and so on. Responses to a detected flame vary based on the installation.

Flame detection methods differ. They include: Infrared detectors, UV/IR detectors, near-IR arrays, infrared thermal cameras, Ultraviolet detectors, and many others.

Circuit Diagram

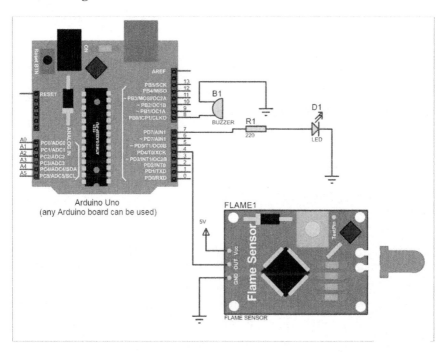

An infrared light sensor is utilized to detect the amount of Infra-red light emitted by the fire. An Op-Amp is then used to assess if any change has occurred in voltage across the IR Receiver, so that if there has been a fire the output pin (DO) will read 0V (LOW), and otherwise it will read 5V (HIGH).

In this project, we are using an IR flame sensor. This sensor utilizes a silicon phototransistor, the YG1006, which is extremely sensitive and has a high speed. Detectors for infrared light can detect wavelengths between 700nm and 1000nm, and have detection angles of 60° or greater. An integrated circuit which contains a photodiode, a resistor, a capacitor, a potentiometer, and an LM393 comparator is called a flame sensor. By adjusting the onboard potentiometer, the sensitivity can be adjusted. With a digital output, the working voltage ranges from 3.3v to 5v DC. On the output, logic high indicates the presence of fire or flame. On the output, logic low indicates the absence of fire or flame.

Applications of flame sensors

- Hydrogen stations
- Combustion monitors for burners
- Oil and gas pipelines
- Automotive manufacturing facilities
- Nuclear facilities
- Aircraft hangars
- Turbine enclosures
- Components Required
- Arduino Uno (any Arduino board can be used)
- Flame sensor
- LED, Buzzer
- Resistor, Jumper wires

45. IoT Based Electricity Energy Meter using ESP12 and Arduino

Every home in the world is equipped with electricity energy meters that measure electricity consumption. At the end of every month, many of us get worried about the high electricity bill and we have to look at the energy meter once in a while. How about being able to monitor your consumption from anywhere in the world and receive an SMS/email when the threshold value is reached? IoT-powered Energy Meters are what we're building here.

An Energy Meter circuit was previously built using the GSM module which provides you with SMS notifications about your bill. Designed using the Arduino and ESP8266 Wi-Fi module, we build a Smart Electricity Energy meter that can send you an SMS/Email of the electricity bill along with real-time monitoring of your energy usage from anywhere and anytime. Our current sensor ACS712 has been used here to determine the energy consumption, and we will learn more about it shortly.

In addition, we will utilize MQTT Dashboard for Android to monitor our Energy usage. Through this project, we will utilize the IFTTT platform to link our Wi-Fi with SMS and E-Mail notifications.

Circuit Diagram

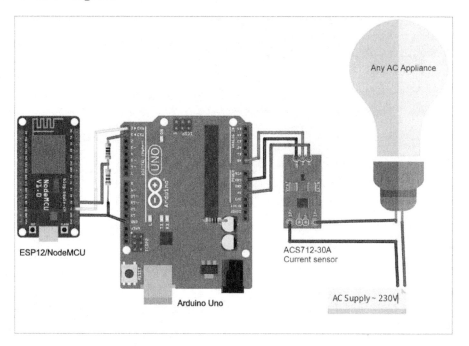

Materials Required:

- Arduino Uno, ESP12/NodeMCU
- ACS712-30Amp Current sensor, Any AC Appliance
- Male-Female Wires

46. Coronavirus Sterilizer Box | Food Mask Sterilizer

The Covid technology revolutionized 2020 for all of humanity. The way it spread rapidly forced us to wear face masks and gloves to protect our skin from everything we touched. Certainly, we can put on a mask when we are outside but what do we do if we bring something home from the store or trade with someone else? The fact that patients and employees exchange files and paperwork with doctors or with each other, cannot be sanitized by applying sanitizers to these outside items.

Circuit Diagram

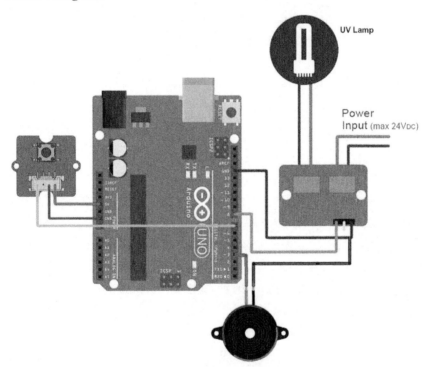

Using an arduino-powered system powered by a smart electronics chip, we solve this huge problem. To solve the problem, we designed an ultraviolet-sanitizing box that has a 60-degree angle. 8 uv tubes are employed by the system in order to achieve this task. All viruses have been killed by UV C in a matter of seconds:

Components

- Arduino Uno
- LCD Display,Buzzer
- Lid Sensor

- UV-C Tubes, Buttons
- Metal Mesh, LED's
- IC's , Resistors
- Capacitors
- Diodes, Transistors
- Transformer
- Base frame, Supporting Frame
- Mounts and Joints
- Screws and Bolts

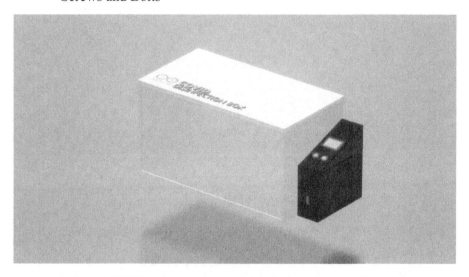

The Arduino COVID Disinfection box has the following Key Aspects

- A 360-degree approach to disinfection

- All Coronaviruses can be deactivated.

- Shutdown and alerts based on timers

- Sterilizes masks, packaged foods, electronics etc.

- Specifying the duration of the sterilization

- Shut off automatically

- Easy To Use

- We use no water and no chemicals | Environmentally friendly

Sterilization starts when the start button on the Arduino controller is pressed and the controller takes user inputs for time setting. This device shuts off automatically after it reaches the sterilization temperature. Another shutoff system also prevents lipids from being opened by users while sterilization is taking place.

Advantages

- No Chemicals or Water Sterilization
- Sterilization at 360 degrees
- Demonstrated to deactivate Bacteria and Viruses
- Sterilization time that can be adjusted
- Untimely opening will result in automatic safety shut off.

Disadvantages

- Since it is not large enough to sterilize large objects, it is not suitable.
- It does not have a battery and is not suitable for car use.

47. Play the Space Race Game using the Arduino and Nokia 5110 Graphic Display

Developing with Arduino is fun, and programming has been that way for years. Everyone out here has used the language they are learning or practicing to develop some kind of game. They have fun while practicing programming in this way. My interest in Arduino has been on the rise ever since I was introduced to it and wanted to do something cool with it. When I saw how smooth an interface could be using a Graphical LCD like the Nokia 5110 along with Arduino, the idea of developing a game came to me. So, you might also enjoy developing your game since it was an effective way to practice programming skills. As a result, in this tutorial, you will learn how to build an entertaining game employing the Arduino microcontroller and the graphics LCD display.

This time around we are going to try a new version of the Snake game using Arduino, which we have named Future Race, in which the player needs to keep their vessel safe from enemy ships by using a joystick.

Game Plan:

The method by which your game would work is very important before we start. A graphics LCD and joystick was the hardware that I chose for my hardware selection. You have likely selected the same option in this tutorial as well.

We have had to plan our entire game inside the 84 * 48-pixel dimensions of the Nokia 5110 display because it doesn't have a lot of free space. The Nokia 5110 LCD has been reprogrammed to be used with the Arduino, as well as the Nokia Joystick for Arduino.

It will be difficult to arrange the gaming area within this space, as well as the scoreboard area, which displays things like score and things. In order to update your screen with the pixel locations, it is very important to know where the pixel locations are.

Circuit Diagram:

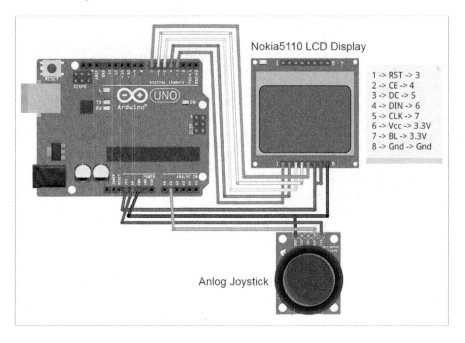

It's very easy to make this game with Arduino; we just need to interface the Nokia 5110 LCD module, and the Joystick to Arduino.

Our game characters need to be decided after we determine the appearance of the game screen. I have designed a game based on a spaceship over a planet and an enemy spacecraft disguised as a planet. So, I used the Nokia LCD's bitmap feature and my spaceship and enemies were displayed on the screen.

A spacecraft will race against the alien spaceships, and have the capability to change lanes to avoid a contact with them. It should never be possible for an alien to occupy more than two tracks at a time and the player should always be able to drive over a free track. Our goal is to finish the Hardware and complete the Programming once the ideas are concluded.

48. Interfacing Tilt Sensor with Arduino

When a tilt sensor is activated, it determines whether the object is upright or tilted, and outputs high or low based on its orientation. In essence, it consists of a mercury ball which moves inside to create a circuit. Therefore, the tilt sensor is able to either turn on or off the circuit according to the orientation.

We are interfacing an Arduino UNO with a Mercury switch / tilt sensor. We are controlling a LED and buzzer based on the tilt sensor's output. The alarm will be triggered upon tilting the sensor. This tilt sensor circuit also demonstrates the workings of tilt sensors.

Material Required

- Mercury Switch/ Tilt Sensor
- Arduino UNO
- Buzzer
- LED
- Resistor - 220 ohm
- Breadboard
- Connecting wires

An Arduino interface for tilt sensors.

A schematic of the easy connection between the sensor and Arduino follows below. Sensor pin VCC is connected to Arduino terminal 5V and sensor pin GND is connected to ground. The DO pin can be connected to any digital pin of the Arduino board.

Circuit Diagram

The Arduino needs 5v dc power to be able to operate the Tilt sensor. The 5V supply and Tilt sensor output is obtained by wires connected to pins 3 and 4 of Arduino. In order to prevent an overcurrent, the LED is connected with the Arduino UNO PIN 2 with a 230-ohm resistor. In addition, the buzzer is connected directly to Arduino UNO PIN 3.

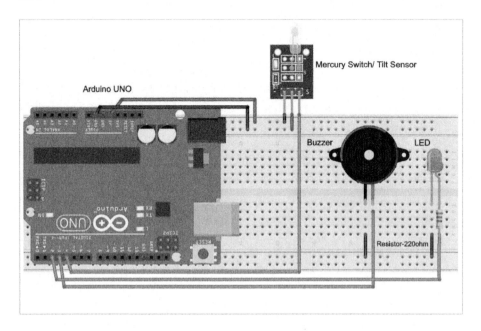

Designed to measure tilt angle, this Mercury switch-based tilt sensor gives high on its output pin. 5V is required to power this device. It consists of input, ground, and output terminals. It is composed of a glass tube containing a liquid mercury ball and two electrodes. As the mercury ball is inclined a certain way, it closes and opens the circuit. Here is how the module works and is organized internally:

Working of Tilt Sensor

CASE 1: NOT TILTED

Initially, when it is in NOT tilted position as shown in the image below, it gives LOW output because of the liquid mercury complete the circuit by connecting the two electrodes. When the output is LOW on-board LED remain ON.

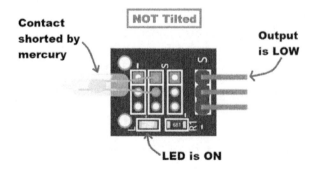

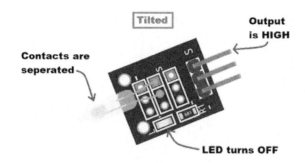

49. Bluetooth Controlled Servo Motor using Arduino

Robots are controlled precisely by using a Servo motor. Using an Arduino UNO and an Android device via Bluetooth, we will show you how to control a Servo motor via Bluetooth connection. Previously we controlled servo via Arduino, this time we will use Bluetooth Module HC-6 to control Servo wirelessly.

Material Required

- Arduino UNO,
- HC-05 or HC-06 Bluetooth module
- Servo Motor,
- Roboremo App from PlayStore
- Breadboard,
- Connecting wire
- HC-06 Bluetooth Module

How it works

Sending data packets to the Bluetooth module is done by the android app. These data packets are then transmitted via serial communication to the Arduino Uno. A servo motor is controlled by Arduino Uno based on the value of the data packet. The flowchart below illustrates how this works.

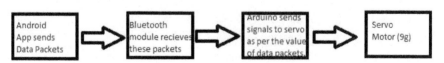

Bluetooth can operate in the following two modes:

1. Command Mode
2. Operating Mode

Command Mode will allow us to change the Bluetooth properties, like the name of the Bluetooth signal as well as the password, baud rate and range of features. This is the mode in which the PIC Microcontroller can transfer and receive data with a Bluetooth module.

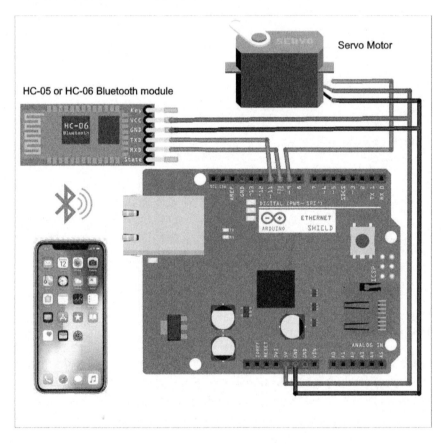

Thus, the Operating Mode will be our only discussion in this tutorial. We will use the default settings for the Command mode. All Bluetooth modules will use a default baud rate of 9600. The Device Name is HC-05 and the password is 0000 or 1234.

50. Controlling Multiple Servo Motors with Arduino

Arduino is great for controlling one or two Servos, but how do we control more than one Servo?

We will be demonstrating how multiple servo motors can be controlled using Arduino. When connected to Arduino supply pins multiple Servo Motors seem to be simple, but they won't work correctly because there is not enough current to drive all the motors. Therefore, you need to supply each motor with a separate power supply, whether from some adapters (5v 2A) or from good quality batteries (9v).

While integrating more than two servos into one Arduino, we all experience current difficulties. There is only one solution to this problem, which is to connect an external power source rated appropriately (that is, I used a 9V supply that was rated for 2A). Powering small Servos can be accomplished by wiring in an external power supply through adapters, RPSs (Regulated Power Supplies), or good quality 9-volt batteries. When using a laptop, you can also connect your USB port to power your Servos. The Arduino ground must be shorted to the external supply ground in order to use the external supply.

Circuit Diagram

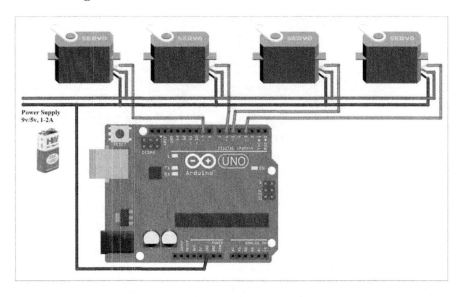

Material Required

- Arduino UNO
- Servo Motor
- Power Supply
- Breadboard
- Connecting Wires

51. Arduino Based Countdown Timer

A timer refers to a type of clock that measures time intervals. Counting upwards from zero is one type of timer when measuring the elapsed time is called a stopwatch. It also has a second option, generally termed a Countdown Timer, which counts down based on the time duration provided by the user.

The following tutorial will provide you with detailed instructions in order to make a Countdown Timer using Arduino. Our implementation does not use the Real Time Clock (RTC) for time synchronization. With the help of the Keypad and 16x2 LCD, the time duration is provided by the user. The buzzer will be used to alert the user according to Zero on the timer.

Material Required

- Arduino UNO
- LCD 16*2
- 4*4 matrix keypad
- Buzzer
- Pushbutton
- Potentiometer (10k)
- Resistor (10k, 100 ohm)
- Connecting wires

Circuit Diagram

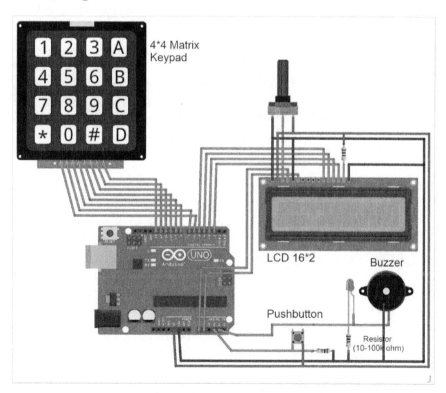

The main controller here is the Arduino Uno. The time duration is fed into the keypad and the countdown is displayed on a 16*2 LCD. To start the time, the pushbutton is pressed. Here is an Arduino tutorial on how to connect a 4x4 keypad with an LCD and a 16x2 LCD with Arduino.

52. Automatic Pet Feeder using Arduino

A Pet Feeder based on Arduino can automatically deliver food to your pet on schedule. Your pet should be fed on time and date set by the DS3231 Real Time Clock module. The device drops or fills the food bowl depending on your pet's eating schedule, so set the time accordingly.

Circuit Diagram

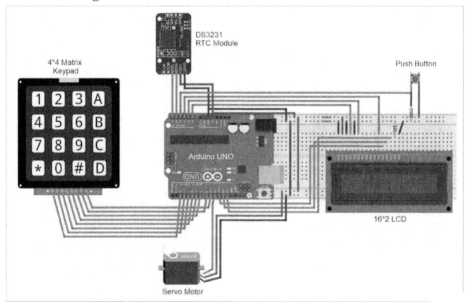

DS3231 RTC Module and Arduino UNO are used in this circuit to display the time on a 16*2 LCD. Also, a servo motor is used to provide the food by rotating the containers and a 4*4 matrix keypad should be used to set the feeding time. Depending on the quantity you want to serve your pet, you can set the rotation angle and duration of dish opening. Aside from the size of your pet, the amount of food you ought to give him also depends on whether he is a cat, a dog, or a bird.

Material Required

- Arduino UNO, 4*4 Matrix Keypad
- 16*2 LCD, Push Button

- Servo Motor
- Resistor
- Connecting Wires
- Breadboard

We have used RTC (Real Time Clock) Module for time and date acquisition in this Arduino based Cat Feeder. With the help of the 16x2 LCD, we made the Stepper control Pet's eating time by using a four-by-four matrix keypad. When the user sets the time, the Servo motor rotates the container and drops the food on the determined date and time. In the video on the end, you can see complete working of the LCD. Date and Time can be displayed on the LCD.

DS3231 RTC Module

RTC (Real Time Clock) module DS3231 works with the DS3231 microcontroller. Many of the Electronics projects rely on it to keep track of the date and time. When the main power is removed from the module or if the MCU has undergone a hard reset, the module will maintain the date and time using the coin cell battery power supply.

This module will always keep track of the date and time once the date and time have been set. In our circuit, we are using the DS3231 to make the pet's owner set the feeding schedule, like an alarm, to the pet's daily food requirements. The clock opens the container gate when the timer reaches the set time and drops the food into the Pet's bowl.

Note: You can also use the RTC IC DS1307 to read the time if you use this module for the first time.

3D-Printed Pet Feeder Model

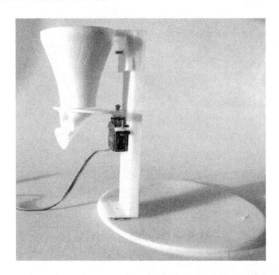

The Arduino Pet Feeder container prototype is printed with a 3D printer.

53. Arduino Based AC Home Appliances controlling with thermistor and relay

If you were sitting in a cold room and you wanted your heater to be automatically turned on, then that might be possible. Usually, when a room temperature increases, appliances are turned on for some time and then off, making the project useful for controlling home appliances according to the temperature. With Arduino, we control our home air conditioning systems based on the temperature. A Thermistor was used to measure temperature in this case. The Thermistor was interfaced with Arduino and the temperature was displayed on LCD.

We will use the Arduino temperature-controlled system in this tutorial to be able to control an AC appliance using a Relay. Displayed on the 16*2 LCD display with connection to the circuit are the current temperature and appliance status.

A variety of components are used in this Home Automation System, including an Arduino board, LCD display, relay and thermistor. Basically, the whole system works by using a relay and a thermistor; as the temperature rises, the relay will turn on and as the temperature drops below the threshold, the relay will turn off.

Relays will also enable and disable the appliance attached to them. CFL bulbs are used as AC appliances in this system.

Circuit Diagram

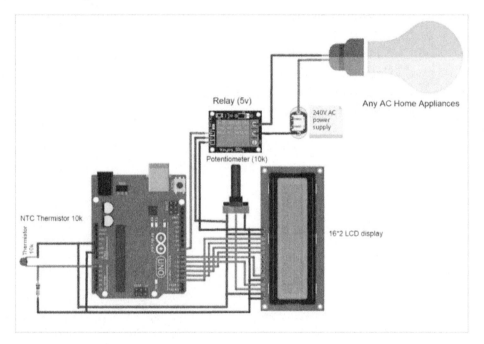

The Temperature based Home Automation System contains components such as an Arduino board, LCD display, thermistor, Relay, and Relay. The relay and the thermistor are key elements in this system. As the temperature increases so does the relay. If it drops below the preset temperature the relay is turned off.

The Relay will also control the home appliance connected with it. For this example, an AC appliance is connected as a CFL bulb. The Arduino board is programmed to trigger the entire triggering procedure and set the temperature value. On the LCD screen, we can see the temperature at every half second, as well as the status of the appliances.

The Arduino Servo Motor library takes care of all electronic properties of the servo, so you just need to enter this angle and there is a function servo1.write(angle); which will rotate the servo to the desired angle.

Material Required

- Arduino UNO
- Relay (5v)
- 16*2 LCD display
- Light Bulb (CFL)
- NTC thermistor 10k
- Connecting wires
- Resistors (1k and 10k ohms)
- Potentiometer (10k)

Thermistor

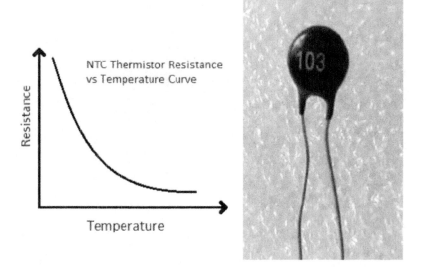

Thermistor is the key component in this circuit, which is responsible for detecting temperature rise. Temperature-sensitive resistors measure resistance by changing according to temperature, called thermocouples. We are being tested with a NTC thermistor.

Both types of thermistors have negative temperature coefficients and positive temperature coefficients. The resistance of an NTC thermistor increases with rising temperature, while the resistance of a PTC thermistor increases with rising temperature.

54. DIY Arduino Inclinometer using MPU6050

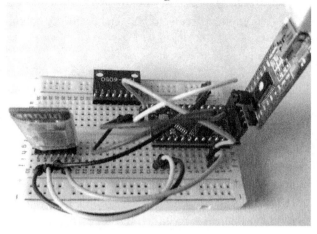

This accelerometer and gyroscope are an integrated circuit (IC) that measures three axes of movement at the same time. Besides the temperature sensor and DCM, the module contains additional features for complex tasks. In the production of self-balancing robots and other remote devices, the MPU6050 is often used. We will build an Inclinometer or Spirit Leveler using the MPU6050 and learn how to use it.

A digital inclinometer or a spirit bubble inclinometer is used to measure inclination, but they can also be used as inclinometers to level a surface. A Digital Inclinometer is being developed in this project and it can be monitored by an Android application. By using a mobile phone for displaying the data from the MPU6050, we can do so without having to look at the hardware; this could be very useful when the MPU6050 is mounted on a drone or inaccessible place.

Materials Required:

- Arduino Pro-mini (5V)
- MPU6050 Gyro Sensor
- HC-05 or HC-06 Bluetooth module
- FTDI board
- Breadboard
- Connecting wires
- Smart Phone

An image of the circuit diagram is shown below for this Arduino Tilt Sensor Project. A breadboard can be used to build the circuit with just three components.

The I2C communication protocol is used by the MPU6050. Hence the SDA pin on the MPU6050 is connected to the SDA pin on the Arduino and its SCL pin is connected to its SCL pin on the Arduino.

The HC-06 Bluetooth Module is connected to pin D11 of the Arduino and pin D10 of D4 of the Bluetooth module, which means the Rx pin and the Tx pin of Bluetooth are connected. Programming an Arduino will enable these pins as Serial pins by configuring D10 and D11. Hence, they are powered via the Vcc pin of the Arduino, and they are powered by the HC-05 module and the MSP6050 module.

Circuit Diagram

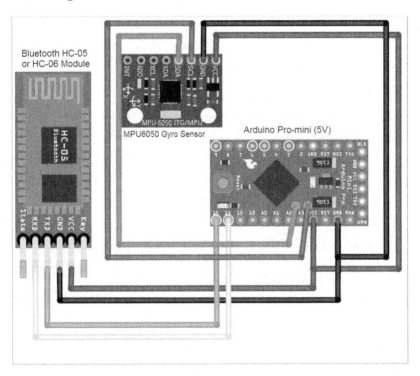

The following circuit diagram shows how Arduino Inclinometer uses MPU6050

Powering your setup:

It depends on your power options. You may use the FTDI programming board, use a battery, or an adapter, but for powering your circuit you'll need a 9volt battery or 12volt adapter. An in-built voltage regulator on the Arduino Pro-mini will convert the +5V external voltage into the preferred 2.4V.

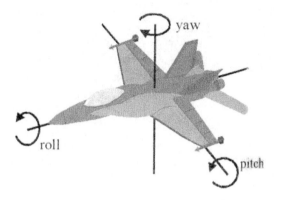

As the breadboard moves, you can observe these values changing as the zeros become values. You should check your connections if they change, otherwise make sure your connection is correct. Look at the three values Pitches, Roll and Yaw as you tilt your sensor and note how they vary according to your tilt. Once the Arduino has been reset, you can take a look at its values in one direction and you will be able to recognize which value changes. Below is an illustration of that.

55. Smart Blind Stick using Arduino

Were you ever talked about the famous American rock climber Hugh Herr? He has broken the limitations of his disabilities; Technology can help people with disabilities live a normal life. He is a strong believer in this. A TED talk given by Herr said "There is no such thing as a disabled person. a person can never be broken". Buildings and technology within our society are broken, disenfranchised, and lacking. It is not necessary for us to accept our limitations. Through technological innovation, we can transform disability". Then, and now, he lived his life by these words, now using prosthetic legs and claiming to live a normal life. Therefore, technology can indeed neutralize human disability; to this end, let us take advantage of the power of Arduino and some simple sensors to create a Blind man's stick that can perform more than just serve blind persons.

Materials Required:

- Arduino Nano (Any version will work)
- Ultrasonic Sensor HC-SR04
- LDR,
- Buzzer and LED
- 7805,
- Push button
- 433MHz RF transmitter and receiver
- Resistors, Capacitors
- Perf board
- Soldering Kit
- 9V batteries

An Ultrasonic sensor will be used on this Smart stick to assess distance from any obstacle. A light detection radio receiver to facilitate remote locating of the man's stick and a wireless RF remote control. Through a Buzzer, the blind person will get all feedback. Of course, you can swap Buzzer out for a vibrating motor, and do even more, just by putting your own creativity into it.

Circuit Diagram:

Two circuits are required to build this Smart Blind Stick. A large portion of the electrical power source will go into the main circuit, which will be mounted on the blind man's stick. This small RF transmitter circuit is intended to locate the main circuit board. The circuit diagram on the main board is shown below:

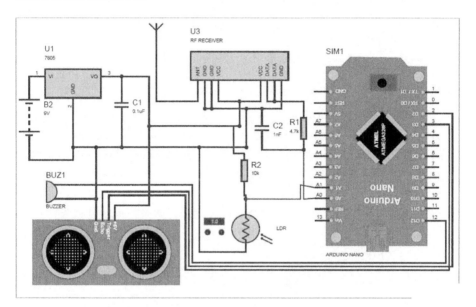

As you can see, all the sensors are controlled by an Arduino Nano. With a 9V battery plugged into the board, a Voltage regulator of 7805 rate voltage to +5V. Powered by 5V, the ultrasonic device is connected to the trigger and echo pins on the Arduino Nano.

Taking advantage of a LDR that will expose the ground through a resistor valued at 10K, Arduino ADC pin A1 detects any difference in voltage across pin A1, which can be used to measure the distance between the plugged-in electrode and the ground. In the output circuit, Pin 12 is connected to the buzzer which reads the signal from pin A0 of the ADC.

RF Remote Transmitter Circuit

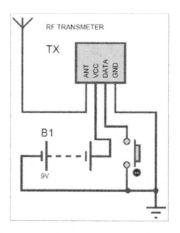

An RF transmitter transmits the missing alert to the smart stick, which receives it via a receiver circuit. A small PCB sub-assembly houses the RF transmitter module.

56. Home Automation Using Arduino with Bluetooth Control

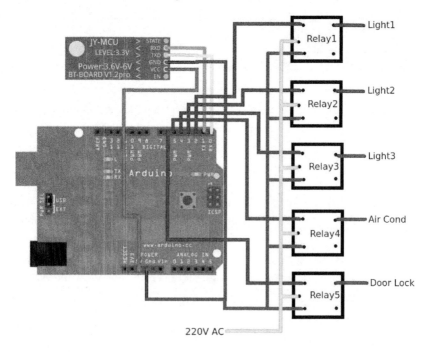

A human's life can be enhanced through technology today. As technology evolves, we live in progressively more advanced times. Automation used to be a science fiction story before, but is not so today. Our home can be awesome if we combine the latest technology with it. A home automation system can be created with the Arduino Uno and Windows 10 to allow home devices to operate on their own automatically.

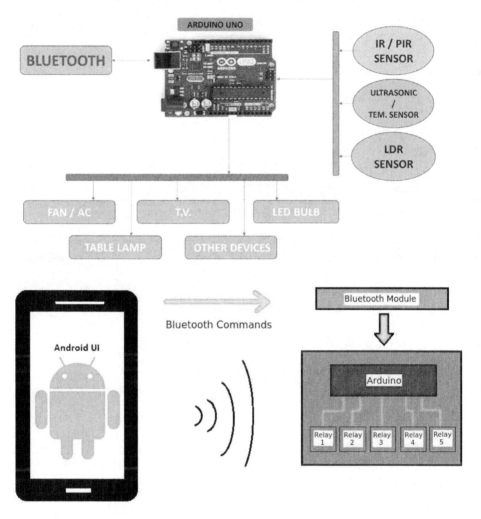

Home automation can do more than ensure the safety of your family and provide easy control of temperature, lighting, and music. Automating your home theater allows you to have perfectly balanced sound and perfect lighting that can be adapted to the time of day or the film you are watching

57. Control your Computer with Hand Gestures using Arduino

Recent market research indicates that the number of wireless computer keyboards is rapidly increasing. We can control certain functions of our computer and/or laptop by using a motion that we call Leap Motion. These laptops are rather expensive, but they are cool. Let us use the Power of Arduino and Python to provide Gesture Control for our Laptop/Computer.

A VLC media player will be controlled based on the position of our hand using Ultrasonic sensors. When you are familiar with this project, however, you are able to do anything just by changing a few lines of code and manipulate your favourite application in your favourite way.

Pre-requisites:

Python has already been used in several Arduino projects before. Assuming you've already set up Python and its serial library, and have executed a few basic projects like blinking LEDs, this is what you can expect. Don't be alarmed, here's a tutorial you can use to learn how to program your led directly using Arduino and Python. Please ensure Python and the Python Serial library are installed before moving on.

Concept behind the project:

The project's concept is extremely straightforward. Our approach is to place two Ultrasonic sensors on our monitor and use Arduino to read the distance between it and our hand. We will then do what the distance reading tells us, based on it. pyautogui is an open-source Python library that allows us to perform actions on our computer. A USB connection is used to connect Arduino to the computer and send commands. Python is run on the computer and Python will read the read data and subsequently perform an action based on the read data.

Circuit Diagram:

The Arduino will connect to the two Ultrasonic sensors and control the computer with hand gestures. Knowing that US sensors require 5 Volts of Voltage, Arduino's on-board voltage regulators are powering them. Besides being connected to the PC/Laptop for powering the board and serial communication, the Arduino can also be used as a computer control system. The connection should look like this once it's finished. You can use your own creativity to stick it to your monitor but I used double sided tape to do so. We can then begin the programming process after securing the device in place.

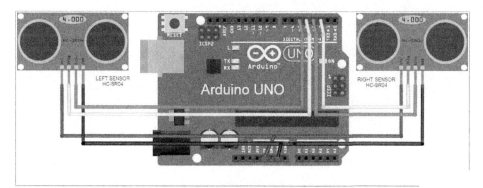

For example, we can program five actions to be controlled by gestures by reading the distance value and adjusting our program accordingly.

Action 1: In VLC player, the video should Play/Pause when both hands are placed in proximity to the sensor.

Action 2: A video should Fast Forward one step when the right hand is held up in front of the sensor at a certain distance.

Action 3: At a particular distance from the sensor, the video should Rewind one step when the left hand is placed before it.

Action 4: When your right hand is placed up in front of the camera at a certain distance, and then your hand is moved towards the camera, and you move away, the video should fast forward and rewind.

Action 5: After placing the left hand close to the sensor, it should increase the video volume and when it is moved away from the sensor, it should decrease the volume.

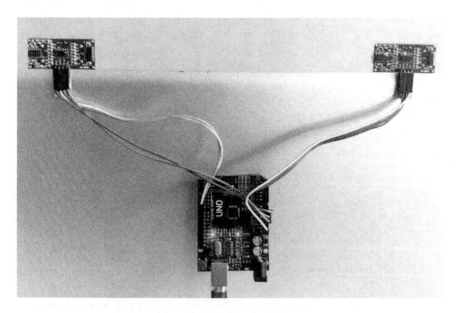

Here, we will see how the program is built to accomplish the above actions. So, just like any other program, we define the I/O pins first as you can see above. Digital pin 2, 3, 4, and 5 are used to power the two US sensors which are powered by +5V pins.

The Arduino's trigger pins are input pins, and the Arduino's echo pins are output pins. Serial communication takes place with a baud rate of 9600 for the Arduino and Python programs.

58. Floor Cleaning Robot using Ultrasonic Sensor with an Arduino

Floor cleaning machines don't do anything new, but they all share the same problem. There are currently no Robots for House cleaning that aren't too expensive for what they do. So today, we are making an Automatic Robotic Cleaning Machine. Its cost will be a small fraction of the one on the market. In the event the Robot detects obstacles it can continue progressing, avoiding obstructions, until the entire room has been cleaned. The floor is cleaned with the help of a small brush on the side of the machine.

Component Required:

- Arduino UNO R3.
- Ultrasonic Sensor.
- Arduino Motor Driver shield.
- Wheel Drive Robot Chassis.
- Computer to Program the Arduino.
- Battery for the Motors.
- A Power Bank to Power the Arduino
- A Shoe Brush.
- A Scotch Brite Scrub Pad.

Note:

A four-stranded wire can be used instead of batteries. That is what we did. If it is not something you plan to use in the real world every day, it is a feasible solution even though it is not elegant or practical. Confirm that the cable's length is sufficient.

Wiring and Connections:

The circuit for this Robotic Home Cleaning Machine is very simple. Mount the Motor Driver shield on the Arduino and connect the Ultrasonic sensor as mentioned below.

How to assemble a floor cleaner robot:

The Arduino must be mounted to the chassis. Assuming your chassis is made of metal, take care not to short circuit anything. Getting a box for the Arduino and the motor controller shield is a good idea. Mount the motors using screws on the chassis and wheels. If the chassis doesn't come with this option from the factory, you can improvise. Epoxy is an option that can work well. Place the shoe brush on the front of the chassis. This was done with M-Seal epoxy and drilled screws; however, you could use any other solution you prefer.

The Scotch Brite scrub pad should be installed behind the brush. It is held in play with a shaft across the chassis, but the mechanism can be improvised. A spring-loaded shaft can be employed to hold it in play. The batteries (or cables) are mounted on the back of the chassis. A battery holder or epoxy can be used to mount the batteries. Hot glue can also be used.

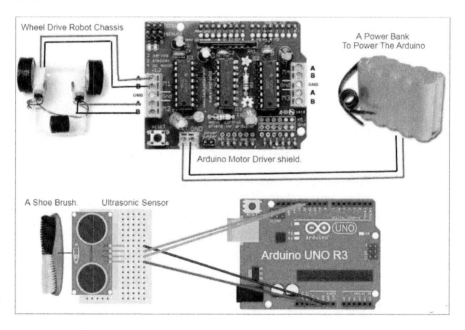

It is connected to ultrasonics Trig pin (attached to pin 12), Ultrasonics Echo pin (attached to pin 13), the voltage pin (connected to the 5V pin), and the ground pin to the ground pin on the Arduino. A power supply and ground pins connect the sensor to the Arduino and allow it to receive power from both. The Trig and Echo pins allow the Arduino to communicate with it, and also serve to send data to and from the sensor. Here you can learn more about how you can interface Ultrasonic sensors with Arduino.

Motor shields ought to have at least 2 outputs, and the direct connections between them and your two motors should be made. The outputs of these channels are normally labelled as "M1" and "M2". Connect the motor shield and the Arduino to the batteries, and your power bank to the power bank. Motor shields should have input channels, so do not cross connect them. Please connect wires to AC adapters if you're using them.

59. Controlling a Stepper Motor using Potentiometer with Arduino

As stepper motors become increasingly popular in electronic products, they will continue to hold a stronghold in the electronics market. Everywhere, stepper motors are used as actuators for easy control ranging from surveillance cameras to complex CNC machines and robots. This tutorial demonstrates the 28-BYJ48 stepper motor, commonly available and cheaply. We'll also explore the ULN2003 stepper module that enables us to interface the 28-BYJ48 with an Arduino controller.

The last project we did was Interface Stepper Motor with Arduino, where you could control the rotation angle of the stepper motor through the Serial Monitor. In this project, we are going to rotate Stepper Motor using Arduino and Potentiometer, the potentiometer will rotate clockwise when you turn it clockwise, and will rotate anticlockwise when you turn it the other way.

Stepper Motors:

Let's take a look at the 28BYJ48 stepper motor.

Its wires are all fancy colours and are not connected to a normal DC motor, it is just the opposite. Why? Before understanding this, we need to know how steppers work and what their specialties are.

A stepper motor does not rotate, but its movements are linear, hence it is commonly referred to as a step motor. Each step will be taken one after the other. A series of coils are embedded in these motors, and these coils have to be wired in an energized manner in order for the motor to rotate. A motor takes steps when each coil is energized, and a series of the energizations makes the motor turn continuously, thus causing it to spin. Here is what these coils in the motor look like to determine exactly where they come from.

A five-lead unipolar coil arrangement can be seen on the motor. Each coil requires an individual sequence of energizing. A + 5V supply will be applied to the red wires while the rest of the wires will be pulled to ground for triggering the respective coils. These coils are energized in a particular sequence using a microcontroller such as Arduino.

Now that I think about it - I have no idea why this motor is called 28-BYJ48. It doesn't appear that this motor has any technical reason for its title; perhaps we should delve further into it. In the picture below we have taken some important technical data from the data sheet of this motor.

Rated voltage :	5VDC
Number of Phase	4
Speed Variation Ratio	1/64
Stride Angle	5.625°/64
Frequency	100Hz
DC resistance	50Ω±7%(25°C)
Idle In-traction Frequency	> 600Hz
Idle Out-traction Frequency	> 1000Hz
In-traction Torque	>34.3mN.m(120Hz)
Self-positioning Torque	>34.3mN.m
Friction torque	600-1200 gf.cm
Pull in torque	300 gf.cm
Insulated resistance	>10MΩ(500V)
Insulated electricity power	600VAC/1mA/1s
Insulation grade	A
Rise in Temperature	<40K(120Hz)
Noise	<35dB(120Hz,No load,10cm)
Model	28BYJ-48 – 5V

Here is an example that shows using the Arduino Stepper Library to control a stepper motor using a potentiometer (or other sensor) on analog input 0. With either unipolar or bipolar motors, the stepper can be controlled via digital pins 8, 9, 10, and 11.

If you are using a unipolar stepper, you will connect the Arduino board to a U2004 Darlington array; if you are using a bipolar motor, you will connect it to a SN754410NE H-bridge.

Circuit Diagram

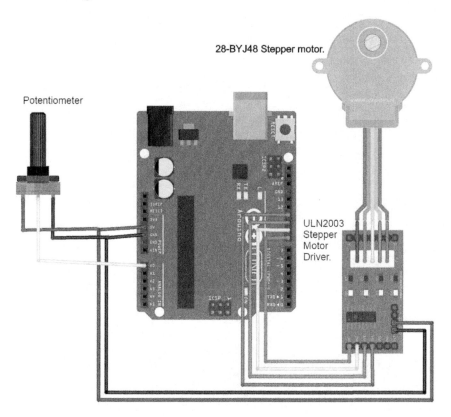

What are the reasons for the need for Driver Modules for Stepper Motors? A driver module is usually required to operate most stepper motors. We cannot drive the motor with the controller module (In our case Arduino) because the controller's I/O pins won't deliver enough current. So, we will use the ULN 2003 stepper motor driver as an external module. Different types of driver modules are used for different types of motors so the rating will change accordingly. For any driver module, the primary function will be to source/sink sufficient current for the motor to operate.

Using Potentiometer and Arduino to control a stepper motor is shown in the circuit diagram above. The ULN2003 driver module and the 28BYJ-48 Stepper motor were used. A driver module connected to the Arduino board's digital pin 8 is used to energize the four coils on the stepper motor. The Arduino 5V pin is used to power the stepper motor. We will rotate the Stepper motor based on the values of a potentiometer connected to A0.

If you are connecting some load to the stepper motor, then power the driver with an external power supply. The motor has been used on the +5V rail of the Arduino Board for demonstration purposes. Make sure the Arduino is connected to the ground of the Driver module as well.

60. Arduino Based 3-Way Traffic Light Controller

An Arduino based 3-Way Traffic Light Controller demonstrates the working of traffic lights which we see around us. This is a simple, yet useful project to help you understand the way traffic lights work. Here we are demonstrating a simpler version of traffic lights that are used in three-sided or way traffic signals. Now let us move on to the project...

Components Required:

- 3 Red LED Lights, 3 Green LED Lights
- 3 Yellow LED Lights, 3n 220ohm Resistors, Breadboard
- Male To Male Connectors, Arduino Uno with Ide Cable

Circuit Diagram

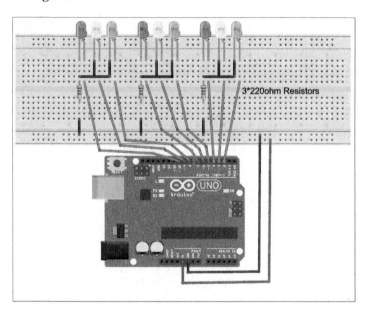

The following circuit diagram demonstrates how to build the Arduino Traffic Light Controller.

This project uses an Arduino to drive traffic lights. A breadboard can easily be used to build it, as detailed in the below steps:

1. Red, Green, and Yellow LEDs should be connected in the breadboard.
2. Attach the 220ohm resistor in series with the negative terminal of the LEDs.
3. Attach your connectors in accordance with their instructions.
4. Make sure that the corresponding pins (2, 3, 4...10) on the Arduino Uno are connected to the other end.
5. The breadboard can be powered using Arduino's 5v and GND pins.

61. Simple Arduino Audio Player and Amplifier with LM386

Adding music or sounds will always make our project look a lot cooler and more appealing. The best way to add sound effects to your project is by investing in an extra SD card module and a normal speaker, especially if you are using an Arduino and you have lots of open pins. Using your Arduino Board, I have created a simple Music Player/Sound Maker. Thank you to the Arduino community for developing some libraries for you to build this quickly and easily. The IC LM386 was also used here to increase the volume and cancel out the noise.

Hardware Required:

- Arduino UNO
- SD Card Reader module
- SD card
- LM386 Audio Amplifier
- 10uf Capacitor (2 Nos)
- 100uf Capacitor (2 Nos)
- 1K, 10K Resistor
- Push buttons (2 Nos)
- Breadboard
- Connecting Wires

Circuit Diagram

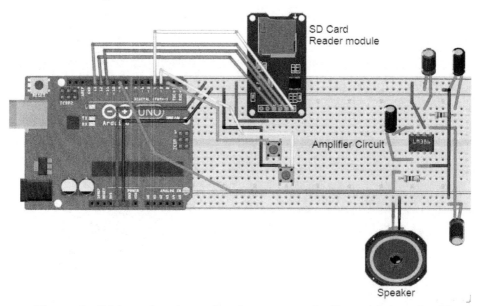

The goal of this project is to play the .wav music files stored on the SD card. Through the LM386 Audio amplifier, we will play these .wav files on a speaker using an Arduino programmed to read them. This project cannot technically be called an Arduino Mp3 Player since this code can only read .wav files, but you still get to hear the music. Alternatively, consider an Arduino music player without SD card if you are looking for a simple alternative

Prepare your audio files with your WAV files:

Audio files in .wav format are necessary for playing sounds from SD cards using Arduino. Due to the inherent limitations of the Arduino Board, only wav format audio can be played. An Arduino mp3 player can be made using many different mp3 shields which are available for Arduino. Alternatively, many websites provide instruments for the conversion of audio files into WAV files on your computer.

Following the steps below will help you convert any audio file to wav format:

Step 1: Go to "https://audio.online-convert.com/convert-to-wav" website.

Step 2: The following format is supported by Arduino. You can experiment with different settings later, however, the following settings were experimentally the best in quality.

Bit Resolution	8 Bit
Sampling Rate	16000 Hz
Audio Channel	Mono
PCM format	PCM unsigned 8-bit

Step 3:

In the website, check the "choose file" box and select the file you will be converting. Then feed the settings into the field. Once done, your conversion should look like the image below.

Upload your audio you want to convert to WAV:

[Choose File] Daavuya - ...al.com.mp3

Or enter URL of the file you want to convert to WAV:

(e.g. http://cdn.online-convert.com/example-file/audio/m4p/example.m4p)

Or select a file from your cloud storage for a WAV conversion:

🌀 Choose from Dropbox   ☁ Choose from Google Drive

┌─ Optional settings ─────────────────────────────

Change bit resolution: [8 Bit   ▼]

Change sampling rate: [16000 Hz   ▼]

Change audio channels: [mono   ▼]

Trim audio: [   ] to [   ]

00:00:00

Normalize audio: ☐

Show advanced options >

PCM format: [PCM unsigned 8-bit   ▼]

[Convert file]   (by clicking you confirm that you understand and agree to our terms)

Step 4: Afterwards, click on "Convert File" and your Audio will be converted into .WAV format. Once the conversion is completed, the .WAV file will be downloaded.

Step 5:

Once you've formatted your SD card, save the audio .wav file onto it. Before adding this file, make sure it is formatted correctly. Keep in mind the name of your audio file as well. You can do the same with your four audio files, selecting any one of them and saving them as 1, 2, 3, and 4. As shown below, I have converted four songs created by a particular digital music converter to wav, mp3, mp4, and mp3 audio formats.

↑ SD ▸ This PC ▸ AISHA (G:)

	Name	Date modified	Type	Size
☆ Favorites				
🖥 Desktop	1	23-06-2017 11:37 ...	Wave Sound	3,660 KB
📥 Downloads	2	23-06-2017 07:35 ...	Wave Sound	5,020 KB
📋 Recent places	3	24-06-2017 10:31 ...	Wave Sound	3,301 KB
	4	23-06-2017 07:40 ...	Wave Sound	4,182 KB
☁ OneDrive				
🖳 This PC				
🖥 Desktop				
📄 Documents				
📥 Downloads				

We interface the Arduino with a SD card reader module since we haven't been able to interface our Arduino directly with some of our audio files. With the SD card and Arduino, communication is accomplished using SPI. Thus, the Module is connected to the Arduino's SPI pins as shown above in the diagram. The following table provides further details.

Arduino	SD card module
+5V	Vcc
Gnd	Gnd
Pin 12	MISO (Master in Slave out)
Pin 11	MOSI (Master Out Slave In)
Pin 13	SCK (Synchronous Clock)
Pin 4	CS (Chip Select)

After the SD card is read, the Arduino will be capable of playing the music on pin number 9. On pin 9, the audio signals generated by the Arduino are not loud enough to be audible much. Therefore, LM386 Low voltage Audio amplifier IC is used to amplify it.

Amplifiers like the one shown above have Gains as high as 200 and the 5V pin of the Arduino is powering the Vdd pin. If you want to adjust the volume, the voltage applied to this pin can be increased/decreased. There are 200 watts of gain amplification in this device, which is ideal for use in low power circuits for LM386.

Additional buttons are also connected to pins 2 and 3 on the Arduino. The switches can play/pause the music and play/skip the next track of a song respectively. The buttons below were used only to demonstrate the song's capabilities; you can play the song whenever desired.

62. Arduino based Bluetooth Biped Bob (Walking & Dancing Robot)
Welcome back to another site where we will build a small robot that can walk and dance. This project encompasses the use of Arduino and open-source software to allow the creation of 2D robotic devices (robots). This robot takes commands from an Android Mobile Phone to walk and dance following predefined actions at the end of the project. You can also control the movement of your robot by using the Serial monitor to control the position and motion of the servo motors. The program is included at the end of the tutorial. This project will be more interesting and cooler if it uses a 3D printer. In the absence of such an item, you may use an online service or take advantage of cardboard to recreate the same thing.

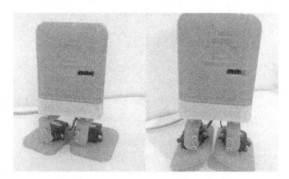

The following are the materials required for building this robot:

- Arduino Nano
- Servo SG90 – 4Nos
- Male berg sticks
- HC-05/HC-06 Bluetooth module
- 3D printer

This 3D printed robotics creation requires the bare minimum number of electronic components to assemble it so that project costs are kept at a minimum. This project is purely experimental and has no immediate real-time applications so far.

Hardware and Schematics:

This Arduino biped robot controlled using a mobile phone has a simple circuit; the complete schematic is shown below.

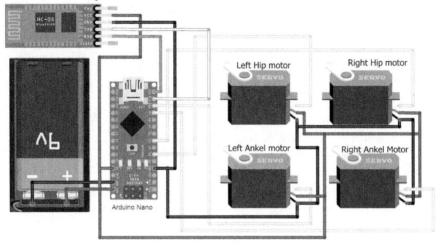

The connections I have made above were made on a perf board. You need to make sure that the circuit also fits into the head of the robot. The result should look something like below once your Perf board is ready.

Assembling the robot:

We can assemble the robot using the completed hardware and 3D printed parts. Make sure the motors are placed at the angles below so that the program works flawlessly before you fix them.

Motor Number	Motor place	Motor position
1	Left Hip motor	110

2	Right Hip motor	100
4	Right Ankle Motor	90
5	Right Hip motor	80

A program given at the end of the tutorial can be used to set these angles. Once you have connected the Arduino to the serial monitor and uploaded the program, enter the following commands in it.

(**Note:** Baud rate is 57600).

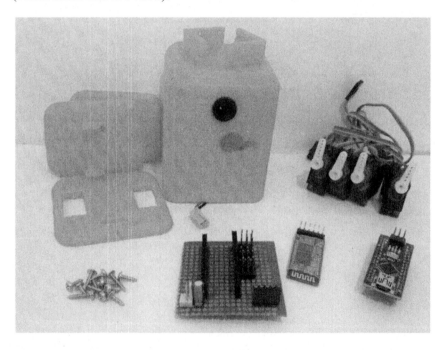

You should see the following in your Serial Monitor after all your motors have been placed.

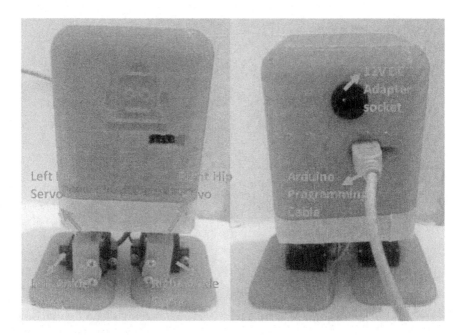

After the motors are set to the corresponding angles, they should be mounted like in the following figure.

63. Arduino Radar System Processing with Ultrasonic Sensor

The aim of this project is to demonstrate the power of an Arduino and Arduino software is used to develop a Surveillance device that transmits information via Bluetooth to an Android application.

Safety and Security have always been a top priority for us. Installing a surveillance camera with night vision, tilting, and panning options will burn a big hole in our pocket. Thus, we should create an affordable device with similar functions but without video.

Using an ultrasonic sensor, it detects objects and can therefore be used during the night as well. We are also mounting the ultrasonic sensor on a servo motor, which is able to scan an area automatically or manually, depending on whether it is set up for automated rotation or whether it is manually rotated via our Mobile app, Our ultrasonic sensors are focused in our preferred direction, allowing us to detect objects nearby. With the US sensor, we will be able to broadcast selected information to our smart phone, similar to a sonar or a radar.

Requirements: Hardware:

- A +5V power supply (I am using my Arduino (another) board for power supply)
- Arduino Mega (You can use anything from pro mini to Yun)
- Servo Motor (any rating)
- Bluetooth Module (HC-05)
- UltraSonic Sensor (HC-SR04)
- Breadboard (not mandatory)
- Connecting wires
- Android mobile
- Computer for programming

Software:

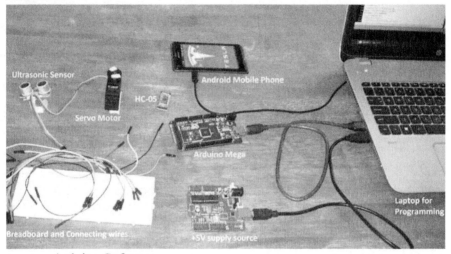

- Arduino Software
- Android SDK
- Processing Android (To create mobile application)

Let's start building the hardware once we have the materials ready. For ease of understanding, I have divided the tutorial into two parts: the Arduino Part and the Processing Part. The tutorial's code is complete and can be used directly by anyone who has no experience with Processing.

The servo motor, Bluetooth module, Ultrasonic sensor and other components all play an important role in the project. As such, beginners should start with some tutorials that cover these components before returning to this one. Here are our various projects involving Servo Motors, Bluetooth Modules, and Ultrasonic Sensors.

In this project, the Arduino is not responsible for powering any components as the servo motor, Bluetooth module and US sensor all draw a great deal of current that the Arduino cannot supply. Therefore, any external +5V power supply is highly recommended. I have used two Arduino boards to share the components when I did not have access to an external +5V supply. A second Arduino mega board (red colour) has been used to power the Servos. I have also mounted the Bluetooth module HC-05 and the ultrasonic sensor HC-SR04 on the Mega. CAUTION: The voltage regulator on the Arduino will be damaged if all these modules are powered with one Arduino board.

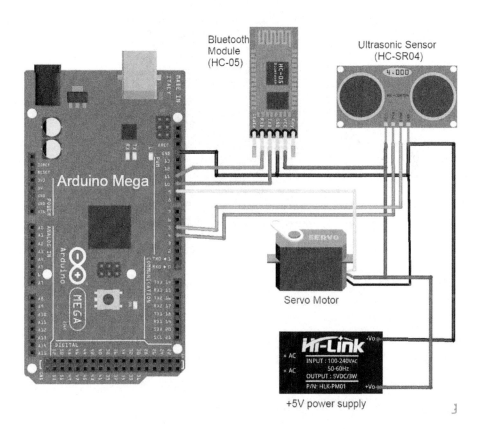

To mount the sensor, I used a piece of junk I had in my junk box, along with double-sided tape. To do the same, you can think of your own idea. Markets also offer servo holders for use with the same type of device.

Android Mobile Application for Ultrasonic Radar:

To install the same application used in this tutorial if you do not want to make your own application, you can follow the steps below.

Figure. Zealotbt App

1. This APK app is compatible with Android version 4.4.2 and above (Kitkat and above). The APK file can be downloaded directly from the link below.

https://circuitdigest.com/sites/default/files/Radar-zealotbt_1.0_apk_file.zip

(App Name: Zelobt)

2. APK files should be transferred from your computer to your phone.

3. Make sure your Android settings allow you to install applications from unknown sources.

4. Install the application.

If the app was successfully installed, you will see "Zelobt" installed as shown below.

At this point, both the hardware and software are ready. Your Bluetooth module should be powered on and paired with your mobile device. You should see your Bluetooth module (HC-05) automatically get connected to your phone once you have paired them. Open the "Zelobt" application we just installed and wait a second.

You will get the following message once the connection has been established:

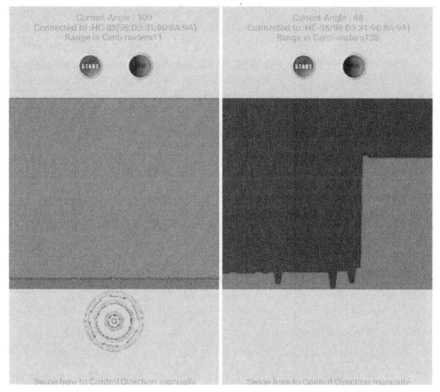

Figure. Radar data in the zealotbt mobile App

The top of the screen shows you that it is connected to: Device name (hardware address). Moreover, it shows the angle of the servomotor and the distance between the US sensors. On the red background, a blue graph is also plotted based on the measured distance. In the blue region, the closer the object, the taller it becomes. A mobile app can be used to control your servo motor, as we mentioned earlier. You can stop the servo from sweeping automatically by clicking the stop button. On the bottom of the screen, you will find a circular wheel that will rotate clockwise or anticlockwise when swiped. If you swipe this wheel, your servo motor will also turn in the same direction.

64. Heart Beat Monitoring over Internet using Arduino and ThingSpeak

The objective of this project is to create a Heart Beat Detection System using Arduino which will detect the heartbeat with the help of a pulse sensor and display the results of the measurement on an LCD connected to the Arduino board. Heart Beats can also be monitored remotely from anywhere in the world via the internet, using the Wi-Fi module ESP8266. With ThingSpeak, you can display the data online, access it when you want and where you want.

Previously, we developed a simple Heartbeat Monitor without displaying results online. Our project uses ThingSpeak for remote monitoring, so it falls under the Internet of Things category.

Components Required:

- Pulse sensor
- Wi-Fi module ESP8266
- Arduino Uno
- LCD
- Bread Board
- 10k potentiometer
- 1k resistors
- 220-ohm resistors
- LED
- Connecting wires

Circuit Diagram and Explanation:

In order to use ESP8266, we need to first connect it to the Arduino. The ESP8266 runs on 3.3V and is not able to function properly if you give it 5V from the Arduino. You need to connect the VCC and CH_PD pins of the Arduino to 3.3V. When we connect ESP8266 directly to the Arduino, its RX pin will not transmit when it operates at 3.3V. Thus, we will need to create a voltage divider so that the 5V can be converted into 3.3V. You can do this by increasing the resistance of three resistors as we did in the circuit. The ESP8266's TX pin is connected to pin 9 of Arduino while its RX pin is connected to pin 10 through the resistors.

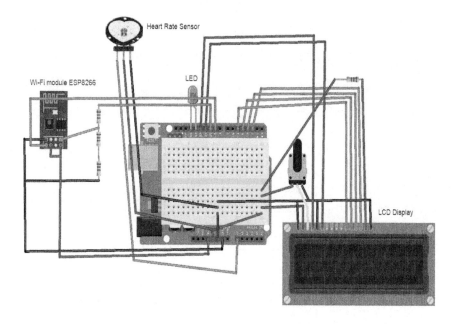

Your projects can connect to the internet and Wi-Fi using an ESP8266 Wi-Fi module. Your projects become very powerful with this device, which is very cheap. In the IOT platform, it is among the most prominent devices because it can be used with any microcontroller. Check out this article to learn how you can use an ESP8266 with Arduino.

Once the Pulse Sensor is connected to the Arduino, it is ready to be used. I love how easy it is to connect the pulse sensor. An Arduino is connected to the pulse sensor through the ground pin and 5V pin. The signal pin of the pulse sensor is connected to the A0 pin.

ThingSpeak Setup:

In regard to IoT projects, ThingSpeak offers a very useful tool. Our systems can be monitored and controlled using ThingSpeak's channel and webpages, which make monitoring and controlling our systems possible. ThingSpeak collects data, analyses it, and develops a response. We have previously used ThingSpeak in Raspberry Pi weather station projects and Arduino weather station projects. The following is a short description of the IoT Heart Beat Monitoring project as it is implemented using ThingSpeak.

Features of ThingSpeak

With ThingSpeak you can aggregate, visualize, and analyze live data streams on a cloud environment. Some of the features that ThingSpeak offers include:

- Connect ThingSpeak to a variety of IoT devices easily using popular protocols.
- Get real-time data from your sensors.
- On-demand access to aggregated data from third-parties.
- Analyze IoT data using the powerful MATLAB programming language.
- Automatically run your IoT analytics in response to schedules and events.
- IoT prototypes can be built without launching servers or creating web-based applications.
- You can use Twilio® or Twitter® to communicate using data that is automatically processed.

Creating an account on ThingSpeak.com is the first step, followed by signing in and clicking on Get Started.

Go to channels once you've created an account to create a channel. Put the name of the Channel and the Fields on the paper. You should also check the box below for the Make Public option before saving the channel. You have now successfully created your new channel.

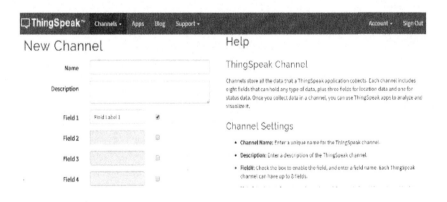

Once you have copied your API key, go to API Keys. It's needed in the code. Examine the full code at the end.

Private View   Public View   Channel Settings   **API Keys**   Data Import /

Write API Key

Key   9QPHPEPZIL8Z9KSV

Generate New Write API Key

Working Explanation:

The pulse sensor must first be attached to any organ of the body where it can readily detect the pulse, like a finger, as shown in the video. As the heart pumps blood into the body, the Pulse Sensor will measure the change in volume of blood. In the same way, the change in blood volume affects the brightness of the light that filters through the organ. Once this change is observed, the Arduino will convert it to heart beats per minute (BPM). Additionally, the LED connected to pin 13 will flash in response to the Heart Beat.

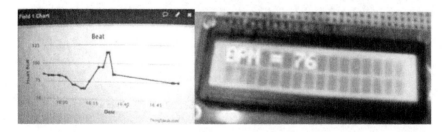

An Arduino will communicate with the ESP8266 through ThingSpeak, which will send data to it. With the help of the ESP8266, you can get the data from the sensor and transfer it online via the network of your router. These readings will appear in a graph format and can be accessed from anywhere with a web browser. In addition to the BPM, the LCD connected will also display it.

65. IoT based Air Pollution Monitoring System using Arduino

This project involves the development of an Internet of Things (IoT) based service that monitors air pollution over the Internet through a web server, and it will sound a warning if sufficient amounts of hazardous gasses like carbon dioxide, smoke, alcohol, benzene and NH3 enter the air at a certain level. On the LCD and on the webpage, we will be able to read the air quality in PPM, so we can easily monitor it. This time the air quality sensor was the MQ135 sensor instead of the MQ6 sensor, which we used previously for making LPG detectors. The MQ135 sensor can detect most harmful gases without affecting their amount.

You can monitor pollution levels in this IOT project using your computer or mobile device no matter where you are. In addition to installing this system anywhere, we can also set up some device that will turn on the exhaust fan or send SMS/email notifications to the user when pollution reaches some level.

Required Components:

- MQ135 Gas sensor
- Arduino Uno
- Wi-Fi module ESP8266
- 16X2 LCD
- Breadboard
- 10K potentiometer
- 1K ohm resistors
- 220-ohm resistor
- Buzzer

Circuit Diagram and Explanation:

In order to use ESP8266, we need to first connect it to the Arduino. You can't use Arduino to power an ESP8266 as it runs on 3.3V, but if you give it 5V, then it won't function properly and might even be damaged. 3.3V should be connected to VCC and CH_PD on Arduino. When connected directly to the Arduino, the RX pin of the ESP8266 works with 3.3V voltage and thus cannot communicate with the Arduino. Thus, we will need to create a voltage divider so that the 5V can be converted into 3.3V.

You can do this by increasing the resistance of three resistors as we did in the circuit. By connecting the ESP8266's TX pin to Arduino pin 10, and its RX pin to Arduino pin 9, you can make the ESP8266 transmit data.

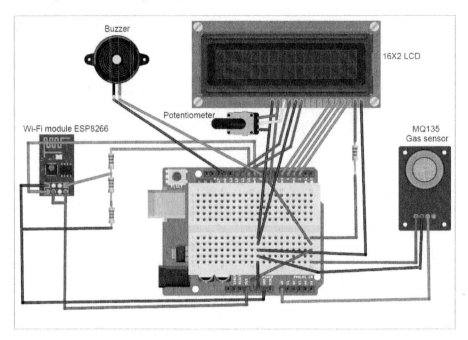

Your projects can connect to the internet and Wi-Fi using an ESP8266 Wi-Fi module. You can create very powerful projects with this inexpensive device. ESP8266 is a leading IOT device, capable of communicating with any microcontroller. Discover more about using ESP8266 with Arduino here.

Our next step will be to connect the MQ135 sensor to the Arduino. The sensor's VCC and ground pins should be connected to the Arduino's 5V and ground, while the sensor's Analog pin should be connected to the Arduino's A0. In addition, we'd like to connect the LCD to the Arduino through pin 8, which is responsible for beeping when the condition occurs.

Working Explanation:

A gas sensor can detect NH3, NOx, alcohol, benzene, smoke, CO2, and a few other gases, so the MQ135 sensor is ideal for our Air Quality Monitoring Project. With Arduino we can detect the pollutants, and we will get their concentration in parts per million. Gas sensors such as

MQ135 provide output based on voltage levels that must be converted into PPM. Therefore, I have used a library for MQ135 to convert the output in PPM, and you can find the details below in the "Code Explanation" section.

Despite being within a safe limit of air quality (350 PPM), the sensor gave us a value of 90 when no gas was close by. It causes headaches, sleepiness, stagnant, stale air, and increased heart rate when it exceeds 1000 PPM and changes can be seen in other conditions when it exceeds 2000 PPM.

The LCD and webpage will display "Fresh Air" when the value is less than 1000 PPM. A buzzer will start beeping every time the value reaches 1000 PPM, displaying "Poor Air, Open Windows" on the LCD and webpage. In the event that it reaches 2000, the buzzer will continue to beep and the LCD and webpage will indicate "Stay away from fresh air".

66. IOT Based Dumpster Monitoring using Arduino & ESP8266

We will build an Internet of Things (IOT) based garbage can monitoring system in this DIY that will let us know when the trash can is full or empty by monitoring the webserver, enabling you to control the trash can from anywhere. Aside from being highly useful, it can also be placed on trash cans in public areas and private homes.

Within this Internet of Things project, ultrasonic sensors are used to detect trash can content. The Ultrasonic Sensor is mounted on top of the trash can and measures how far the trash is from the sensor. Based on the size of the trash can, a threshold value can be set for the distance between the trash and the sensor.

When the distance is less than this threshold value, the trash can will be full of garbage, and a message "Basket Full" will be printed on the webpage. If the distance is greater than this threshold value, however, the container will be empty. The threshold value has been set to 5 cm in our program code. A Wi-Fi module called ESP8266 is used to communicate between the Arduino and the webserver. On a local web server, we demonstrated our Garbage Monitoring System.

Components Required:

- Arduino Uno (you can use any other)
- ESP8266 Wi-Fi module
- HC-SR04 Ultrasonic sensor
- 1K Resistors
- Breadboard
- Connecting wires

Circuit Diagram and Explanation:

In order to use ESP8266, we need to first connect it to the Arduino. You cannot power the ESP8266 with 5V from an Arduino or it won't function properly and may get damaged. It runs on 3.3V. 3.3V should be connected to VCC and CH_PD on Arduino. When connected directly to the Arduino, the RX pin of the ESP8266 works with 3.3V voltage and thus cannot communicate with the Arduino. A voltage divider will be needed, so we will be using three 1-k resistors in series. In the circuit diagram below, you will see the RX is connected to pin 11 of the Arduino, along with the TX, as well as the TX of the Arduino is connected to pin 10.

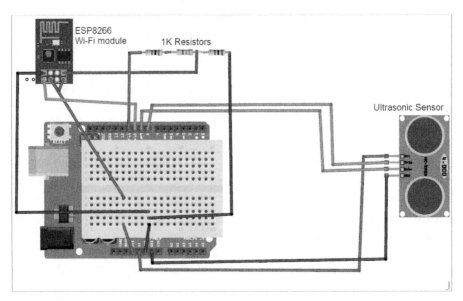

HC-SR04 ultrasonic sensor now needs to be connected to the Arduino. Ultrasonic sensors connect to Arduino boards in a very simple manner. An ultrasonic sensor's VCC and ground should be connected to the Arduino's 5V and ground. You should connect pin 8 and pin 9 of the Arduino to the TRIG and ECHO pins of the ultrasonic sensor, respectively.

DEMO OUTPUT

In the Serial Monitor, you can view the IP address of the code after it has been uploaded.

The output is shown below if you type in this IP address into your browser. For a second look at whether the trash can is empty, you must refresh the page again.

67. Arduino based Vehicle Tracker using GPS and GSM

We are taking GPS one step further in this project by tracking the vehicle using GPS and GSM. With a few hardware and software changes, this system could also be used for Accident Detection Alerts, Soldier Tracking, and many more.

Vehicle tracking consists of tracking the location of the vehicle using GPS coordinates (latitude and longitude). GPS coordinates represent the location of a point. A system like this is a great choice for outdoor applications.

In order to track Cabs/Taxis, stolen cars, school/college buses, etc., this type of Vehicle Tracking System Project is widely used.

Components Required:

- Arduino
- GSM Module
- GPS Module
- 16x2 LCD
- Power Supply
- Connecting Wires
- 10 K POT

GPS Module and Its Working:

With the Global Positioning System, you can find the position of any place on the planet in exact UTC time (Universal Coordinated Time). GPS stands for Global Positioning System. Vehicle tracking systems are primarily built with a GPS module as the key component. Using this device, satellite coordinates are received every second from the earth, as well as time and date.

Tracking position data is sent in real time via GPS module, and all the information is formatted in NMEA (see the screenshot below). We only need one sentence in the NMEA format, which consists of several sentences. Starting from $GPGGA, this sentence contains coordinates, times, and other relevant information. The GPS fix data is known as the

GPGGA, or Global Positioning System Fix Data. Read more about GPS data and its string here.

Counting the commas in $GPGGA allows us to extract the coordinates for this string. Consider how Latitude and Longitude can be found from a string stored in a $GPGGA array; after two commas Latitude can be found and after four commas Longitude can be found. Latitudes and longitudes from the array can now be inserted into other arrays.

Below is the $GPGGA String, along with its description:

$GPGGA,104534.000,7791.0381,
N,06727.4434,E,1,08,0.9,510.4,M,43.9,M,,*47
$GPGGA,HHMMSS.SSS,latitude,N,longitude,E,FQ,NOS,HDP,altitude,
M,height, A, checksum data

Identifier	Description
$GPGGA	Global Positioning system fix data
HHMMSS.SSS	Time in hour minute seconds and milliseconds format.
Latitude	Latitude (Coordinate)
N	Direction N=North, S=South
Longitude	Longitude (Coordinate)
E	Direction E= East, W=West

FQ	Fix Quality Data
NOS	No. of Satellites being Used
HPD	Horizontal Dilution of Precision
Altitude	Altitude from sea level
M	Meter
Height	Height
Checksum	Checksum Data

Circuit Explanation:

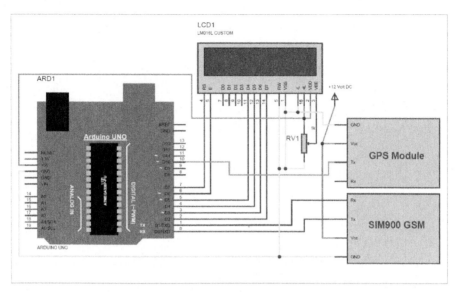

A Vehicle Tracking System uses a simple circuit where TX pin number 10 of the Arduino is connected directly to Tx pin number 9 of the GPS module. By using the Software Serial Library here, pins 10 and 11 have been enabled for serial communication and have been set to Rx and Tx respectively, leaving the RX pin of the GPS Module open.

By default, serial communication is limited to Pin 0 and 1 of the Arduino board. However, the SoftwareSerial library enables serial communication on almost any pin of the board. In order to power the GPS Module, a 12-volt power supply is used.

Rx and Tx pins of the GSM module are wired directly to pins Rx and Tx of the Arduino. A 12v power supply is also required for GSM modules. Pin numbers 5, 4, 3, and 2 of the Arduino are connected to the LCD's data pins D4, D5, D6 and D7. The RW pin of the LCD is connected directly to ground. Command pins EN and RS are connected to pins 2 and 3 of Arduino. The LCD can also be controlled by the potentiometer by setting the contrast or brightness.

Working Explanation:

This project uses an Arduino board along with a GPS module and GSM module to control the whole process. GSM module is used for sending GPS coordinates via SMS to the user. GPS receiver detects the location of the vehicle. Furthermore, a 16x2 LCD allows status messages and coordinates to be displayed. This module was integrated with the GPS module SKG13BL and the GSM module SIM900A.

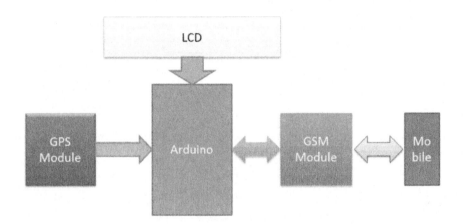

Creating our hardware is the final step in programming our vehicle. The hardware is now ready to be mounted on our vehicle and powered up. Our vehicle will receive a message stating "Track Vehicle" as soon as we send it to the tracking device. In projects like these, we have incorporated prefixes (#) and suffixes (*) to indicate the beginning and the end of the string. Similarly, we did the following in these projects: Wireless Notice Board and Home Automation With GSM

The sending GSM module receives the message data, which it sends to Arduino, which reads it and extracts the main message.

It will be compared with a predefined message in Arduino. Once any match occurs, the Arduino reads the coordinates by reading GPS module data and extracting $GPGGA String, which it sends via the GSM module to the user. The location of the vehicle is specified in this message.

68. Snake Game on 8x8 Matrix using Arduino

From the beginning of the mobile phones, Snake has been incredibly popular. Black and white mobile phones were initially available and became extremely popular. Cell phones have changed this game dramatically as well, which has led to a range of graphical and colorful versions being available now.

Figure. Arduino Snake Game Project

Besides Snake, DIY electronics projects are also popular among students and hobbyists. Keeping it simple and yet providing all its functions is what we will be demonstrating today in the Arduino Snake Game.

Components Used:

- Arduino UNO
- 8x8 LED Dot Matrix Display
- Shift Register 74HC595
- 16x2 LCD
- POT 1K
- Push Buttons
- Connecting wires
- Bread Board
- Power Supply

Working Explanation:

A complex game like this requires a lot of work. Fortunately, we have simplified it in this tutorial for you. Our LCD screen displays the snake and its food dot, the 8x8 red colour Dot matrix displays the score, 5 push buttons to initiate the game and an Arduino UNO controls the entire process. An 8x8 LED Dot Matrix Display pin diagram has been provided below, along with its original image:

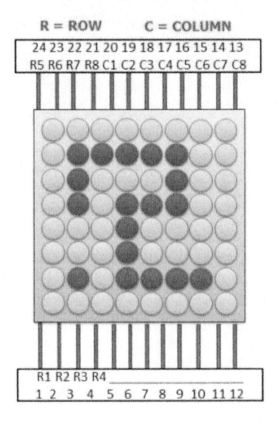

Circuit Diagram

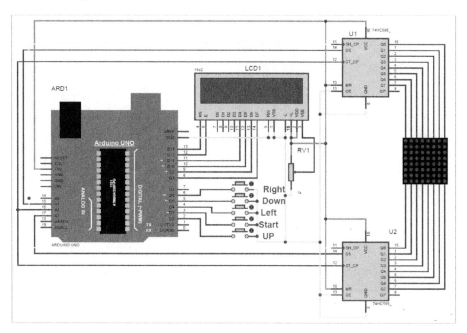

Project Snake's circuit is rather complicated. Shift Register 74HC595 is used in this example to connect the dot matrix display. For driving the columns, one shift register is used while the other drives the rows. On Arduino, pin number 14 and 16 are connected directly to the control pins for both registers, the Column Shift Register (SH, ST). Pins 15 and 17 of Arduino are directly connected to the DS pins of column shift registers and rows shift registers, respectively. Game controls are connected at pins 3, 4, 6, 2 and 5. Left and right directions are linked at pins 3, 4 and 6, up and down directions are connected at pin 5. Our hardware also includes an LCD that displays scores. There is a direct connection between pin 13 and pin 12 for RS and EN. A ground wire runs directly from the RW pin to pin 11 of the Arduino, and data lines from d4-d7 are connected to pins 8, 9, and 10 of the board. Circuit diagrams are used to show the rest of the connections.

After we power the circuit up, the LCD displays a "Press Start to Play" message and a welcome message. A second dot matrix display appears with two snakes and a single food dot, and the score is displayed as zero on the LCD.

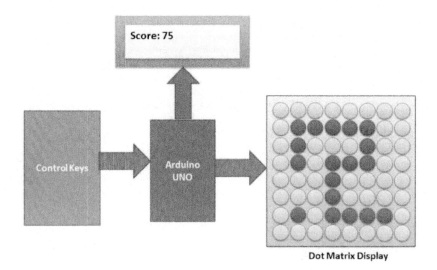

Dot Matrix Display

The game can now be started by pressing the middle button and the snake automatically moves upwards. In order to move the snake, the user must press the direction keys around the middle button. In this case we have used five push buttons (left, right, up, down, and start) respectively.

Once the snake reaches the food dot or eats the food, its score will increase by five points and its length will increase by a dot (LED) every time, making it faster than before. The game would end whenever a snake struck any wall, reached the end of the LED matrix, or reached the end of the game mat. Once the user presses the start key, the game must be started again.

69. Prepaid Energy Meter using GSM and Arduino

Electricity Energy Meters with prepaid balances are a solid idea because they allow you to refill them just like we do on our mobile phones. This project involves the use of Arduino and GSM modules to create an automated system. This system allows electricity balances to be recharged through SMS messages. If the system is unbalanced or low, it can stop the power supply to the house. And this system will automatically send users updates on their mobile devices, such as low balance alerts, cut off alerts, resume alerts, and recharge alerts, depending on the energy meter readings.

Working explanation:

Using an Arduino and the power meter's calibration LED, we have interfaced the energy meter with Arduino. Our CAL LED only needs to be connected to an Arduino by means of an Optocoupler IC.

Components used:

- Arduino
- GSM Module
- 16x2 LCD
- Analogue Electricity Energy Meter
- Optocoupler 4n35
- Resistors
- POT
- Connecting wires
- Bulb and holder
- SIM card
- Power supply
- Mobile Phone

As soon as the system comes on, it reads previous rupee values from EEPROM and restores them into variables; it compares the value with the predefined one and decides whether to proceed. Use relays to switch on the electricity of a house or office if the available amount is more than 15 rupees, for example. Once the balance falls below 15 rupees, Arduino sends a SMS to the phone of the user informing them of the low balance and asking them to recharge soon. The Arduino turns off the electricity supply of the home when the balance falls beneath 5 rupees and sends a SMS alerting the user of a 'Light Cut' and requesting him to recharge soon. Here you can find information on the GSM module and AT commands used to send and receive messages.

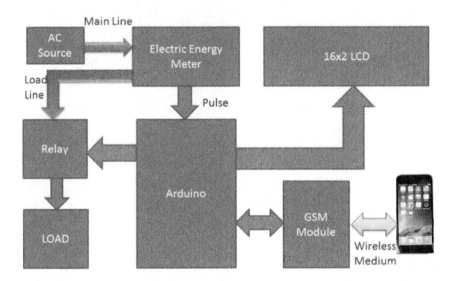

Now that our system can be recharged through our cell phones, we can do so simply by sending a SMS to it. We would send #45* if we want to recharge 45 dollars, here the # and * indicate the sum to be recharged. Upon receiving this message, the system extracts the recharge amount to update the system balance. In the video at the end, you will see how the system turns on the electricity in the house or office.

Circuit Description:

A schematic of the project circuit connections is shown; an Arduino UNO processor has been used to process all the components. Unit status and remaining balance are displayed on a liquid crystal display. LCD pins RS, EN, D4, D5, D6, D7 are connected to Arduino digital pin number 7, 6, 5, 4, 3, 2. GSM pins Rx and Tx are directly connected to Arduino pins Rx and Tx respectively. An adapter powered by 12 volts is used to power a

GSM module. On pin 12 of Arduino, a relay is used to switch electricity through the ULN2003 relay driver.

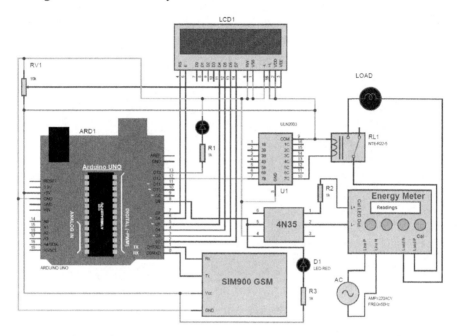

How to Connect Energy Meter with Arduino:

An Analogue Electricity Energy Meter must first be purchased by the user. Once it has been opened, the user can locate the terminals of Pulse LEDs and Cal LEDs (cathode and anode). Once you have soldered two wires in each terminal, remove them from the meter and close it. Then tighten the screws. Now the LED's anode terminal must be connected to pin number 1 of the optocoupler. On an optocoupler, pin number two is connected to the cathode terminal, and pin number four should be directly connected to ground. In the pin number 5 of the optocoupler is an LED and Pull-up resistor. A similar terminal should be connected to Arduino pin 8 as well.

The aim of this project is to gather information about the usage of energy by a specific consumer or user, using a wireless communications system (not requiring a visit to the consumer's home or office), and the system is called AMR (Automatic Meter Reading). AMR would involve remotely accumulating meter readings at a location through a wireless telecommunications system, instead of individuals visiting the site physically and taking notes.

70. Clap Switch using Arduino

Using ARDUINO UNO as a platform, we will prototype a Clapper circuit using the ADC concept. In order to detect sound and generate a response, we are going to use a MIC and Uno. Clap ON Clap OFF switches the device by using clapping sound, however it does not work in reverse. The 555 Timer IC was previously used to build the Clap ON Clap OFF switch and Clap ON Clap OFF switch.

In case of clapping, there is a peak signal in the microphone that is much higher than normal. That signal is sent to the amplifier via a high-pass filter. ADC converts this high voltage signal into a number using an amplification circuit. In other words, the ADC reading for the UNO will peak at that time. The project is described in detail below. When the peak is detected, the LED on the board will be toggled.

MIC is a transducer that detects sound, converting audio energy into electrical energy. Hence sound is represented as a changing voltage with this sensor. A device like this is used mostly for recording or detecting sounds. All mobile phones and laptops have this type of transducer. A typical MIC looks like this

A typical MIC appears like, A typical MIC can be found in all mobile phones and laptops.

A condenser mic's polarity can be determined in several ways.

There are two terminals for MIC, one is positive, the other is negative. Using a multimeter, it is possible to check the polarity of the microphone. The positive probe of the Multimeter (the meter must be in DIODE TESTING mode) must be connected to the positive terminal of the MIC, and the negative probe must be connected to the negative terminal of the MIC. On the Multimeter, if the positive (MIC) terminal is at the negative terminal, it indicates the positive (MIC) terminal is at the negative terminal. The negative terminal has two or three soldering lines connected to the metal case. The positive terminal is similar, with one soldering line connected to the metal case. You can also check whether the connection between its metal case and the negative terminal is intact using continuity tester, in order to discover the negative terminal.

Components Required:

- Hardware:
- ARDUINO UNO, power supply (5v), a condenser mic (explained above)
- 2N3904 NPN transistor,
- 100nF capacitors (2 pieces), one 100uF capacitor,
- 1K Ω resistor, 1MΩ resistor, 15KΩ resistor (2 pieces), one LED,
- And Breadboard & Connecting wires.
- Software: Arduino IDE

Circuit Diagram and Working Explanation:

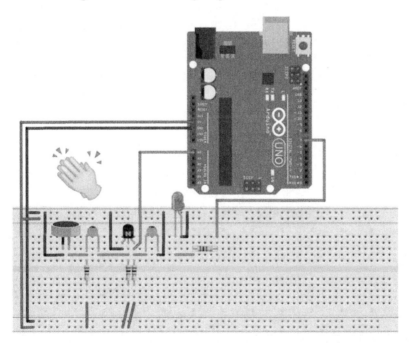

In this figure, you can see the circuit diagram for the clapper project

There are four main parts to the process, namely: Filtration, Amplification, Analog-Digital conversion, and programming to control the LED.

When sound is detected, the microphone can convert it into voltage that is proportional to the level of sound. We would assign a higher value to a higher sound, and a lower value to a lower sound. In order to filter this signal, it is first fed into a High Pass Filter. This filtered value is then fed into the transistor to produce an amplified output, which is delivered through the collector. ADC0 of the UNO receives this collector signal, which is then converted to a digital signal. The LED is programmed to turn on with every increment of ADC channel A0, coupled into PIN 7 of PORTD.

There are four stages in each project:

1. Filtration:

In the first instance, we will talk briefly about R-C High Pass Filters, which have been used to filter out noise. There is a single resistor and a single capacitor in this simple device. Keeping the circuit simple is all we need for this circuit, so we won't get bogged down in the details. Unlike low pass filters, high pass filters allow high frequency signals to pass through their input to output. In other words, input signals appear at the filter output if their frequency exceeds the filter's prescribed frequency. For now, we are not designing an audio amplifier, so we do not need to worry about these values. Here is the circuit for a high pass filter. A transistor then amplifies the voltage signal after passing through the filter.

2. Amplification:

In order to drive the voltage of MIC, we need a transistor amplifier. Since the voltage of MIC is too low, it cannot be fed to the UNO for ADC (Analog to Digital Conversion). The voltages of MICs are amplified here with a single transistor amplifier. ADC0 of the Arduino receives the amplified voltage signal.

3. Analog to Digital Conversion:

There are six analog to digital converter channels on the ARDUINO. You can use any or all of them as analog voltage inputs. This means that input voltages within the range of 0-5 volts are translated into integer values within the range of 0-1023 using the UNO ADC of 10 bits. So, for every

(5/1024= 4.9mV) per unit. We need to use the ADC channel of ARDUINO UNO in order to transform analog signals into digital signals, such as the following:

Reference values for ADC channels on the Arduino UNO are set to 5V. Therefore, we can provide feedback voltages of up to 5V on any input channel for ADC conversion. We have an instruction that enables us to change the reference value, as some sensors provide voltages of 0-2.5V, so with a 5V reference, the accuracy is reduced. The analog reference value can be changed using the "analogReference()" method.

The ADC channel 0 reading can be performed by directly calling the function "analogRead(pin);", where "pin" represents the pin to which the analog signal was connected in our circuit, for instance "A0". By adding this instruction to the digital readout instruction "int sensorValue = analogRead(A0);", the value from the ADC is taken and converted into an integer for storage in the memory of the UNO.

4. Program Arduino to Toggle the LED on each Clap:

When the MIC is working properly, we get normal signals, so we also get normal values in the UNO. The MIC provides a peak upon clapping; thanks to this, we have a peak digital value in the UNO, the LED can then be programmed to toggle ON when the peak is present. Thus, the LED illuminates with the first clap and stays on. Once the LED has been turned off, it will remain off until the next clap. Thus, we have a clapper circuit.

71. Bluetooth Controlled Toy Car using Arduino

Following the development of a few popular robotic projects like line following robots, edge avoiding robots, DTMF robots, gesture-controlled robots, etc. This project involves developing an Android-based application that uses Bluetooth technology to control a robot car.

Components

- Arduino UNO, DC Motors
- Bluetooth module HC-05
- Motor Driver L293D
- 9 Volt Battery and 6-volt battery
- Battery Connector, Toy Car

Android-based mobile devices can control Bluetooth-enabled cars instead of buttons, gestures, and other traditional control methods. In this case, I could control the car with an Android phone by simply touching buttons forward, backward or left and right. Here, the Android phone transmits data to the car's Bluetooth module, which acts as the receiver. In order to move in the required direction like forward and reverse, turning left and right, and stopping, an Android phone will transmit commands via Bluetooth to the car.

Working Explanation

A toy car was used in this project to demonstrate the process. This RF toy car has steering features that can be moved left and right. This car's RF circuit was replaced by an Arduino circuit we purchased after buying it. Both the front and rear of this car are equipped with DC motors. An engine on the front of the car gives the car direction, such as turning left or right. Rear-wheel drive energy is used to propel the car forwards and backwards. The Arduino UNO is used to control the entire system, with Bluetooth modules receiving directions from Android phones.

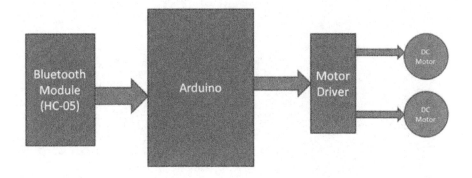

In the Bluetooth mobile application for Android, the car is driven by buttons touched. Getting started with this project requires first downloading Bluetooth apps from Google Play.

The apps that should work correctly include any that support or can send data. These are some examples.

- § Bluetooth Spp pro
- § Bluetooth controller

It is necessary to open the app once it is installed and then search for the Bluetooth device and choose it. Using the Bluetooth controller app, we have set up the keys.

Download the Bluetooth Controller and install it.

1. Turned ON mobile Bluetooth.
2. Now open Bluetooth controller app
3. Press scan
4. Select desired Bluetooth device

Press the set buttons on the screen to set the keys. Keys can be set by pressing the "Set" button and setting them according to the following picture:

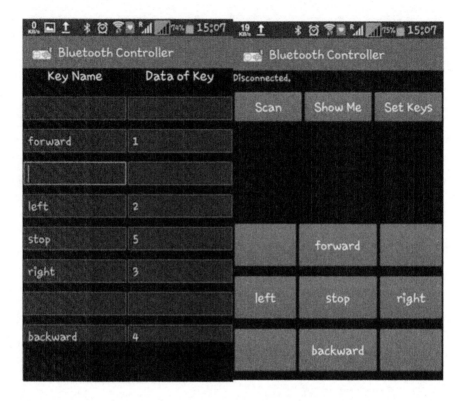

Press OK after you have set the keys. The Bluetooth controller app starts moving forward when we touch the forward button, and the car keeps moving forward until we hit the next command.

The car moves backward when we touch the backward button in the Bluetooth controller app and continues to move backward until the next command is given.

In the app, we can tap the left button to cause the car to move in the left direction. In addition, it continues moving left until the next command is given. When the front motors are operating in this condition, the tires will turn in the left direction, whereas the rear motors will run in the forward direction.

If we touch the right button on the Bluetooth controller app, the car will start moving in the right direction and it will continue to move until the next command is received. Under this condition, the motors on the front side move the wheels in the right direction, while the motors on the back move the vehicle forward. We can stop the car by touching the stop button.

403

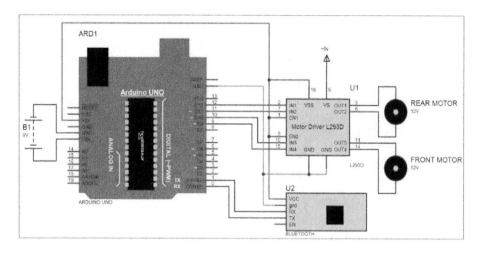

A Bluetooth-controlled car circuit diagram is shown in the above figure. To drive the car, a motor driver is connected to Arduino. Arduino's digital pin numbers 12, 11, 10 and 9 correspond to the motor driver's input pins 2, 7 and 15. This circuit uses two DC motors and a 6-volt battery to power the motors. One motor is connected to the output pins 3 and 6 of the motor driver, while the other motor is connected to pins 11 and 14. RX and TX pins of the Bluetooth module are connected directly to the TX and Rx of the Arduino. The Bluetooth module's VCC and GND pins are connected to Arduino's +5 volt and GND. An Arduino's Vin pins are powered by a 9V battery.

72. Automatic Water Level Indicator and Controller using Arduino

We will use ultrasonic sensors to measure the water level in this Arduino based automatic water level controller and indicator project. A fundamental principle of ultrasonic distance measurements is based on ECHO. After impacting on an obstacle, sound waves travel back to their source as ECHO.

We must then only calculate the sound's outgoing and returning times after striking the obstacle, in other words, their traveling time. In addition, we can calculate the distance and get a result from it. The water pump is automatically turned on when the tank water level drops, so that we can use this concept in our water controller project. For a simplified version of this project, you can check out this simple water level indicator circuit.

Components

- Arduino Uno
- Ultrasonic sensor Module
- 16x2 LCD
- Relay 6 Volt
- ULN2003
- 7806, PVT
- Copper wire
- 9-volt battery or 12 Volt Adaptor
- Connecting wires

Working of Automatic Water Level Controller

Working on this project is very straightforward. This module uses ultrasonic waves to generate sound waves which are reflected by the water in the tank and senses the sound waves as ECHO. In order to send a signal to the ultrasonic sensor module, we have to trigger Arduino to transmit it, and then we will wait for the ECHO to arrive. Arduino measures the time between triggering and receiving ECHOs. Using the following formula, we can calculate the distance using the sound speed of 340 m/s:

Distance= (travel time/2) * speed of sound

Sound travels at an average speed of 340m per second.

We can compute distances from a sensor to the surface of the water using these methods. In order to determine water level, we first need to determine depth.

Effort must now be put into determining the total length of the water tank. By subtracting the actual distance from the tank from the total length, we can calculate the water level by subtracting the distance from the tank's length. In the next step we'll need to calculate the distance between the water level and the LCD display. We can then convert the distance into a percentage. Below is a block diagram that explains the complete workings of the water level indicator.

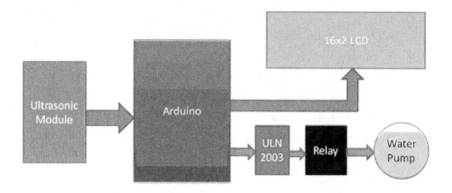

The circuit diagram for the water level controller below shows that pins 10 and 11 of the Arduino are connected directly to the Ultrasonic sensor module's "trigger" and "echo" pins. Four-bit mode is used to connect a 16x2 LCD to the Arduino. In addition to the 3 control pins of Arduino RS, RW and En, GND pins 5 and 6 are also connected through ULN2003 to the buzzer at pin 12, while pin 8 of Arduino is wired through ULN2003 to operate the water pump. The relay and the remaining circuit are powered by a voltage regulator 7805.

Water level indicators measure and manage the level of water in multiple different systems, including swimming pools, cooling towers, and pumps and tanks. They act as a basic flow regulator and optimise the performance of a system by controlling water flow.

Applications and Uses of Water Level Indicators

There are several applications for water level indicators, including:

- Water level can be controlled in water tanks using this device
- Activate/deactivate pumps automatically
- Suitable for factories, commercial buildings, apartments, and homes
- Measuring the level of fuel in tanks
- Controlling the level of an oil tank
- A low-level alarm and a high-level alarm
- Managing the level of the pool water
- Switches between life stations

- Monitoring the level of leachate
- Controlling the level of water in cooling towers
- Pump level control for sewage systems
- Fluid monitoring via remote control
- A mechanism to control water levels
- Control panel for pumps
- Monitoring of the stream at the individual level
- Pumps for storing water
- Tsunami warnings and monitoring sea levels
- Controlling and monitoring batches of processes
- Controlling irrigation systems

A Water Level Indicator and Water Alarm Has Many Benefits

Indicators and alarms for water levels provide several benefits, such as the following:

- The installation process is simple
- There is very little maintenance required
- You are alerted when the water level is either too high or too low
- Alarms for low and high temperatures
- The compact design
- Water levels are automatically adjusted
- Reduce your electricity and water consumption to save money
- By keeping tanks from overflowing, we can prevent roof and wall leaks
- Manual labor is reduced to a minimum with automatic operation
- Easily maintains multiple operations with a small amount of energy
- Provides information about water levels in any type of tank or reservoir
- It is easy to hear a water alarm because it is loud

Circuit Diagram and Explanation

An Ultrasonic sensor module was placed on top of the water tank in the circuit to demonstrate the mechanism. In this sensor module, a distance will be measured between the sensor module and the water surface, and the distance will be displayed on an LCD screen as "Water Surface in Tank is:". In other words, we are displaying an empty space of volume or distance for water rather than its level. As a result of this feature, this system can be applied to any water tank. An Arduino will run a relay to turn the water pump ON when empty water levels reach about 30 cm. A

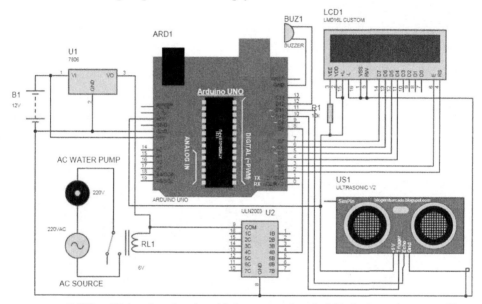

green LED will begin glowing if the water level falls below the cut-off level and the motor is turned on.

If the empty space is within 12 cm of the Arduino, the relay is turned off and the display shows "Tanks are full" and "Motors are off". During this time, the relay status LED will also turn off and the buzzer will beep.

73. Tachometer using Arduino

RPM is calculated by the Tachometer, which counts rotations per minute. The mechanical tachometer and the digital tachometer are separate types of instruments. Using an IR sensor module for object detection, we will design a digital tachometer based on an Arduino board. The infrared (IR) transmitter emits IR rays, which are reflected to the IR receiver, and the

IR module outputs a pulse which is detected during the start of the program by the Arduino controller. There are 5 seconds of continuous counting.

Following the given formula, the Arduino calculates the revolutions per minute for a minute.

RPM= Count x 12 for single object rotating body.

This project is demonstrated using ceiling fans. Therefore, we have made the following changes:

RPM=count x 12 / objects
Were
Object = number of blades in fan.

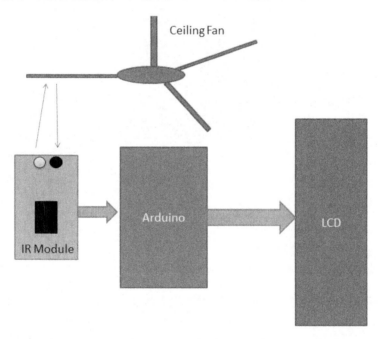

Required Components

- Arduino
- IR sensor Module
- 16x2 LCD
- Push button
- Bread board

- 9-volt battery
- Connecting wires

Circuit Diagram and Explanation

The Arduino Pro Mini is connected to an IR sensor, a buzzer and a LCD in the tachometer circuit. IR sensor module generates the reading pulse that Arduino controls. IR sensor module calculates RPM from detected objects and displays the value on the LCD.

Sensors use infrared light to detect objects. Inbuilt potentiometers on the IR module allow us to adjust the sensitivity of the sensor. They are designed to detect or receive infrared rays and are composed of an IR transmitter and a photodiode. This Line Follower Robot explains that infrared rays are transmitted through IR transmitters, and they reflect back when they hit any surface. An Arduino receives the output of the photodiode through a comparator, which compares the photodiode's output voltage to a reference voltage.

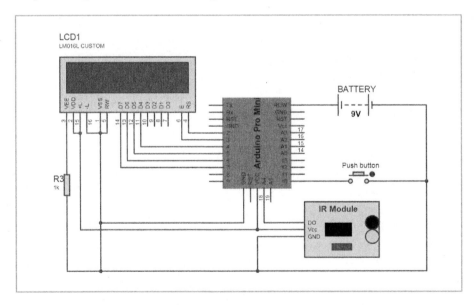

The Arduino Pro Mini is connected to an IR sensor, a buzzer and a LCD in the tachometer circuit. Arduino controls the entire process, including reading the pulses generated by the IR sensor module based on object detection, calculating RPM, and sending RPM values to the LCD. It uses an inbuilt potentiometer to set the sensitivity of this sensor. We can set the sensitivity of this sensor by the inbuilt potentiometer on the IR module. They are designed to detect or receive infrared rays and are composed of an IR transmitter and a photodiode. This Line Follower Robot explains that infrared rays are transmitted through IR transmitters, and they reflect back when they hit any surface. An Arduino receives the output of the photodiode through a comparator, which compares the photodiode's output voltage to a reference voltage.

74. Automatic Room Light Controller with Bidirectional Visitor Counter

We can often find visitor counters in stadiums, malls, offices, and class rooms. What do they do with the lights when nobody is present? How do they turn them on or off? Using Arduino Uno, we have developed an automatic light control project that also tallied visitors in the room in a bidirectional manner. There is a lot of fun and learning to be had with the project for hobbyists and students.

Components

- Arduino UNO
- Relay (5v)
- Resisters
- IR Sensor module
- 16x2 LCD display
- Bread Board
- Connecting Wires
- Led
- BC547 Transistor

This project uses Arduino to interface sensors, motors, and other components with a visitor counter. This counter can count people in both directions. You can use this circuit to count who enters a building, mall, home, or office. By incrementing the count when a person exits the hall, the number of persons left the hall can be counted. Sensors as well as gates of parking areas are examples of other public places where sensors can be used. And it depends on where they are placed in the mall/hall.

Sensors, controllers, counter displays and gates comprise the four parts of this project. An interruption would be detected by the sensor, and its input would be used by the controller to increase or decrease the counter based on whether a person entered or exited. A 16x2 LCD screen displays the counting through the controller.

We set a delay for the other sensor so that it won't work if the IR sensor is interrupted by an object present in the room.

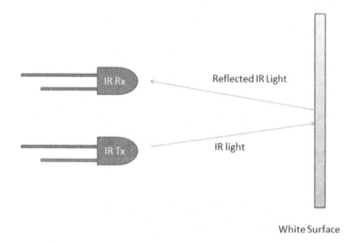

White Surface

Circuit Explanation

A visitor counter circuit consists of the following sections: sensors, controls, displays, and drivers.

Sensor section: Two IR sensor modules with LED's, potentiometers, comparators (Op-Amps), and IR diodes were used in this chapter. Infrared sensors sense objects and cause a change in voltage at the comparator's second terminal. A potentiometer is used to measure voltage at the comparator's first terminal. This is then compared with the output voltage by the comparator and a digital signal resulted. Here in this circuit, two sensors are being compared using two comparators. A comparison is performed with LM358. LM358 has two Op-amps built into it.

Control Section: Throughout the process of this visitor counter project, Arduino UNO is being utilized. A digital pin 14 and a digital pin 19 are connected to the outputs of comparators. A relay driver circuit drives a relay by sending commands to Arduino from the LED control circuit. You can learn how to operate a relay with Arduino with this tutorial if you are having problems working with relay.

Display section: A 16x2 LCD screen is provided in the display section. During this time the number of people will be counted and the lighting status will be shown. Suitable relay driver/section: The relay driver section consists of a BC547 transistor and a 5-volt relay used to control the light bulb. Since the Arduino will not supply enough current and voltage to operate the relay, a transistor is used instead. Our relay driver circuit was added to provide enough voltage and current to work the relay. This transistor drives a relay connected to the Arduino and turns the light on/off accordingly.

Visitor Counter Circuit Diagram

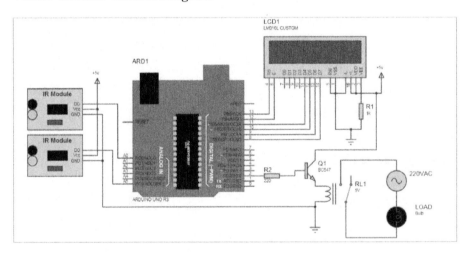

The pins 14 (A0) and 19 (A5) of the Arduino digital board interface directly with the outputs of IR sensors.

At digital pin 2, there is a Relay driver transistor. A four-bit LCD is connected. In the LCD, the clock and data pins are connected directly to pins 13 and 12. A direct connection is made also between the Arduino D11-D8 and LCD pin D4-D7 respectively.

Additionally, this project can be equipped with a GSM modem so that the operation can be controlled remotely by SMS. This would allow the equipment to know the status and to be adjusted accordingly. Using simple microcontrollers to design an automatic room controller is the subject of this article. Therefore, it would be wise to implement this type of home automation system for energy savings.

75. Electronic Voting Machine using Arduino

Despite the fact that we have covered some other electronic voting machines here previously using RF and AVR microcontrollers, we are quite familiar with voting machines. A voting machine made using an Arduino controller has been created in this project.

Components

- Arduino Uno
- 16x2 LCD
- Push button
- Bread board
- Power
- Connecting wires

Circuit Diagram and Working Explanation

Four different candidates have been assigned four push buttons in this project. Despite the ability to increase the number of candidates, we have decided to limit it to four candidates to better understand. Every time a voter presses one of four buttons, the voting value will be incremented by one. The results will be displayed after the voting is complete. In order to show the total number of votes for each candidate, Arduino calculates the total votes and displays them on the LCD display.

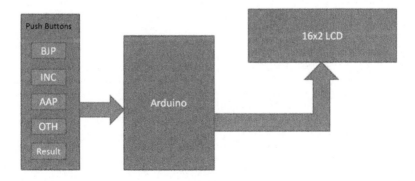

Arduino, push buttons and LCD are used in this project, which is a fairly simple circuit. Arduino controls all the processes, including reading the buttons, incrementing votes, creating results, and displaying them on the LCD display. There are five buttons here, the first one showing BJP, the second showing INC, the third showing AAP, the fourth representing OTH, and the last button is for calculating and displaying results.

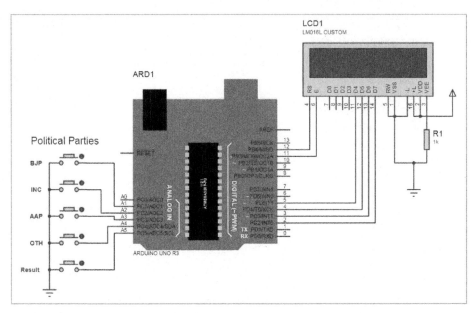

A5-A5 on the Arduino have direct connections to pin 15-19 of the buttons. Four-bit mode is used to connect a 16x2 LCD to the Arduino. On the Arduino board, pins 12, GND, and 11 serve as control pins for RS, RW, and En, and pins 5, 4, 3, and 2 serve as data pins.

76. Humidity and Temperature Measurement using Arduino

Temperature and humidity are widely used as indicators of environmental conditions. This project will use an Arduino board to measure ambient temperature and humidity, displaying the results on a 16x2 LCD. This Celsius scale thermometer and percentage scale humidity measure project uses DHT11 temperature and humidity measurements in combination with Arduino undo. Another project that I worked on previously involved designing a digital thermometer based on the temperature sensor LM35.

There are three main parts to this project: in one, a humidity and temperature sensor (DHT11) detects the humidity and temperature. Second, it determines the temperature and humidity according to DHT sensor data and converts them into percentages and Celsius values. The third component is an LCD display that displays humidity and temperature.

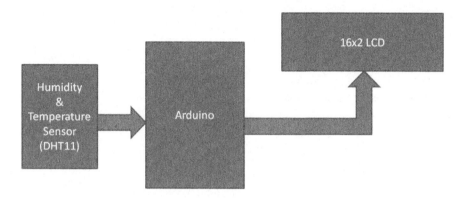

Serial communication is used in working on this project. An Arduino first sends a start signal to the DHT module, which then transmits temperature and humidity data back to the Arduino. Two humidity and temperature measurements are collected and extracted by Arduino and sent to a 16x2 LCD.

The DHT11 sensor module was used in this project. An integrated humidifier and thermometer with a calibrated digital output are featured on the module. The DHT11 sensor module provides a digital output signal that is calibrated to measure humidity and temperature. DHT11's high accuracy and long-term stability guarantee high reliability and long-term stability. Incorporated into the 4-pin single row package is an eight-bit microcontroller that has an 8-bit resistive humidity and temperature measurement component that is cost-effective, has a fast response time, and is available in a 4-pin single row package.

Single wire serial communication is the method used by the DHT11 module. A pulse train of data is transmitted by this module over a specific period of time. An initialization command with a time delay is required before data can be sent to the Arduino. And the total processing time is four milliseconds. In this process, there are 40 bits of data transmitted, and the format is as follows:

Eight-bit integral RH + eight-bit decimal RH + eight-bit integral T + eight-bit decimal T + an eight-bit checksum.

Complete Process

In order for DHT11 to be detected, Arduino sends a 18s delay high to low start signal. Once the data line is pulled up, the Arduino waits for DHT to respond. A low-voltage response signal will then be sent by the DHT to the Arduino after 80s, when it detects the start signal. In addition, DHT controllers pull up the data lines and keep them for 80s so that DHT can arrange and send data.

A low voltage level on the data bus indicates that DHT11 is sending a response signal. After that is completed, the DHT again prepares the data lines for transmission by pulling up the 80s. Each bit of data is sent by DHT to the Arduino as a 50s low voltage signal, and whether the bit is a "0" or a "1" depends on the amount of high voltage signal.

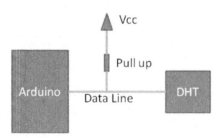

It's important to make sure the resistor value is cranked up because, if the DHTS is being installed at a distance of 20 meters, 5K pull-up resistors are recommended. Whenever the DHT is placed beyond 20 meters, a suitable pull-up resistor must be used.

A huge problem with humidity is also the sensitivity of other products to moisture, such as pharmaceuticals. In fact, humidity and temperature can drastically change the properties of the product and cause it to become useless, which is why items such as medical pills and dry powders are stored at precisely controlled conditions.

Circuit Diagram and Explanation

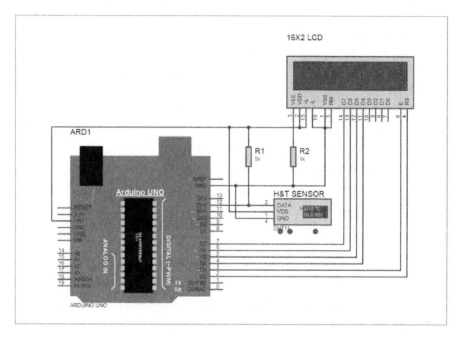

The temperature and humidity are displayed on the LCD directly connected to the Arduino in 4-bit mode. There are five LCD pins connected to the Arduino digital pins 2, 3, 4, 5, and 6. Additionally, RS, EN, D4, D5, and D7 are located in the LCD. Additionally, a 5k pull-up resistor is connected to digital pin 12 of the Arduino to connect the DHT11 sensor module.

77. Automatic Door Opener using Arduino

Automatic door openers are typically found in shopping malls and commercial buildings. Whenever someone approaches the entrance, the door is opened and then closed after a while. PIR sensors, Radar sensors, Laser sensors, Infrared sensors, etc. are all examples of systems that can be created according to various technologies. The same concept was tried in this project with an Arduino based on a PIR sensor.

The door is opened or closed using a PIR sensor that detects the infrared radiation emitted from the human body. An infrared sensor detects changes in the infrared energy when a person approaches the door and responds by opening the door when a person approach. This signal is passed on to Arduino Uno, which subsequently activates the door.

Circuit Components

- Arduino UNO
- 16x2 LCD
- PIR Sensor
- Connecting wires
- Bread board
- 1 k resistor
- Power supply
- Motor driver
- CD case (DVD Trolley)
- PIR Sensor

It detects any change in heat and makes sure the output PIN is HIGH whenever it detects any change. IR motion sensors are sometimes called Pyroelectric ones.

It is worth noting that all objects emit some infrared rays when heated. In addition, our bodies produce infrared because they are warm. Detecting small variations in infrared is possible with PIR sensors. Infrared is produced by friction between an object and the air, so when it passes through the sensor's range, it is caught by PIR.

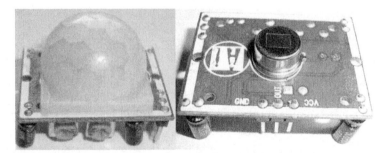

Figure shows the Pyroelectric sensor (rectangular crystal behind the plastic cap) that is at the heart of the PIR sensor. Among the components used to create PIR sensors were BISS0001, a micropower PIR motion sensor IC, resistors, and capacitors. Input signal from sensor BISS0001 is processed by BISS0001 IC to result in a HIGH or LOW output pin.

Pyroelectric sensors are divided in half, so that they sense the same level of infrared no matter how fast the motion is. PIRs begin reacting when somebody enters the first half of the room, and the output pin goes high once the infrared level is larger in one half than the other.

There are multiple Fresnel lenses inside a plastic cap covering the pyroelectric sensor. As a result, the lens covers a wide range so that the sensor can cover as much area as possible.

Circuit Diagram and Explanation

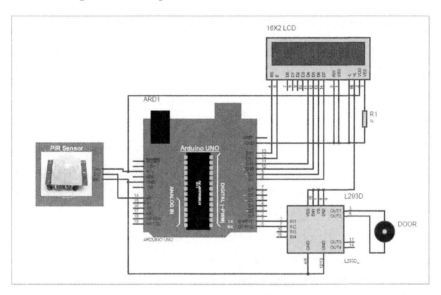

The above diagram illustrates the connections needed to build an Arduino-based door opener. An infrared sensor, based on the PIR principle, is used to detect human motion, which has three terminals: Vcc, GND, and Dout. Located at pin 14 (A0) of Arduino Uno, Doubt is directly connected to it. An LCD with a resolution of 16x2 is used to display the status.

The LCD's RS and EN pins are connected to the Arduino's digital pin numbers 13, 12, and 8 while its D0-D7 pins are directly connected to digital pins 11, 10, 9, 8, respectively. The Arduino pins 0 and 1 are connected to the L293D motor driver to open and close the gate. In this circuit we are using a motor to move the gate.

78. LPG Gas Leakage Detector using Arduino

Leaking LPG may be a disaster even though it is an essential need of every household. LPG leak detection is done by various products that detect the leakage and prevent any mishappening. An LPG gas detection alarm is developed using an Arduino. The circuit buzzes if there is a leak in gas and that triggers a signal from the system. This system is extremely easy to construct, and anyone with programming and electronics skills can do it.

The LPG gas was detected using an LPG sensor module. Whenever LPG leaks, it sends a HIGH pulse to the DO pin, which Arduino stays in continuous contact with. A 16x2 LCD displays the message "LPG Gas Leakage Alert" when Arduino detects a HIGH pulse from LPG Gas module. The gas detector module beeps repeatedly until no gas is detected in the environment, leading to the buzzer being activated. The LCD displays a "No LPG Gas Leakage" message when the LPG gas detector outputs a LOW signal to the Arduino.

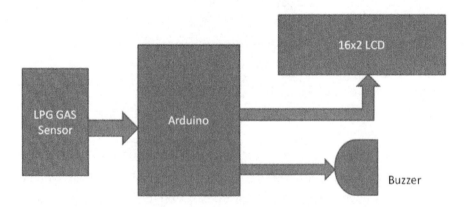

Components Used

- Arduino Pro Mini
- LPG Gas sensor Module
- Buzzer, BC 547 Transistor
- 16x2 LCD, 1K resistor

- Bread board
- 9-volt battery, Connecting wires

LPG Gas Sensor Module

In this module, we find a MQ3 sensor, which actually detects the presence of LPG, and a comparator (LM393), which compares the sensor's output voltage with the reference voltage. When LPG gas is present, it will emit a HIGH output signal. Potentiometers are also used to control the sensitivity of gas sensors. In addition, it can be made with LM358 or LM393 and MQ3, which can be accessed by microcontrollers and Arduinos quite easily. There is also a "LPG Gas Sensor Module" readily available on the market.

Circuit Diagram and Description

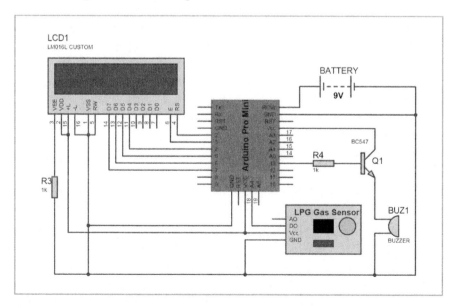

As you can see from the schematic diagram above, it has an Arduino board, an LPG GAS Sensor Module, a buzzer, and a 16x2 LCD module. This system is controlled by Arduino, which reads the gas sensor's output, sends messages to the LCD and activates the buzzer. This sensor module has an inbuilt potentiometer that we can use to set its sensitivity.

DO, pin 18 (A4), of the LPG sensor module is connected directly to Arduino's Vcc and GND pins. A MQ3 sensor detects LPG gas in the LPG gas sensor module. In order for the heater to heat up, the MQ3 sensor will require some electrical power, and it may take up to fifteen minutes for it to get ready for detecting LPG gas.

An analog to digital converter circuit converts the output of MQ3 to a digital signal. Four-bit mode is used to connect a 16x2 LCD to Arduino. Arduino pin 2 and GND are directly connected to pins RS, RW and En while pins 4, 5, 6 and 7 of the Arduino are connected to the data pins. Through a binary NPN BC547 transistor coupled to pin 13 of the Arduino, a buzzer is connected.

79. IR Controlled DC Motor using Arduino

Students and hobbyists are increasingly using Arduino Microcontrollers in recent years. Since Arduino is easy to use and has a smooth learning curve, everyone uses it to make any project. Many Arduino projects are also available on our website, from basic interface modules to more complex robotic modules.

Required Components:

- Arduino UNO
- 5V-relay module
- DC motor
- IR sensor module
- Breadboard
- Connecting wires

IR Sensor, Relay Module and DC Motor are three basic components that we will use in our project today. Arduino will be used to control an electric motor with the IR sensor. In this case the IR sensor reads the output from the IR sensor and makes the relay high when it detects an object in front of it. As IR Sensor detects any objects in front of it, DC Motor will also be ON if relay is connected to it.

Circuit Diagram and Explanation:

It is a simple circuit for controlling this DC Motor with an IR Sensor using Arduino.

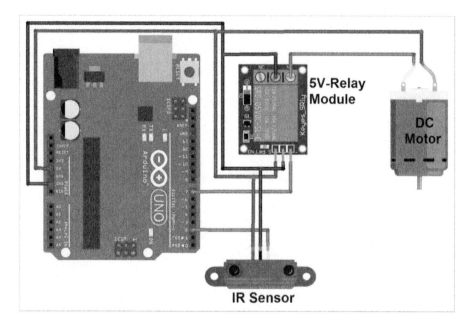

On the circuit, the output of the IR sensor module is connected to pin 2 of the Arduino and the input of the relay module to pin 7. The relay is additionally connected to a DC Motor. Project management is straightforward in this case. The IR sensor will turn on the output pin whenever it detects a movement in front of it. Arduino reads the IR sensor's output pin, so pin 7 goes high to activate the relay module, and Arduino reads pin 1 as well. Upon activation of the relay, the DC motor will begin to rotate.

The output of the IR sensor remains low when nothing is in front of it, and the DC motor remains in off state, as well. With the potentiometer mounted on the module itself, the IR sensor's sensitivity can be adjusted. The sensitivity of the sensor simply means the distance at which the object can be detected.

80. DC Motor Speed Control using Arduino and Potentiometer

Electric motors are the most commonly used motors in robotics and electronics projects. Various methods exist for controlling DC motor speed, but in this project, we are using PWM to control DC motor speed. This project uses a potentiometer for controlling the speed of the DC motor. By rotating the knob of the potentiometer, the speed can be modified.

Pulse Width Modulation:

The PWM technique, also known as pulse width modulation, is used to control voltage or power. Applying 5 volts to a motor will cause it to move at a certain speed, and if we reduce a charging voltage by 2 volts, or applying 3 volts to the motor, the motor speed will also decrease. In the project, PWM is used to control the voltage using this concept.

Material Required

- Arduino UNO
- DC motor
- Transistor 2N2222
- Potentiometer 100k ohm
- Capacitor 0.1uF
- Breadboard
- Jumping Wires

Working and Circuit Diagram

We use a 100K ohm potentiometer to change the duty cycle of the PWM signal in this circuit to control the speed of the DC motor. Connecting the 100K ohm potentiometer to the Arduino UNO's A0 analog input pin, and connecting the DC motor to the PWM pin 12 of the Arduino, creates a simple controller to oscillate a DC motor. Using an Arduino program only requires that the voltage be read from analog pin A0. By using the potentiometer, the voltage can be varied at the analog pin. A duty cycle is then adjusted as necessary after doing some calculations.

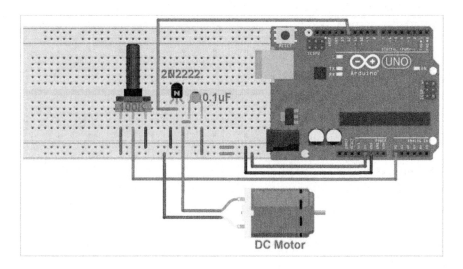

DC Motor

The HIGH time, for example, will be 768ms (256-1024) and the LOW time, 256ms when we input 256 values to the analog input. It is only implied that 75% of frequency oscillation is being observed by our eyes. High frequency oscillation is almost imperceptible to our eyes, which makes the motor appear to run continuously with 75% of speed. This is how the speed can be controlled using a potentiometer.

81. DIY Smart Vacuum Cleaning Robot using Arduino

Robotic vacuum cleaner with four wheels that intelligently avoids obstacles while also vacuuming the floor. Robot Roomba, which appears in the image below, inspired the idea of this vacuum cleaner.

Required Components:

I think we already know what our Automatic Vacuum Cleaner Robot is, but now we need to make it real. Thus, let's find the best position for our execution to begin. The first step in building our concept robot would be to determine the following:

- Microcontroller type
- Sensors required
- Motors required
- Robot chassis material
- Battery capacity

Let's now consider each of the above points. By doing so, you will have the opportunity to build not only this home cleaning robot but also any other robot that strikes your imagination.

Required Components lets list them down

- Wooden sheets for chassis
- IR and US sensors
- Vacuum cleaner which runs on DC current
- Arduino Uno
- 12V 20Ah battery
- Motor driver IC (L293D)
- Working tools
- Connecting wires

Circuit Diagram

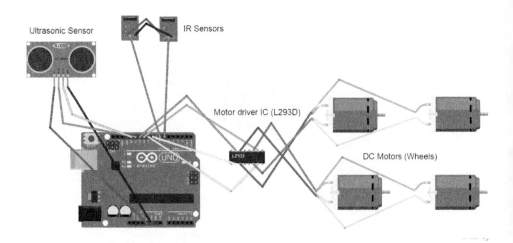

Building and Testing the Robot:

The most critical component of robotic placement is the vacuum cleaner. The vacuum must be tilted at the angle in the photo so that it can provide effective vacuum action. Vacuum cleaners are not controlled by Arduino; they are powered on directly when the robot is powered on.

We found that the wooden work was the most exhausting part of building our robot. For the sensors and vacuum cleaner, we will have to drill holes in the wood and carve them.

Whenever you have the motor and the motor driver in place, it is recommended to Test Ride your robot before connecting the sensors.

Passionate energy for learning and working.

Once you've verified that everything works properly, attach the sensors to Arduino using the circuit diagram provided at the end. On top and on both sides of the robot, I have added an Ultrasonic sensor and two IR sensors. On the L293D, the heat sink is fitted to prevent the IC from overheating.

There are also some extra parts you can add.

We used a BLDC fan to create the vacuum and had it enclosed in a box. Those who are on a tight budget can adopt this strategy. Similarly, this approach looks good but isn't efficient.

Detailed code for this robot vacuum cleaner is located below. Your robot can get started once you've connected the Arduino and loaded the program. These comments explain how a program works. The following video will show you the robot in action.

Additionally, I plan to completely 3D-print the parts in the next version. It will also have some cool features and complex algorithms for covering the entire carpet area and will also be easy to use and compact. You can look forward to future updates.

82.Robot Car controlled by a mobile phone using a G-Sensor and Arduino

In this project, we will use a mobile phone's G sensor to control a robot car and you will be able to tilt the phone to control it. The G-Sensor Controlled Robot will also be controlled by Arduino and the RemoteXY app. A smartphone app called RemoteXY is used to control the Robot from the Smartphone. It will also be possible to control Robot by both tilting the phone and the joystick when the interface has a joystick.

Gravity sensors or Gravity sensors are acceleration sensors in smartphones that allow them to know the screen orientation. As the Gravitational force moves in X, Y, Z directions, the accelerometer senses how the screen rotates in accordance with it. In modern mobiles, the orientation of the screen is determined by a Gyroscope sensor that is a lot more sensitive and accurate. The Robot car in this project will follow the angle that the phone is tilted in. For example, if we tilt the phone forward then it will move forward. The car will then move backward when the tilt is lowered. A G sensor is used in most car games in Mobile, too, so the car moves accordingly.

Required Components:

- Two-wheel robot car chassis
- Arduino UNO
- L298N Motor Controller
- HC-06 Bluetooth module (HC-05 will work too)
- Power supply or Cells
- Connecting wires

Creating Interface for Robot using RemoteXY app:

- You will need to access the following link in order to create the interface for controlling the robot car with RemoteXy.
- http://remotexy.com/en/editor/ the webpage will look like this

Circuit Diagram

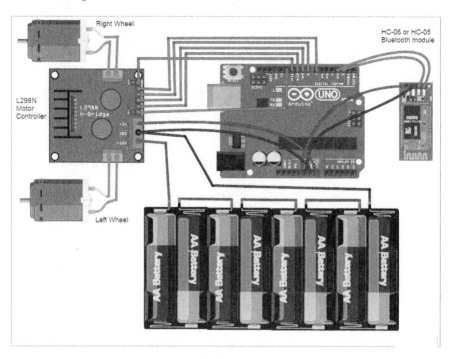

Put the switch button and joystick into the mobile interface from the left side of the screen. By pressing the button, you'll turn on Pin 13 on the Arduino, which is internally connected to the car, and by pressing the joystick, you'll control it. After you have placed the switch and joystick, you will see the following webpage.

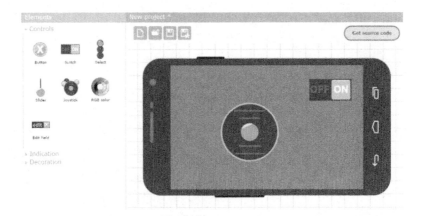

After that, we will need to connect the G sensor enable/disable button to the joystick, to enable us to move the Robot Car with the phone by tilting it left, right, up and down. The G sensor can be turned on and off using that button, and the car can be controlled using the joystick when the G sensor is disabled.

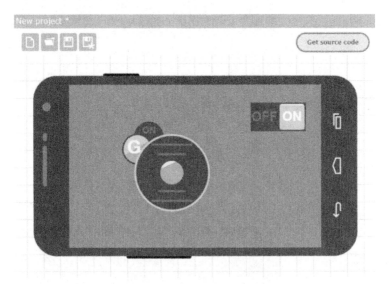

Click the joystick you placed on the interface to place the G sensor enable/disable button. You will see the properties section on the left, and at the end, there is an option to place the G sensor button near the joystick, so you can place it wherever you like. This is what the webpage will look like after this.

You should then click the "Get source code" button and save it on your computer. Download the library from here http://remotexy.com/en/library/ and save it into the Arduino library directory. Make sure that the downloaded code is error-free by compiling it. These are not the actual Robot code, but rather the code that helps to utilize the Arduino with the App. Download the app from here http://remotexy.com/en/download/ or. You can download RemoteXY from the Google Play Store on your Android smartphone.

Circuit Diagram and Explanation:

The L298N motor controller needs to be interfaced with the Arduino first. Motor controller pin ENA and ENB should be connected to Arduino pins 12 and 11, respectively. The motor can be controlled with these two pins via PWM. Our car can be sped up or slowed down using these pins. To connect the IN1, IN2, IN3 and IN4 to the Arduino pins 10, 9 and 8, follow the steps below. The motors will rotate both clockwise and anticlockwise with these pins.

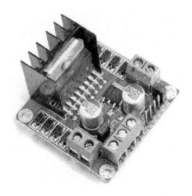

Battery positive and negative should be connected to 12V and ground on the motor controller to power the motor. To connect the Arduino to the motor controller, connect the motor controller's 5V and ground lines to the Arduino Vin and ground lines.

If you have an HC-06, you can connect it to the Arduino, but if you have an HC-05, it will work too. The 5V and ground of the Bluetooth module should be connected to the Arduino's 5V and ground. After that, connect the RX pin of the Bluetooth Module to pin 3 of the Arduino and the TX pin to pin 2 of the Bluetooth Module. You can also learn about Bluetooth controlling a toy car with an Arduino using Bluetooth Controlled Toy Car.

83. Weight measurement using Arduino, the HX711 Module, and a load cell

The Load Cell and Weight Sensor HX711 will be connected to the Arduino to measure weight. The weight of an item is displayed by an automated weight machine in many shops. Users place the item on the platform and the machine displays the weight. Therefore, there is a weighing machine that has been built with Arduino and Load cells, which is capable of weighing up to 40kg. Further increase of the limit is possible by using more capable load cells.

Required Components:

- Arduino Uno
- Load cell (40kg)
- HX711 Load cell Amplifier Module
- 16x2 LCD
- Connecting wires
- USB cable
- Breadboard
- Nut bolts, Frame and base

Load Cell and HX711 Weight Sensor Module:

Load cells are electronic transducers that create an electrical signal from force or pressure. Indirectly related to the force applied is the magnitude of the electrical output. During application of pressure, strain gauges in load cells deform. When the strain gauge is deformed, the effective resistance changes, so electrical signals are generated. Four strain gauges are typically used as part of a Wheatstone bridge to form a load cell. These load cells can weigh up to 40kg, and come in different ranges like 5kg, 10kg, 100kg and even more. Here, we are using a Load cell that can weigh up to 40kg.

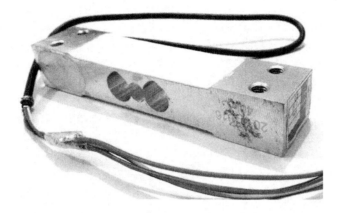

Because the load cell has an output voltage in the range of a few millivolts, these signals require further amplification, hence the HX711 Weighing Sensor is required. An HX711 chip is used in the HX711 Weighing Sensor Module, which is an A/D converter with 24 high-precision channels. Two analog input channels can be programmed in the HX711 for gains up to 128 by programming them. So the HX711 module outputs the low electrical signal from the load cells which is then amplified and digitally converted before being fed to Arduino to calculate weight.

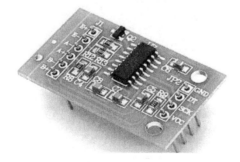

Four wires are used to connect the load cell to the HX711 Amplifier. Red, black, white and green/blue wires make up these wires. Wire colors may vary slightly from one module to another.

- RED Wire is connected to E+
- BLACK Wire is connected to E-
- WHITE Wire is connected to A-
- GREEN Wire is connected to A+

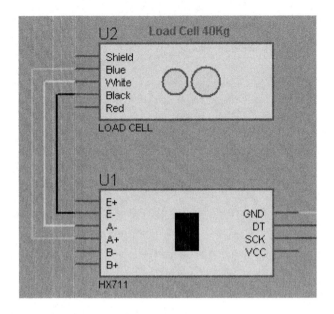

Fixing Load Cell with Platform and Base:

Weights may be applied directly to the load cell without the Platform step. Although the clamp can simply be attached to the plate without a base, a platform should be attached for putting large objects on it, which should be fixed to a base so that it stands still. Therefore, the frame or platform is necessary in order to place the weight measuring equipment. Furthermore, a load cell needs to be fixed to a base using bolts and nuts. The base is made out of a hard board, which has been covered with hard cardboard. Once the connections are made according to the schematic, you are ready to go.

Circuit Explanation:

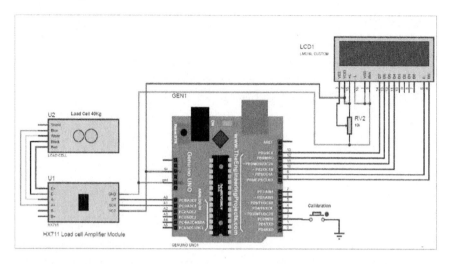

Schematic and connections are provided below for this project. Pin numbers 8, 9, 10, 11, 12 and 13 of Arduino are connected to 16x2 LCD pins RS, EN, d4, d5, d6, and d7 respectively. Arduino's A0 and A1 pins are connected directly to the DT and SCK pins of HX711 Module. Circuit diagrams of the HX711 module and load cell connections have also been explained earlier.

Working Explanation:

It is easy to execute this Arduino weight measurement project. In advance of discussing details, this system needs to be calibrated for accurate weight measurements. A calibration process starts automatically when the system is powered up. In case the user wishes to calibrate it manually, he or she can use the push button. The following code describes how we created a void calibrate() function for calibration purposes.

When calibrating the load cell, wait for the LCD display to appear once 100 grams of load is placed on the cell as demonstrated in the picture below. You should put the 100g weight over the load cell when the LCD reads "put 100g" and then wait for it to appear on the LCD. Upon completion of the calibration procedure, the process will take a few seconds. Any weight can be put over the load cell after calibration (maximum 40kg) and the calculated value will appear over the LCD in grams.

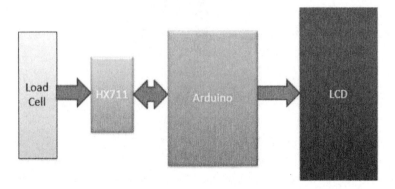

Arduino was used to manage the entire process in this project. HX711 Load Amplifier Module receives the weight signal from the load cell in the form of an electrical analog voltage. Using the HX711 ADC, a 24bit input signal is amplified, and then digitally converted into a 24-bit output, which is then fed to the Arduino. After the data from HX711 has been calculated by Arduino, the weight values are converted into grams and displayed on LCD. The calibration of the system is accomplished by pushing a button. In order to facilitate the process, we created an Arduino program.

84. Automated Plant Irrigation System Using Arduino with Message Alerts

It is always difficult to leave our plants unattended if we are going out of town for a few days. Our plants require regular watering. We are making an Arduino-based Automated Plant Irrigation System, which sends out messages to you as well as automatically provides water to plants.

Water is provided to the plant through a water pump if the soil moisture level drops due to a low moisture level detected by the soil moisture sensor. Once the system detects sufficient soil moisture, it automatically turns off the water pump. An update on the status of the water pump and soil moisture is sent to the user whenever the water pump is turned on or off via the GSM module. Farms, gardens, homes, etc, would benefit all from this system. No human intervention is required because this system is completely automated.

Required Components for Arduino Plant Watering System Project

- Arduino Uno
- GSM Module
- Transistor BC547 (2)
- Connecting wires
- 16x2 LCD (optional)
- Power supply 12v 1A
- Relay 12v
- Water cooler pump
- Soil Moisture Sensor
- Resistors (1k, 10k)
- Variable Resistor (10k, 100k)
- Terminal connector
- Voltage Regulator IC LM317

GSM Module:

Using the SIM800 GSM module, we have used it here. Customers as well as hobbyists can easily embed the SIM800's quad-band GSM/GPRS module. GSM/GPRS 850/900/1800/1900MHz performance for voice, SMS, data is provided by SIM900 GSM Module, while SIM800 GSM Module employs an industry-standard interface. Slim and compact, the SIM800 GSM Module follows a modern design aesthetic.

Quad - band GSM/GPRS module in small size.

- GPRS Enabled
- TTL Output

Circuit Explanation:

The homemade soil moisture sensor probe used in this system allows us to measure moisture levels in the soil. As shown in the following image, a copper clad board was cut and etched to make the probe. There is a direct connection between the probe and Vcc, and the other probe terminal is attached to BC547's base. Sensor sensitivity is adjusted using a potentiometer connected to the base of the transistor.

This Automatic Plant Watering System is controlled entirely by an Arduino. Directly connected to the digital pin D7 of Arduino is the soil sensor circuit's output. The sensor circuit uses a LED, which indicates whether moisture is present in the soil by its ON state and whether it is not present by its OFF state.

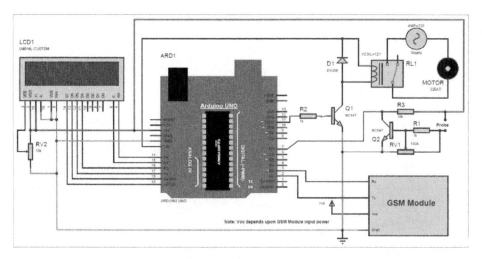

An SMS can be sent to the user using the GSM module. As you can see, here we are using a GSM SIM800 card, which is a device that directly gives and takes TTL signals (to be used by any GSM module). The SIM800 GSM module is powered by the LM317 voltage regulator. It is recommended to read the data sheet of the LM317 before using it, since voltage rating is very sensitive to that. 3.8 to 4.2 volts is its operating voltage rating (please use 3.8 volts when operating it). An example of a circuit diagram for the power supply of a TTL sim800 GSM module is shown below

A SIM900 TTL Module should be used with 5V, and a SIM900 Module should be used with 12v in the DC Jack slot on the board.

The 220VAC small water pump is controlled by a 12V Relay. An Arduino digital pin 11 is connected to the BC547 transistor, which drives the relay.

Status and messages are also displayed on an optional LCD. Several LCD pins are directly connected to the Arduino, including RS, EN, and D4-D7, which are directly connected with the Arduino on pins 16, 17, 18 and 19. In this case, Arduino uses the LCD library built into the board to drive a 4-bit LCD display.

Working Explanation:

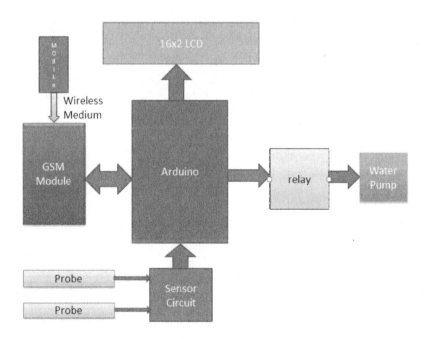

A Plant Irrigation System like this is pretty straightforward in terms of how it works. The first thing to point out is that the system is completely

automated, and it does not require any manual labor. A GSM module sends alert messages to the cell phone of the user based on the Arduino's handling of the entire process.

The Irrigation System with Arduino and a Soil Moisture Sensor is shown on the following block diagram: When soil contains moisture, conduction occurs between the two probes of the Soil Moisture sensor, resulting in transistor Q2 remaining in the triggered/on state, and Arduino Pin D7 remaining low. The Arduino sends the SMS message "Soil Moisture is Normal" when it detects the LOW signal at D7. The water pump is still in an off state because the motor switched off.

Transistor Q2 will become off if no moisture is present in soil, and Pin D7 will become high. A message is then sent to the user stating that "Low Soil Moisture has been detected" and Arduino turns on the water motor. Motor turned ON". The soil will automatically turn off the motor when the moisture content is sufficient.

85. Making calls and sending messages with Arduino and GSM modules

Microcontrollers sometimes have difficulty communicating with the GSM Module, specifically for functions such as SMS, calls, and texting. With the help of the Arduino, we will build a simple mobile phone. The GSM Module involved in this project can make and receive calls, as well as send and receive SMS, and the Arduino phone also has a Microphone and Speaker so you can talk over it. Besides interfacing with the GSM Module, the project will be able to run any phone's basic functions by using all the necessary code on the Arduino.

Components Required:

- Arduino Uno
- GSM Module SIM900
- 16x2 LCD, 4x4 Keypad
- Breadboard or PCB
- Connecting jumper wire
- Power supply
- Speaker, MIC
- SIM Card

Working Explanation:

Arduino Uno is used to control all the features of this Arduino Mobile Phone Project, as well as to interface all the components. An alphanumeric keypad is used to make all kinds of inputs, such as entering mobile numbers, typing messages, making and receiving calls, and sending and receiving SMS. The GSM Module communicates with the network in order to make and receive calls and messages. As well as ICs and speakers, a 16x2 LCD shows messages, instructions, alerts, and a MIC picks up the voice call and ring sound.

Using the same keypad for both numbers and alphabets, alphanumeric is a way to enter data. Check out the Code in Code section below for the Arduino code to accept the 4x4 keypad interface as well.

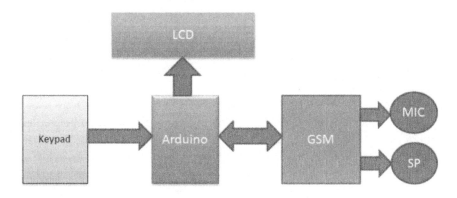

It is easy to work on this project. We will use an alphanumeric keypad to handle all the features. For a full understanding of the process, please check out the code and demo video below. In this section, we will describe all four features of the following projects.

The Arduino Mobile Phone has the following four features:

1. Make a Call:

If you want to call someone from your Arduino Phone, you have to press the 'C' button, and then enter their Mobile Number. An alphanumeric keypad is used for entering the number. Again, we need to press 'C' once the number has been entered. As soon as Arduino receives the AT command, it will attempt to make the call to the number entered:

ATDxxxxxxxxxx; <Enter>   where xxxxxxxxx is entered Mobile
Number.

2. Receive a Call:

Getting a call is a very straightforward process. In the event that a call is
made to your GSM module SIM number, then your system will display an
"Incoming... The LCD will display the incoming number of the caller. The
only thing we need to do now is press 'A' to attend this call. When we press
'A', Arduino will be programmed to send the following command to GSM
module:

ATA <enter>

3. Send SMS:

Our Arduino based mobile phone allows us to send a SMS by pressing the
B key. In order to send an SMS, we must enter the Recipient Number,
which is 'to whom' we should send the SMS. The LCD now asks for a
message once we have entered the number and pressed 'D'. Once we've
typed our message, we need to hit 'D' to send it, like we do on a traditional
mobile phone. When we've done that, we should be able to send an
SMS. An Arduino sends a SMS by sending the following command:

AT+CMGF=1 <enter>
AT+CMGS="xxxxxxxxxx" <enter>   where: xxxxxxxxxx is entered
mobile number And send 26 to GSM to send SMS.

4. Receive and Read SMS:

In addition, this feature is easy to use. SIM cards are used to receive SMS,
which are then stored in GSM cards. With Arduino, the UART
transmitting SMS information is continuously monitored. If you see the
SMS symbol (look at the video at the end) on the LCD, you need to press
'D' to read the SMS. As shown in the example below, the SMS Received
indicator shows that:

+CMTI: "SM" <SMS stored location>
+CMTI: "SM",6. 6 refers to the SIM card location where the message is
stored.

Arduino extracts the SMS storing location and sends a command to GSM to read the SMS when it receives this indication that an SMS has been received. Afterward, the LCD will show a 'New Message Symbol'.

AT+CMGR=<SMS stored location><enter>
AT+CMGR=6

Next, Arduino receives the stored message from GSM and before reading this message it shows it on the LCD, and then after reading the messages it clears the 'New SMS symbol' on the LCD.

Note: There is no coding for the microphone and speaker.

Circuit Diagram and Explanation:

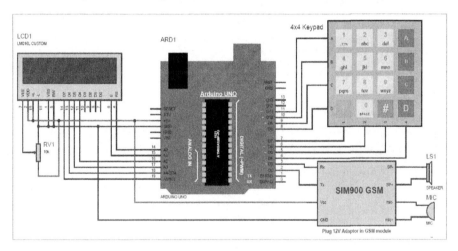

Diagram showing how GSM SIM900 and Arduino can be interconnected is shown above. Pin 14 is connected to pins 15, 16, 17, 18, 19 of Arduino, while pins EN, D4, D5 and D6 are connected to pin 16 of the LCD. (Ground of Arduino and GSM are connected.) The RX and TX pins of the GSM module are directly connected to Arduino's pins D3 and D2. Row pins R1, R2, R3, R4 of the 4x4 keypad are directly connected to pins 11, 10, 9, 8 of Arduino, and column pins C1, C2, C3 are directly connected to pins 7, 6, 5, 4 of Arduino. The MIC pins of the GSM Module are directly connected to mic+ and mic-, and the speaker pins are directly connected to pin SP+ and SP- for the GSM Module.

86. Fingerprint Based Biometric Attendance System using Arduino

The presence of students in an office or school is typically marked by attendance systems. The attendance management system has greatly improved over the years, from marking attendance manually in attendance registers to using high-tech applications and biometric systems. Other electronic attendance system projects that we covered in previous projects included RFID, AVR, and 8051 microcontrollers. We used an Arduino to take attendance records and use a fingerprint module to take attendance data. The system will become more secure for users if it uses a fingerprint sensor. A biometric attendance system based on fingerprints is described in the next section of the article.

Required Components

- Arduino -1
- Finger print module -1
- Push Button   - 4
- LEDs -1
- 1K Resistor -2
- 2.2K resistor -1
- Power
- Connecting wires
- Box
- Buzzer -1
- 16x2 LCD -1
- Bread Board -1
- RTC Module -1

Project Description:

A fingerprint attendance system circuit includes a Fingerprint Sensor module that operates by recognizing a person's fingerprint. This allows the system to authenticate the person or employee. Four push buttons are being used here: Up/Down, Delete, Enroll. A key has three functions: ENROLL, DEL, and END. A new user is enrolled into the system by using the ENROLL key. The user must then press the ENROLL key when enrolling a new finger. LCD will then ask the user for an ID and where the fingerprint image is to be stored. In this case, the user may press ENROLL again to return to the first step if he or she does not want to go any further.

The ENROLL key behaves as the Back key this time. Enrollment and backtracking are both possible with the ENROLL key. As well as downloading attendance data over the serial monitor, the enroll key is also used for enrollment. A similar double function is provided by DEL/OK, since the user must select finger ID using UP and DOWN after enrolling a new finger. After pressing the DEL/OK key (this time it acts like OK), the user can proceed to selecting the ID. Deleting data from the EEPROM of Arduino is accomplished by the Del key.

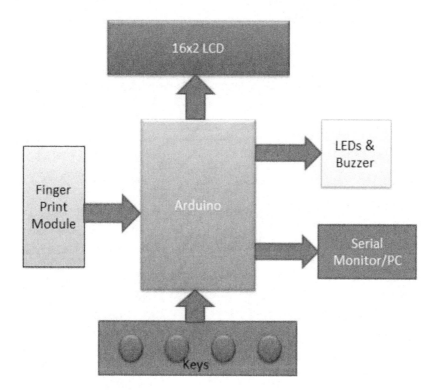

The fingerprint sensor module captures an image of the finger's print and uses that to create an equivalent template. It then saves the template as selected by Arduino into its memory. A fingerprint image is captured, the fingerprint is converted into templates, and the finger is stored as an ID using Arduino.

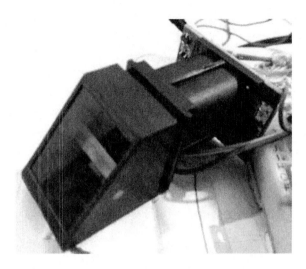

Fig.FingerPrint module

Our fingerprint module has a yellow LED that we have added to indicate that it is ready to take a fingerprint image. Additionally, buzzers are used to indicate various things. This system is controlled by an Arduino; it controls the entire thing.

Working of fingerprint-based attendance systems

It is a relatively simple project, working with fingerprint attendance systems. With the help of push buttons, the user first needs to register his or her fingerprints. The user must press ENROLL to save the fingerprint in memory by ID name and then the LCD will ask for the user's ID name. As a consequence, an ID must now be entered by using the UP/DOWN keys. Press the OK button (DEL) once the user has selected the ID. In order to use the fingerprint module, LCD now asks the user to place their finger there. As a result, the user must now place his finger over the fingerprint module in order for it to generate an image. Once you take your finger off the fingerprint module, the LCD will ask you to repeat the process. As soon as the user places his finger again, the module takes an image and converts it into a template which is stored by selecting the ID into the fingerprint module's memory. By now, the user has been registered and can use the fingerprint module to feed attendance. The system will allow all of the users to enrol in the same way.

The user now needs to press the DEL key if he/she wants to delete the stored fingerprint or ID. LCD will then prompt you for the ID to be deleted after pressing the delete key. After selecting an ID, the user must press the OK key (the same key as DEL). When the fingerprint is successfully deleted, the LCD will let you know.

Circuit Diagram

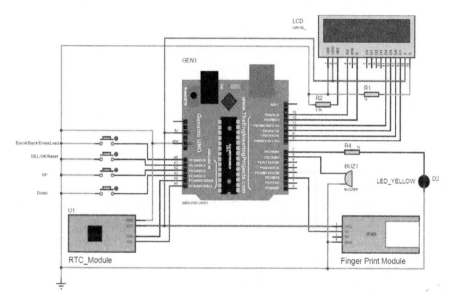

In the above diagram, we can see that this fingerprint-based attendance system project involves a fairly simple circuit. An Arduino controller controls the entire process, push buttons for enrolment, deletion, selection of IDs, and attendance, LEDs for indication, and an LCD to display the message to users.

It can be seen in the circuit diagram that the push button is directly connected to pin A0 (ENROL), With respect to ground, pins A1(DEL), A2(UP), and A3(DOWN) of an Arduino are connected to one k resistor, and pin D7 of the Arduino is connected to the yellow LED via a 1k resistor. Arduino's Serial pins D2 and D3 (Software Serial) are directly connected to the RX and TX of the fingerprint module.

Power is supplied by a 5v supply to an Arduino board with a fingerprint module. The pin A5 is also connected to a buzzer. In this example, a 16x2 LCD is configured in 4-bit mode, with D4, D5, D6 and D7 connected directly to digital pins D13, D12, D11, D10, D9, and D8 of the Arduino.

How Attendance works:

After placing his finger over the fingerprint module, the user will see that the fingerprint device is captured and that it is searching if any recorded ID is associated with these fingerprints. Upon detecting a fingerprint ID, the LCD will display Attendance registered, while a buzzer will burst out once and the LED will turn off until a new input can be entered.

We have also implemented a Time and Date module with the fingerprint module. The system keeps track of the time and date continuously. In this context, Arduino automatically grabs time and date from a user's finger when they place it over the fingerprint and saves them in the allocated memory slot.

This system allows us to create five user spaces for 30 days. When the RESET key in Arduino is pressed and once the program is enrolled, the key will download information from the Arduino EEPROM over the serial monitor.

Memory Management:

Our Arduino UNO comes equipped with 1023 byte of memory of which 1018 byte are available for data storage, and we have taken five days' attendance data from the Arduino UNO. In addition to recording time and date, every attendance recording will be 7-bytes in size.

As a result, total memory requirements are

5*30*7=1050 so here we need more 32 bytes

However, if four users are used, then we need

4*30*7=840

Here, we have taken the memories of five users to demonstrate this project. The 5th user's attendance records will be unable to be stored since we will not be able to store 32 bytes of data each time. Change some lines in the code to make it work with four users.

Fingerprint sensors are commonly used in mobile, lock and unlock, on a mobile display, on a phone screen, in security systems, attendance systems, and security locks.

87. Generating Tones by Tapping Fingers using Arduino

We will use Arduino to build an entertainment system in this project. Creating random sounds out of the pen or table is an ingrained habit for all of us. There's no doubt that doing this at least once is not considered good manners, but we're all used to doing it. Therefore, I decided to take it one step further by using Arduino's tone-playing abilities. With this project you will be able to tap on anything conductive and generate tones, like playing the Piano on your palm, and create your own rhythms.

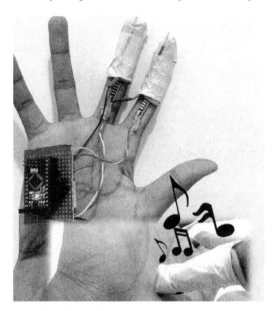

Components required:

Below is a list of materials required for this project. There is no need to stick to the list. You can build it based on your own design once you understand the basic idea.

- Arduino Pro Mini
- Piezo Speaker
- Flex Sensor
- Finger Gloves
- 10K Resistors
- BC547 Transistors
- 9V Battery

Circuit Diagram and Explanation:

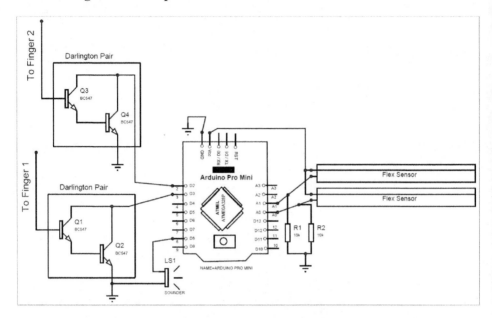

During the development of this project, we used a total of four sensors: two flex sensors and two Darlington pairs functioning as a touch sensor. Secondly, we have attached two 10k resistors R1 and R2 to the Flex sensor as pull-down resistors. Using one finger to generate three distinct tones based on how much it has bent, the Flex sensor here makes use of this technology. This means that two fingers can generate six different sounds.

Darlington Pair:

It is important that we understand what Darlington is and how it relates to our project before we move forward. The Darlington pair can be defined as two bipolar transistors connected in a way that in case of current amplification by the first transistor, the current is amplified further by the second transistor. The following image shows a pair of Darlington:

This circuit consists of two BC547 transistors whose collectors are tied to their respective collectors and whose emitters are connected to the bases of their respective transistors, as shown above. A small signal applied to the first transistor base will bias the second transistor base, which means that the circuit functions as an amplifier.

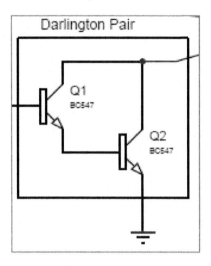

Our body serves as a ground for the second transistor so the transistor becomes biased whenever our bodies touch the base of the transistor. In order to make this project a success, we utilized this knowledge to build the touch sensor.

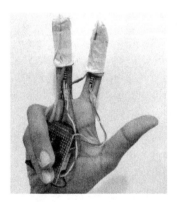

Two Arduino interrupt pins, numbers 2 and 3, are pulled high using internal pull-up resistors. After the Darlington switch closes, these pins will be grounded. The interrupt will be triggered every time the wire touches the base of the transistor (1st transistor) on the Arduino.

I added a flex sensor that alters the tone according to how much the finger is bent, so I can generate more tones using fewer fingers. I have programmed the system to produce three different tones for each finger depending on how far it is bent (flex sensor). Having access to more tones at your fingertips is possible by increasing the number.

In order for the board to fit easily in my palms, I made it on a perf board, however you can also build it on a breadboard. It is important that you touch the ground of the circuit during the course. You should have something similar to this once you've soldered everything

As displayed above, I have secured the Darlington pair wires and the flex sensor with two finger gloves. While playing your tone, you can come up with a better idea (if possible) to secure the earphones in place.

Working:

You can then mount them on your fingers once the hardware is ready. Ensure that you are touching the ground at some point on the circuit. You should now be able to hear the tone by touching any conductive material or your body. The taps can be played at different intervals, at different positions, to create your own melody.

88. The Arduino and Thingsboard are used to create a biometric attendance system based on IoT

With this project, we are aiming to create a smart, efficient and engaging attendance system by integrating IoT into the boring one. The vast majority of modern attendance systems store data on a micro-SD card, which must be accessed by computer software via a PC. This project is about building a biometric attendance system using Arduino that can scan a fingerprint. If a touch is successful, the data is sent to ThingsBoard via the ESP8266 wireless module and logged there. It is capable of displaying all of this information on the ThingsBoard dashboard, allowing authorities to easily view and analyze information while not requiring direct physical access to the hardware. By following the link, however, it is also possible to build the conventional Attendance system without involving the Internet of Things, and the Fingerprint sensor can be further used in further biometric applications such as Voting Machines and Security System.

Preparing the ESP8266-01

This project will use both the AT command mode and the programming mode of the ESP8266. The ESP8266 module can be powered with a LM317 regulator and the Tx and Rx pins can be hooked up to the FTDI board as shown below.

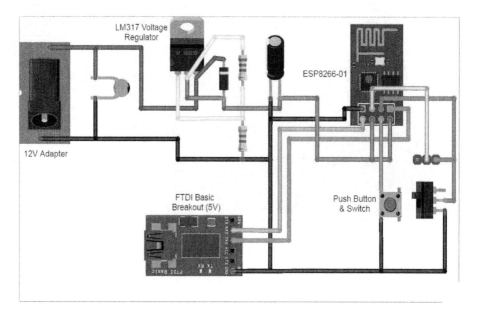

Hardware Required

- Arduino UNO
- 16x2 LCD Display
- Arduino Wi-Fi Shield
- ESP8266-01
- GT511C3 Fingerprint sensor (FPS)
- 12V Adapter

In AT command mode, a toggle switch toggles the ESP8266 into AT commands, and in programming mode, a push button can reset the module. Every time you upload code to the ESP8266, it must be reset.

Circuit diagram

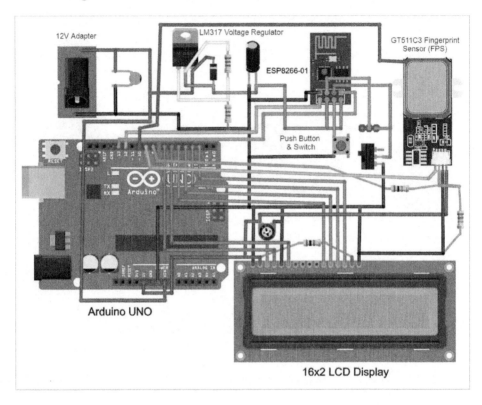

89. Real Time Face Detection and Tracking Robot using Arduino

Have you ever wanted to develop a robot while tracking your face by just using an Arduino and without having to learn programming languages such as OpenCV, Visual Basic and C#? If you're interested in learning more about how we can implement face detection with Arduino and Android, read on. In this project, you'll move the mobile camera with the help of servos to follow you around.

Using an Android Mobile Phone offers the advantage of not having to invest in a camera module, and all of the image detection is done on the phone itself, so you do not need an Arduino-based computer for this. Our Bluetooth Module communicates wirelessly with mobile devices using the Arduino Uno.

Processing Android was used to create the Android application used in this project. You can either download the APK file (see below for details) or install the application directly from the Processing Android website. Alternatively, you may use the Processing Code provided in the Tutorial to create a more interesting Android Application. Our previous Processing projects will give you more information about Processing.

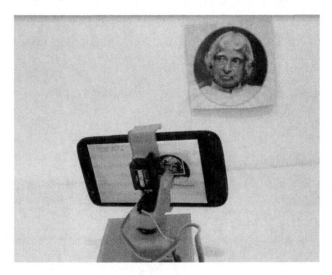

After following this tutorial, you will be able to build a Mini Tilt and Span Robotic Arm with the capability of tracking and moving along with your face. This (with further advancement) can be used to record vlog videos or even take selfies using the front and rear cameras on your mobile phones. The exact centre of the screen is positioned exactly where your face is. Therefore! How does that sound? The Demo Video at the end of this article shows how it works. Let's figure out how to do it...

This project has been designed to be as simple as possible, anyone with a basic understanding of hardware or programming can use these guidelines to make it work in no time. However, once you make it, I suggest you dig deep into the code so you can get a real understanding of how it works.

Materials Required:

- Arduino Nano
- Servo motor SG90 – 2Nos
- Android Phone with decent camera
- HC-05/HC-06 Bluetooth Module

- Computer for programming
- 3D printer (optional)
- 9V Battery

Two servo motors are used in the circuit, one for moving the mobile phone left and right, and another for tilting it up and down. As a result, the Arduino Nano will instruct the servo to move in the direction requested by the Bluetooth module (HC-05). All of the circuit components are powered by a 9V battery.

I have soldered these on a small Perf board, but you can connect these easily on a breadboard.

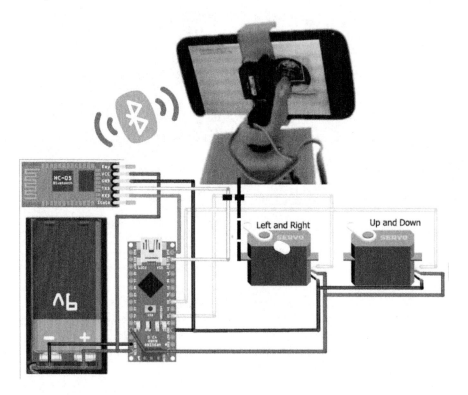

Setting up your Android Application:

Earlier I mentioned that this Android application is the brain behind the project. Processing Android was used to develop this android application. The steps below will show you how to download and launch the application directly on your smartphone.

Download the APK file from here

http://bit.ly/face_tracking_download (Server 1) or
https://drive.google.com/file/d/1SrPrcxjs8jOFUDYYw_FaHrk01cteqD8n
/view?usp=sharing (Server 2)

Circuits such as those shown above should be powered on.

Look for the Bluetooth module named **"HC-05"** in your phone's settings

The name should always be **"HC-05"**, as only then the application will work if you haven't named it anything else.

Use the password **"1234"** or **"0000"** to pair with your Bluetooth module.

The application will now launch in portrait mode. Across the top of the screen, you will see your camera screen and "Connected to: **HC-05**".

The top left corner of your screen will also display the pixel's position when you move your camera over a face.

By adding some additional advancements for which you won't have to code your own Android application, you can take this Arduino Face Tracking Project to the next level. You might think that creating an Android application is a complicated thing, but trust me, it's very easy with processing. With your own creativity, you can make any advancement you want.

Working:

Then, once our hardware, code, and Android application are ready, we can start the building process. Simply power your Arduino and open the android application.

The HC-05 Bluetooth module (must be called HC-05) will automatically connect to the application when it detects a face. In order to use our mobile holder, simply place the phone in the holder and sit back. As your phone's servo motors move, you should notice your face cantered on the display. Your mobile phone will now follow your movements when you move within the camera's range.

90. Arduino Touch Screen Calculator using TFT LCD

Building projects with Arduino is always easy and makes them more appealing. Arduino libraries and shields made it really easy to program an LCD screen with touch screen capability.

We will use a 2.4" Arduino TFT LCD screen in this project to build an Arduino Touch Screen calculator that can perform basic arithmetic operations like Addition, Subtraction, Division and Multiplication.

Materials Required:

- Arduino Uno
- 2.4" TFT LCD display Shield
- 9V Battery.

Getting to know the TFT LCD Screen Module:

2.4" TFT LCD Modules come in many varieties, so it is important to understand how they work before we proceed with the project. Here is what the pinouts look like for a 2.4" TFT LCD screen.

These boards will perfectly fit into any Arduino Mega or Uno board, as can be seen from the photo above. In the table below are some small classifications of these pins.

TFT Pinout:

1	2	3	4	5	6	7	8	9
VCC	GND	CS	RST	D/C	MOSI	SCK	BL	MISO

ILI9341 TFT

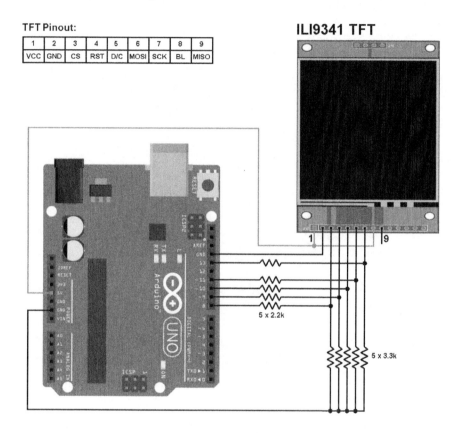

There are four basic classifications for pins, namely LCD Command Pins, LCD Data Pins, SD Card Pins and Power Pins. We do not need to understand the details of how these pins work since the Arduino library will handle them. Using the Arduino program, we can display the images on the TFT LCD screen by loading them into an SD card, and this image can be displayed on the SD card slot at the bottom of the module.

The Interface IC is another important aspect of the kit. There are many types of TFT modules on the market, from the original Adafruit TFT LCD module to inexpensive Chinese knockoffs. If your Adafruit shield works perfectly on a Chinese breakout board, it may not work the same way on your Adafruit shield. As a result, it's essential to know what kind of LCD display you have in your hand. It is the vendor's responsibility to provide this information. If you are using a cheap clone like mine, you are almost certain to be using the ili9341 driver IC.

Calibrating the TFT LCD Screen for Touch Screen:

It is essential for you to calibrate your TFT LCD module if you intend to use the touch screen functionality. If you touch one place on an LCD screen but the TFT responds at another, for instance, you might not be able to use it. You need to calibrate each board separately because the results won't be the same for each of them.

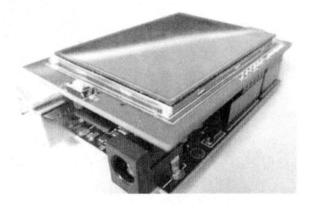

Using the calibration example program (which comes with the library) or a serial monitor is the best way to calibrate.

TFT LCD Connections with Arduino:

Arduino shields that have TFT LCD screens are ideal. The LCD screen will slide perfectly into the Arduino Uno once you push it directly on top of it. Cover the TFT LCD screen's Programming terminal with a small piece of insulation tape as a matter of safety. Here is an example of how the LCD will look when it is assembled on the UNO.

How to Program

To get our Arduino calculator code to work, we're using the SPFD5408 library. With this library, our LCD TFT Module can readily work with Adafruit's LCD TFT Module.

Note: It is vital that you have this library installed in your Arduino IDE for the program to compile correctly.

91. Arduino Motion Detector using PIR Sensor

Many projects have always required motion detection or movement tracking. With the help of the PIR Sensor, it has become easy to detect movement from people or animals. This project will demonstrate how a PIR sensor can be connected to a microcontroller like an Arduino. The Arduino will be interfaced with a PIR module so that whenever movement is detected, a buzzer and LED will beep. In order to build this project, you'll need the following components.

Materials Required:

- PIR Sensor Module
- Arduino UNO (any version)
- LED
- Buzzer
- Breadboard
- Connecting Wires
- 330-ohm resistor

PIR sensor:

Infrared passive sensors are referred to as PIR sensors. Using this sensor, humans and animals can be detected without incurring high costs. In addition to the pyroelectric crystal, the sensor also has a Fresnel lens to enhance the range of the sensor. A pyroelectric crystal is used to track heat signatures of living organisms (humans, animals). As shown below, we can also set the sensor's working by adjusting the options provided by the PIR sensor modules.

Sensor sensitivity and trigger time of the sensor may be controlled using the two potentiometers (orange color). It is essentially the Dout pin that is present between the Vcc and GND pins of the sensor. A 3.3V power supply may also be used, but the module operates on 3.3V. Additionally, there is a trigger pin setup on the left side of the module that can be used to make it work in two different ways. In one mode, the "H" key is pressed and in the other, the "I" key is pressed.

A person will be detected within range when the Dout output pin goes high (3.3V) and will go low at a certain time (time is controlled by potentiometer). It does not matter if the person remains inside the range or has left the area, the output pin will stay high. In our project, our module is being used in the "H" mode.

As long as a person remains within the limits of the sensor range, the output pin Dout will go high (3.3V).

Note:

Depending on your PIR sensor vendor, potentiometers and pins may be positioned differently. Pinouts can be determined by following the Silk screen

Circuit Diagram and Explanation:

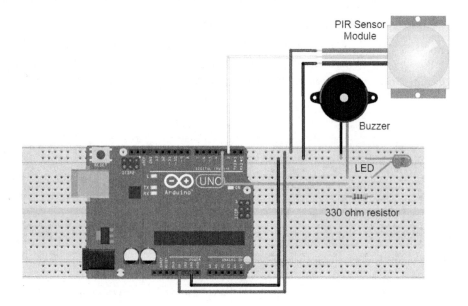

The below image shows the schematic for the Arduino PIR motion detector project by combining it with an LED/Buzzer and a PIR unit.

Our 5V rail of the Arduino is used to power the PIR sensor. On the Arduino, the second digital pin is connected to the output pin of the PIR Sensor. The Arduino INPUT pin will be connected to this pin. A buzzer and LED are then connected to the 3rd pin of the Arduino. In this case, the output pin of the Arduino will be used. An output at the 3rd pin will be triggered by an input at the 2nd pin if an Arduino is programmed to do so.

92. Interfacing Hall Effect Sensor with Arduino

The use of sensors has always been crucial to any project. It is these that create the digital/variable data that is used by electronics to process the real-time environmental data. The market offers many types of sensors, and you can choose one that suits your needs. We will use an Arduino to create a project that uses Hall sensors, also known as Hall effect sensors. Using the magnet sensor, you can determine the magnet's pole as well as detect its magnetic field.

Magnets are detected for what reason? Perhaps you'd like to know. Actually, there are a number of applications that use Hall Effect sensors, but most of us probably are unaware of them. The speed of rotating machines or bicycles can be measured using this sensor. BLDC motors also utilize this sensor to track the Rotor Magnet position and immediately activate the Stator coils accordingly. Let's learn how to add another tool to our arsenal by learning how to interface Hall effect sensors with Arduino. Some projects involving Hall sensors are as follows:

As part of this tutorial, we will utilize Arduino interrupts to detect a magnet near a Hall sensor and flash an LED. We will use interrupts in our tutorial as well, since Hall sensors will typically only be used with interrupts due to their applications that require high reading and executing speeds.

Materials Required:

- Hall Effect Sensor (any digital version)
- Arduino (Any version)

- 10k ohm and 1K ohm Resistor
- LED
- Connecting Wires

Hall Effect Sensors:

Several things should be kept in mind before we dive into the connections for Hall Effect sensors. Digital Hall sensors and analog Hall sensors are the two main types of Hall sensors. As opposed to the digital Hall sensor, which detects whether a magnet is present or not (0 or 1). The analog Hall sensor, on the other hand, can detect the strength of or the distance from the magnet, based on its output. Because these are the most common digital Hall sensors, this project will only focus on them.

By its name, Hall Effect sensors work on the basis of the "Hall Effect". Having carried out this experiment the law states that when current flows perpendicular to the direction that the current is flowing, a voltage can be measured at the angle at which the current flows. It will be possible for the hall sensor to detect magnets around it using this technique. I'm done with theory, let's move onto hardware.

Circuit Diagram and Explanation:

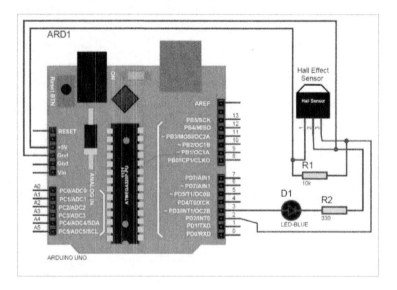

This circuit diagram demonstrates how to connect a Hall sensor to an Arduino.

This Arduino circuit diagram for a Hall Effect sensor is quite straightforward as you can see. It is when we try to figure out hall sensor pin numbers that we usually make mistakes. When positioned face-on, the Vcc and Ground pins are on the left, followed by the Signal pin.

As we mentioned earlier, we will use interrupts, which is why pin 2 of the Arduino is connected to the output pin of the Hall sensor. Magnets are detected by switching on the Pin, which is connected to an LED.

Arduino Hall Effect Sensor Working:

You can now upload the Arduino code once you have created your code and hardware. A 9V battery has been used to power the entire setup. Power can be provided by any preferred source. You will see the LED light up as soon as you place the magnet close to the sensor and it will turn off as soon as you remove the magnet.

Note:

Hall sensors are pole sensitive, which means that each side of the sensor can either detect only the North Pole or only the South Pole, only one side of the sensor can detect both poles. Thus, if you bring the north sensing surface close to the south pole, the LED will not glow.

Throughout the sensor, we bring the magnet near to it, causing it to change its state when we do that. An interrupt pin is triggered by this change, which then calls the toggle function, which changes the variable "state" from 0 to 1. In this way, the LED will illuminate. Once the magnet is moved away from the sensor, the sensor output will again change. We notice that this changes again by using an interrupt statement and thus the variable "state" is set to zero. The LED will darken if the switch is turned off. Each time you approach the sensor with a magnet, the same happens.

93. Automatic Call answering Machine using Arduino and GSM Module

Across the world, we are all reliant on mobile communications as our primary way to communicate. Although we have all encountered situations when we were unable to answer our calls, they were either important personal calls or business calls that changed our lives. Due to the fact that you could not answer the call at that time, you might have missed that opportunity.

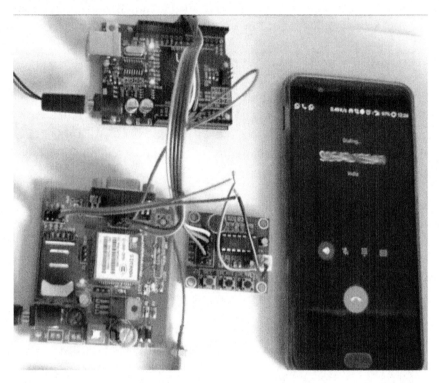

A number of Arduino and GSM modules will be used in this project in order to create an Automatic Call Answering Machine to solve the problem. If you are switching to a new number or going on a long pilgrimage, remember this next time, or just record your voice stating your reason for absence while on vacation or enjoying a well-deserved break and Your recordings will be automatically played to all the people on this machine when you call them. Your business numbers can also be used for answering customer calls during off-hours. Sounds interesting right? So let us build it.

Materials Required:

Although it seems complicated, it is really easy to build, you just need the following components to get started

- Arduino Uno
- GSM module – Flyscale SIM 900
- ISD 1820 Voice Module
- 12V adapter to power GSM module
- 9V battery to power Arduino
- Connecting wires

Before we actually proceed into the project, let us get familiar with the GSM module and ISD 1820 Voice Module

Fly Scale SIM900 GSM Module:

GSM modules are extremely useful to us in our project, especially when we want to access the system remotely. In such a module, phone calls could be placed and received, SMS messages could be sent and received, and GPRS Internet connections could be made, for example.

An USB-to-RS232 adapter is included with GSM modules, which can be plugged directly into a computer or to a microcontroller using either the TX or RX pins. A microphone or a speaker can also be connected to other pins besides MIC+ and MIC-. Power for this module can be provided by a 12V adapter through a regular DC barrel jack.

Upon inserting your SIM card into the module, the LED should automatically become active. During the next minute or two, you will see a red (or other color) LED flashing every 3 seconds. Therefore, a connection was established between the Module and the SIM card. Getting started is easy once you have connected the module to a phone or microcontroller.

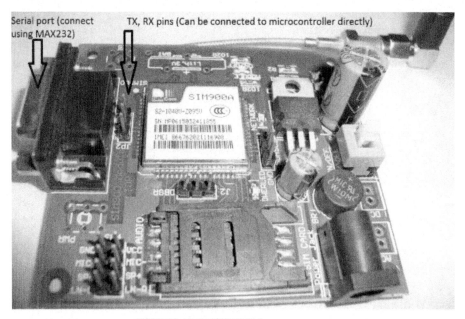

GSM Module SIM900A

ISD1820 Voice module:

With the ISD 1820 Voice module, you can easily integrate voice announcements into your Projects. A 10 second audio clip can be recorded in this module, and you can play it when needed. An example of the device is shown below. The module comes with a microphone and a speaker (8-ohm, 0.5W).

Powered by berg sticks on the left, the modules operate on +5V. Rec, PlayE, and PlayL are the three buttons on the bottom of the screen. Click the corresponding button. Recording your voice is as simple as pressing the Rec button. By selecting PlayE, you will be able to play it. You can play the voice by pressing and holding the PlayL button. On the left, we see pins that are used to interface with a microcontroller. ESP8266/Arduino pins, which can handle 3V-5V, can act as direct drivers. In our project, we control the PLAYE pin on the Arduino module with the D8 pin.

Circuit Diagram and Explanation:

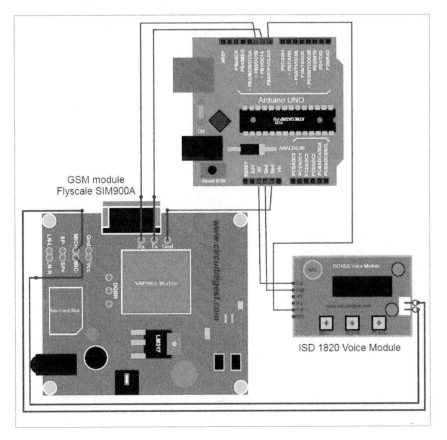

The circuit diagram above describes in detail this automatic voice call answering machine project. There are a lot of simple connections to be seen. The GSM module is powered by a 12V 1A adapter, while the Arduino runs on a 5V battery. We can play back our voice recordings on the voice module whenever we press the rec button on the voice module and then push P-E. In this case, the microphone of the GSM module will be used to capture the audio. Unlike the GSM module, the voice module has a microphone pin that is connected to the speaker pin on the GSM module.

In order for the Arduino and the GSM module to communicate, you must use a serial connection. A chain is connected between the Arduino's X and Y pins. In this way, Arduino will have the ability to communicate with the GSM module. The Arduino requests that the GSM module answer a call when it is received by the GSM module. The Arduino demonstrates that the call is active by turning pin 8 high for 200ms (connected to pins P-E on the voice module).

94. Smart Blind Stick using Arduino

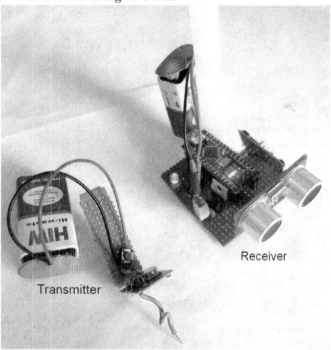

Has Hugh Herr ever caught your attention? His disability has not held him back; he is a staunch believer in the ability of technology to provide the same opportunities for disabled people as the able-bodied. Herr said in a TED talk that human do not have disabilities. There is no such thing as a broken person. We have a broken and disabled built environment and technology. Through technological innovation, we the people do not have to accept our limitations and can transfer them. In truth, he was living his life by these words, today he wears prosthetics to walk and claims a normal existence. Therefore, technology does indeed have the ability to neutralize human disability. With this in mind, let's build a blind man's stick that can do more than just assist the visually impaired.

Its ultrasonic sensor will detect the distance from an obstacle, its LDR will detect lighting conditions, and its RF remote will allow the blind man to find his stick remotely. Using a Buzzer, all feedback will be given to the blind man. The buzzer can certainly be replaced with a vibrating motor and you can advance a lot further using creativity.

Materials Required:

- Arduino Nano (Any version will work)
- Ultrasonic Sensor HC-SR04
- LDR
- Buzzer and LED
- 7805
- 433MHz RF transmitter and receiver
- Resistors
- Capacitors
- Push button
- Perf board
- Soldering Kit
- 9V batteries

Circuit Diagram:

Two separate circuits are required for this Arduino Smart Blind Stick Project. It consists of the main circuit, which is mounted on the stick by the blind man. There will also be a small relay for locating the main circuit, which is an RF transmitter. As seen in the following circuit diagram, the main board consists of:

As can be seen, all the sensors are controlled by an Arduino Nano. With a 7805-voltage regulator, a 9V battery provides power to the entire board. Powered by 5 volts, the Ultrasonic sensor's trigger and echo pins are connected to the Arduino nano's pins 3 and 2 as shown in above diagram. LDRs are connected to resistors of 10K, creating a potential divider, whose differential voltages are read using Arduino ADC pin A1. Reading the RF receiver signal from A0 is done using the ADC pin. Pin 12 of the board is connected to the buzzer, which provides the board's output.

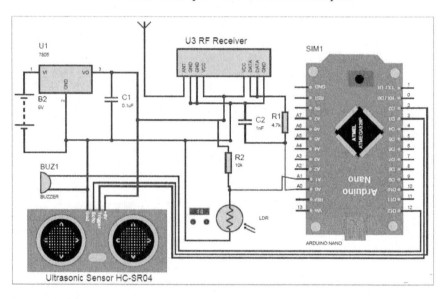

The goal of this project was to develop an ultrasonic blind walking stick that utilized Arduino. There are 30 million permanently blind people and 285 billion people with some form of vision impairment according to WHO.

As soon as you notice them, you will realize that they are unable to walk without the assistance of someone else. They require assistance to get to their destination. As a result, they have more challenges to face in everyday life. Blind sticks allow people to walk with greater confidence. In this stick, the object in front of the person is detected and a response is given either through vibrations or commands. This allows the individual to walk fearlessly. We can help them overcome their difficulties with this device.

Below is a circuit diagram of the RF remote. The workings of this system are also discussed.

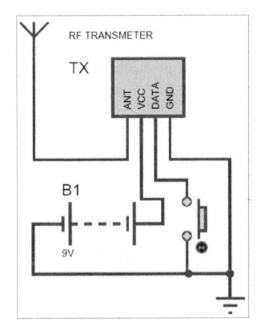

Fig. RF transmitter Circuit

I have modified a remote-control circuit to make it function using a small hack. It usually takes two MCUs or an encoder and decoder to use this 433 MHz module. We rely on the receiver and transmitter to detect if any signals are being transmitted in our application. Thus, ground or Vcc is connected to the Data pin of the transmitter.

An RC filter is used to pass the data pin from the receiver to the Arduino. The example below illustrates this. Now, the Receiver continually outputs the same ADC value whenever the button is pressed. It is impossible to observe this repetition without pressing the button. To detect whether the button has been pressed, we write an Arduino program that checks for repeated values. Therefore, that is how Blind people can track their sticks. You can learn about how RF transmitters and receivers work by visiting this page.

All connections were soldered using a perf board so that it would be intact with the stick. A breadboard can also be used to make them.

95. Arduino Metal Detector

Metal Detectors are used in various places to detect metals that are dangerous, such as airports, shopping malls, cinemas, etc. We have previously made a very simple Metal detector without a microcontroller; now we incorporate an Arduino to make the Metal Detector. The coil and capacitor that will be used in this project will be responsible for detecting metals. We have built this metal detector project using an Arduino Nano. All electronics lovers should find this project very interesting. A very loud buzzer will start beeping the moment the metal detector detects it.

Required Components:

- Arduino (any)
- Coil
- 10nF capacitor
- Buzzer
- The 1k resistor
- 330-ohm resistor
- LED
- 1N4148 diode
- Breadboard or PCB
- Connecting jumper wire
- 9v Battery

Working Concept:

Any time there is current passing through the coil, a magnetic field is generated around it. Magnetic fields generate electric fields when they are changed. The Faraday Law states that due to the Electric field, a voltage is generated across the coil that opposes the change in magnetic field. The result is an increase in current, causing the voltage to oppose the change in magnetic field. The Inductance value is measured in Henrys using the following formula

$L = (\mu o * N2 * A) / l$
Were,
L- Inductance in Henries
μo- Permeability, its $4\pi*10-7$ for Air
N- Number of turns
A- Inner Core Area ($\pi r2$) in m2
l- Length of the Coil in meters

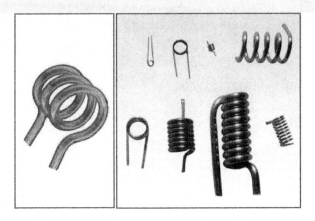

Any metal that comes into contact with the coil causes the coil to change its inductance. The type of metal determines the change in inductance. Non-magnetic metals have a smaller magnetic moment, while iron has a greater magnetic moment.

Inductance value changes drastically depending on the core of the coil. As you can see in the figure below, the inductors have an air-cored core, so there is no solid core in these inductors. This is basically just a lot of coils lying around. No matter what the inductor generates, its magnetic field flows in nothing or air. Inductors with low inductances are used in these applications.

When the values of a few microHenry are required, these inductors are used. If your value is greater than a few milliHenry, then this is not the right choice. An inductor with ferrite core can be seen in the figure below. Despite the large inductance values of these Ferrite Core inductors.

In this case, the coil wound within the inductor is air cored, so when a metal object is brought to the coil it serves as a core. Inductance of the coil changes or increases greatly when this metal acts as a core. By adding a metal piece to the LC circuit, a significant amount of inductance is introduced, altering the overall impedance or reactants of the circuit.

In this Arduino Metal Detector Project, we need to figure out how to detect metals by measuring the inductance of the coil. Thus, we did this by using the LR circuits (Resistor-Inductor Circuits) that we described previously. A coil with about 20 turns has been used here with a winding of around 10 cm in diameter. A tape roll has been used to wind up wire on, and the wire has been wound around it.

Metal Detectors are used to detect land mines, detect weapons such as knives and guns at airport security checkpoints, conduct geophysical prospecting, archaeology and treasure hunting.

Circuit Diagram:

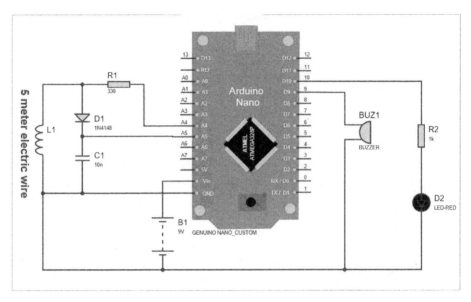

The whole Metal Detector Project has been controlled by an Arduino Nano. Indicators such as LEDs and buzzers are used for metal detection. For the detection of metals, coils and capacitors are used. Reduced voltage is also achieved by using a signal diode. Additionally, a resistor is used to limit the current flowing through the Arduino pin.

Working Explanation:

The metal detector on this Arduino is a little challenging to use. The high pass filter of the LR is fed the block wave or pulse generated by the Arduino. Therefore, each transition will be marked by short spikes caused by the coil. Having a coil with a high inductance result in pulses with a shorter pulse length. We can measure the inductance of a coil with the help of these shock pulses. Due to the very short duration of the spikes (approx. 0.5 microseconds), it is very difficult to successfully measure inductance with that.

The capacitor we used instead of this, is charged by rising impulses or spikes. The capacitor was charged with a few pulses so that A5 on the Arduino can read its voltage. This capacitor's voltage is read using ADC by Arduino. Cap Pin was made the output pin as soon as the voltage was read and set to low, quickly discharging the capacitor. About 200 microseconds are required to complete this process. The measurement was repeated and the resulting average was taken to produce the best results. Using that method, we can calculate Coil's approximate inductance. Using the result, we transfer the data to LED and buzzers to see whether metal is present. The complete code that follows this article will help you understand how the program works.

At the end of this article, you will find the full Arduino code. We will use two Arduino pins in this project, one to generate block waves that will be fed into the coil, and the second to read voltage from the capacitor. We have also connected LEDs and buzzers to two other Arduino pins besides these two.

96. Arduino Based Fire Fighting Robot

It is estimated that between 2010 and 2014 more than 1.2 lakh deaths were caused by fire accidents in India, according to the National Crime Records Bureau (NCRB). While there are many precautionary measures taken to prevent Fire accidents, they do sometimes occur as a result of natural disasters or human error. Human resources will be used to extinguish a fire in the event of a fire breakout so that people can be rescued. It is very much possible that humans can be replaced with robots for fighting fires thanks to the advancements in technology, especially robotics. Firefighters would be more effective, and they would also avoid endangering people on the job. The goal of this tutorial is to create an Arduino Fire Fighting Robot, which will detect fire and start the water pump automatically

This project will teach you how to make a simple robot that can pump out water around a fire and move towards it to put it out. Once you understand the following robotic basics, it will be easier for you to build more complex robots. Okay, let's start at the beginning.

Material Required:

- Arduino UNO
- Fire sensor or Flame sensor (3 Nos)
- Servo Motor (SG90)
- L293D motor Driver module
- Mini DC Submersible Pump
- Small Breadboard
- Robot chassis with motors (2) and wheels (2) (any type)
- A small can
- Connecting wires

Working Concept of Fire Fighting Robot:

The Arduino is the main processor of the project. For detecting fire, we are using the Fire sensor module (flame sensor) as shown below.

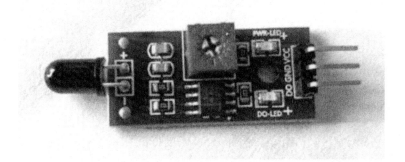

It's possible to see that these sensors are equipped with an IR receiver (Photodiode), which is used to detect fire. This is impossible, how is it possible? An infrared receiver on the sensor module will be able to pick up this light from the fire when it burns. Using an Op-Amp, we then monitor the voltage change across the IR Receiver, so if there is a fire, our output pin (DO) will be 0V (low) and if there is none, our output pin will be 5V (high).

To determine in which direction the fire is burning, we use three sensors located in three directions on the robot.

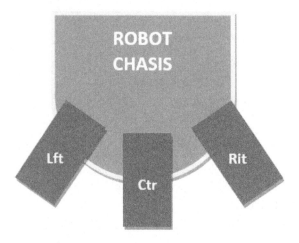

By using the L293D module, we can drive our motors close to the fire once we know the direction in which the fire is coming from. We must use water to put out a fire when near one. The water is carried in a small container, a 5V pump is also tucked inside, and the entire device sits atop a servo motor so that the water can be sprayed from any direction. Now that we have the connections, let's move on

As a profession, firefighting is an important one, but it is very dangerous. Robots are designed for that reason, so that they can find a fire before it rages out of control. The system could be used to reduce victims' injury risks by working with fire fighters.

Firefighting Robots are compact and portable emergency response robots that assist firefighters, especially in highly dangerous environments where people cannot enter, in fighting high-rise fires

Circuit Diagram:

On the following page you'll find the complete schematic for this Fire Fighting Robot. It is either possible to connect each connection to upload the bot to verify its functionality or you can assemble the bot completely. After that, connect the devices. It's very simple to make both connections and you should have no trouble doing it.

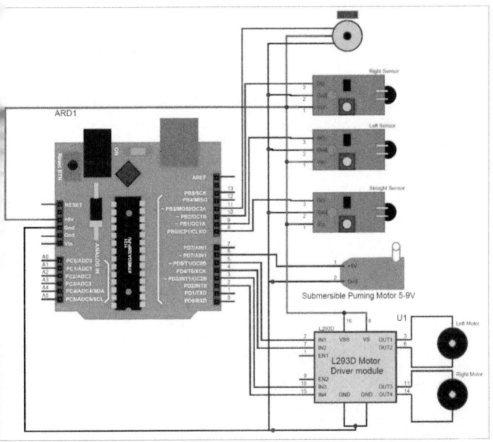

The container that I am using might not be the same for the robotic chassis that you are using. Set up the pumping system then according to your own creativity. It will, however, continue to be the same code. My pump is housed in a small aluminum can (cool drinks can) that I filled with water and set it in place. In order to control the direction of the water, I assembled the whole can on top of a servo motor. I built my robot in a way that looks like this.

Servo fins were made by hot gluing the bottom of the container to the servo motor, and servo motors were attached to the chassis by nuts and bolts. The container just needs to be placed on top of the motor, then the pump inside it can be triggered to force water outside via the tube. Using the servo to rotate the whole container, the water can be directed in any direction.

97. Interfacing Joystick with Arduino

When we hear the word Joystick, we immediately think of the game controller. The same applies here, and you can use it for gaming as well. The technology is not only useful for gaming, but also in DIY electronic projects. X and Y planes of this joystick are controlled with separate potentiometers. Through the potentiometer, it can receive voltage and send it to Arduino as a number. The number changes as we move the joystick shaft (which actually is the potentiometer pointer).

We simply control four LEDs via the Joystick in this Circuit by interfacing it with the Arduino. A motorized joystick is a device used to move the shaft of the joystick. 4 LEDs indicate the direction of motion of the shaft. Besides the joystick, it possesses a push button you can use to control other functions, or you can leave it untouched. The joystick also has a LED, which, when pressed, turns on as soon as the joystick button is pressed.

Circuit Diagram

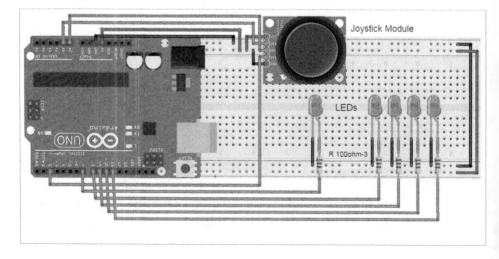

Material Required

- Arduino UNO
- Joystick Module
- LEDs-5
- Resistor: 100ohm-3
- Connecting wires
- Breadboard

Joystick Module

Joysticks come in a variety of shapes and sizes. In the following figure you can see a typical joystick module. The joystick module provides Analog Outputs, which change voltage with the direction the joystick is pointed. Through interpreting these voltage changes with a microcontroller, we can determine the direction of the movement. Joysticks have been interfaced with the AVR and Raspberry Pi in the past.

See how there are two axes on this joystick module. The X-axis is horizontal, and the Y-axis is vertical. A potentiometer or potentiometer is mounted on each axis of JOYSTICK. As the pots are driven out, the midpoints are represented as Rx and Ry. These pots get their points based on Rx and Ry. Rx and Ry work together as a voltage divider when the Joystick is in standby.

Whenever a joystick is moved horizontally, a change in voltage occurs at the Rx pin. A similar change in voltage occurs at the Ry pin when the pin is moved along the vertical axis. Therefore, we have four directions of joystick output connected to two ADCs. A voltage difference between the pins occurs when the stick is moved in either direction

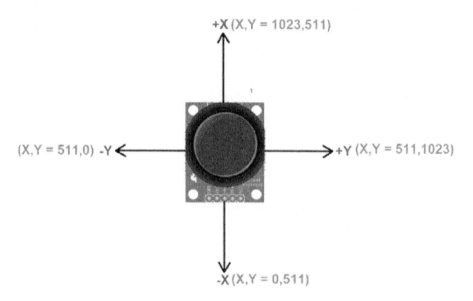

+X (X,Y = 1023,511)

(X,Y = 511,0) -Y ←→ +Y (X,Y = 511,1023)

-X (X,Y = 0,511)

Using this Joystick module, we are going to connect it to the Arduino UNO, which comes with an inbuilt ADC (Analog to Digital Converter) mechanism

Controlling LEDs using Joystick with Arduino

The Arduino code has been uploaded to it, and the components have been connected according to the circuit diagram. Now we can control the LEDs using the joystick. The four LEDs can be turned ON in each direction

according to the Joystick shaft movement.

One potentiometer is used for movement along the X axis, and another for movement along the Y axis, in the Joystick. The potentiometers are powered by 5 volts from the Arduino. We can see here how driving the joystick will change the voltage value and the analog values corresponding to Analog pins A0 and A1. We are reading the analog values of the X and Y axes from the Arduino and turning ON the LEDs in accordance with the joystick movement.

98. Arduino RFID Door Lock

The RFID door lock mechanism can be seen in many hotels and other places that don't require a key to unlock the doors. The key is provided to you, and by simply inserting it into the RFID Reader box, you will hear a Beep and see a blink of LEDs, unlocking the lock. Any door can be fitted with this RFID door lock, which can be easily made and installed at home. It is simply a door lock that operates when the door is turned on by a voltage (typically 12 volts).

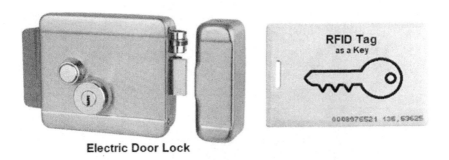

Electric Door Lock

The relay in this project is used to control the Electric Door Lock. RFID tags will be used as keys, so the Arduino and the relay will be used to trigger the lock. You will be alerted about the wrong card if you place it near the RFID reader. Start by reading about RFIDs working and how it can be interfaced with an Arduino.

Material Required:

- Arduino UNO
- EM-18 Reader Module with Tags

- Relay 5v
- LED
- Buzzer
- Connecting wire
- Resistors

EM-18 RFID Reader:

A radio frequency identification system uses radio waves to identify objects. It is possible to read the RFID card number by using a RFID reader, which embeds a unique ID in the RFID card. The EM-18 RFID reader operates at 125 KHz and can be powered with a 5V power supply. While it comes with a built-in antenna, it also comes with an on-chip antenna. Besides Weigand output, it provides serial output as well. There is a range of approximately 8-12cm. Data and stop bits for serial communication are 8 bytes, 9600bps. There are many applications for wireless RF identification, for example

RFID Based Attendance System,

- Security systems,
- Voting machines,
- E-toll road pricing

RFID Reader Module   RFID Tags

In ASCII format, EM-18 RFID readers provide 12 digit output. In a card number, the first 10 digits are the number of the card; the final two are the result of XORing the number of the card. To check for errors, two digits are added to the end.

Arduino RFID Door Lock Circuit Diagram

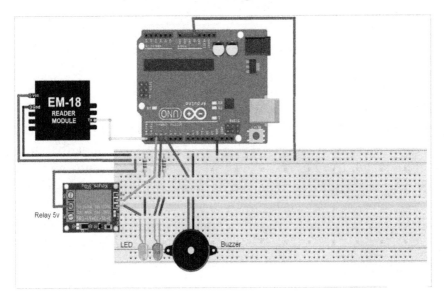

Working of Arduino Based RFID Door Lock

RFID systems are composed of two components: RFID tags and RFID readers. Integrated circuits are used to store data, and antennas are used to transmit the data to RFID readers. RFID tags consist of an integrated circuit and an antenna. RFID tags are powered by RF signals whenever they are in range of RFID readers. The tags transmit data serially when they are powered by RF signals. Afterwards, the RFID reader reads the data and transmits it to the Arduino microcontroller. Following that, different tasks are performed in accordance with the microcontroller's code.

The value of the RFID tag has already been saved in the code of our circuit. As a result, the relay gets activated when that tag gets within the range. To demonstrate the power of a relay, a LED has been connected. However, you can replace the LED with an Electric Door Lock to guarantee the lock will open whenever a relay is activated.

If another RFID card is scanned, the buzzer will start beeping because it's the wrong RFID tag. For this reason, the door lock system relies on the fact that an RFID tag is required for it to open. It is possible to adjust the delay in codes for when the relay itself gets deactivated after 5 seconds and when the door is closed after 5 seconds.

99. An introduction to Brushless DC Motors (BLDC) and how to control them on an Arduino

We have always enjoyed building things and getting them to work as we wanted. It would definitely be an anxiety pump for hobbyists and hardware tinkerers to build something that could fly. Absolutely! Among the various aircraft I refer to are gliders, helicopters, planes, and primarily multi-copter aircraft. Due to the community support available online today, it has become very easy to build one on your own. The BLDC motor is a feature common to all things that fly, but what is it? What is the purpose of it in order to fly? How does it differ from other software? Is there a way you can interface your motor with your controller and buy the right motor? What are ESCs and why do we need them? These are just a few questions you can get answered in this tutorial.

The main purpose of this tutorial is to control the speed of a 2112/13T sensorless BLDC outrunner motor (commonly found in drones), using an ESC (Electronic Speed Controller).

Materials Required

- A2212/13T BLDC Motor
- ESC (20A)
- Power Source (12V 20A)
- Arduino
- Potentiometer
- Understanding BLDC Motors

BLDC motors operate smoothly, which makes them common in ceiling fans and electric vehicles. BLDC motors, on the other hand, are equipped with three wires, thus forming three phases. Hold on... what!!??

BLDC motors still operate by using pulsed waves, though they are classified as DC motors. The DC voltage from the battery is converted into pulses by the electronic speed controller (ESC), and the motor receives the pulses via its three wires. Current can only enter and leave the motor through two phases at a given time, so that one phase powers the motor and the other phase delivers power.

When the motor is in this position, the coil inside is energized, and therefore the magnet on the rotor aligns itself with the energized coil. A motor is rotated by energizing the next two wires and then turning them by the ESC. In order to function, the coils need to be energized according to their order of energization and their speed depends on its speed. The remainder of this article will discuss ESC in greater detail.

A BLDC motor can be classified in several ways, some of which are more common than others.

A BLDC motor can be installed in the in-runner or out-runner: In runner BLDC motors work just like any other motor. In other words, the motor shaft rotates, but the casing is stationary. BLDC motors with outrunners are the opposite in that the coil inside remains fixed while the casing rotates along with the shaft. A major advantage to the use of out-runner motors is that the outer part of the motor (the one that rotates) turns into the tyre rim, so it is not necessary to have a coupling mechanism. A motor without runners tends to have more torque than those with in runners, which makes them a best choice for EVs and drones. Also, the one we are using here is an outrunner type.

Note:

For the sake of this tutorial, let's skip a different type of motor called the coreless BLDC motors, which are also used for pocket drones. They work on a completely different principle, so we'll skip it for now.

Sensorless and sensor-loaded BLDC Motors: To ensure continuous rotation of a BLDC motor, feedback must be provided. That is, the ESC must know which magnets are where and on which pole in order to power the stator appropriately. An inside hall sensor can be used to obtain this information, or the motor can also be left open to collect this information. ESC receives the information from the hall sensor about the magnet.

Motors like this are used in electric vehicles and are known as sensors-based BLDC motors. Second, we can use the back EMF generated by the coils when the magnets cross over them. This method does not require any additional hardware or wires; the phase wire itself is a feedback mechanism for measuring back EMF. We use this method in our motors, as well as in drones and other flying projects.

Why do Drones and other multi-copters use BLDC Motors?

Drones come in many forms, from quadcopters to helicopters and gliders, all of which have one thing in common: hardware. What are BLDC motors? Why do they exist? Compared to DC Motors, what is the purpose of using BLDC motors, which are a bit more expensive?

One important reason for this is the very high torque generated by these motors, which is important for gaining thrust or losing thrust rapidly in order to launch or land a drone. As well as having these motors as out runners, they are offered as out runners as well, enhancing their thrust. Our drone will stay steady in mid-air due to the smooth vibration less operation of the BLDC motor.

BLDC motors have a powerful to light weight ratio. In order for drones to perform well, they need motors that are both powerful (high speed and torque) and lightweight. In order to match the performance and torque of a BLDC motor with a DC motor, the motor would have to be twice as heavy.

Why do we need an ESC and what is its function?

In order to generate the phases for BLDC motors, DC voltage from the battery has to be converted to pulses using a controller. The term Electronic Speed Controller refers to this device. Controllers have the role of energizing the phase wires so that the BLDC motors rotate. To do this, the coil is energized when the magnet crosses the wire and the back EMF is detected. It is beyond the scope of this tutorial to investigate all the hardware brilliance found in the ESC. The speed controller and the battery eliminator are a few other features.

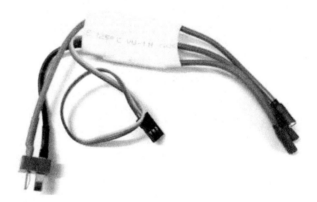

Speed control using PWM: The ESC can read the PWM signal connected to the orange wire to control the speed of the BLDC motor. This motor functions very much like servo motors, the pulse width modulation signal provides a 20ms period, and the duty cycle may be varied to vary the motor's speed. Our Arduino program can utilize the same servo library to control the position since the same logic applies to the servo motors. Here's how you can use Servo with Arduino.

Battery Elimination Circuit: Almost all ESCs feature a Battery Elimination Circuit (BEC). This circuit eliminates the need for a separate battery for the microcontroller; it will provide a regulated +5V to the Arduino, so there is no need for a separate power supply. It is normal for this voltage to be regulated by one of a number of circuits, and on cheap ESCs, you'll usually hear linear regulation, but there are also ones that use switching circuits.

Every ESC comes with a firmware program installed by the manufacturer. In terms of ESC firmware, traditional firmware, Simon-K, and BL-Heli are some of the more popular options. As we mentioned earlier, this firmware can also be customized by users, but we won't go into too much detail about this in this tutorial.

Arduino BLDC Motor Control Circuit Diagram

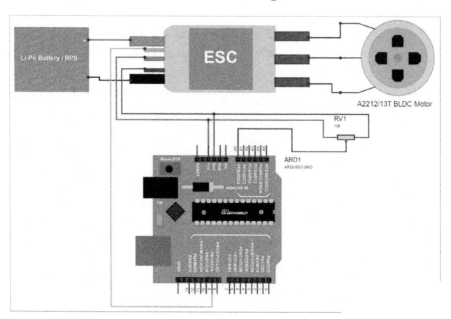

BLDC motors can be easily connected to Arduinos via a straightforward interface. A minimum 12V and 5A source of power is required for the ESC. My RPS has been used in this tutorial, but you can also use a Li-Po battery because it's just as powerful. Connect the three phase wires of the ESC to the three phase wires of the motors, there is no specific order in which the wires should be connected, you can connect them in any order.

Controlling BLDC Motor with Arduino

The circuit diagram should be followed and the code uploaded to the Arduino. The ESC should be powered up.

Make sure you mount the BLDC motors securely, or they will jump around when they are rotating. In the event that the throttle signal is not within the threshold limits within a few seconds after you start your setup, your ESC will make a welcoming tone and keep beeping. The beeping tone will stop when the POT from zero is gradually increased. The motor will start spinning more slowly as you increase the PWM signal beyond the lower threshold value. Once the voltage reaches the upper threshold limit, the motor will stop due to a lack of power. The more voltage you provide, the more speed you will see. Once you have completed the process, you can repeat it.

100. Automatic Medicine Reminder Using Arduino

It is always our intention to keep our dear ones in good shape when it comes to health. The question is, what will happen when people get ill and forget to take their medications.

Right? We'd be concerned, wouldn't we? Hospital patients need to be reminded to take their medicine on time, but it's difficult to do so because there are so many of them. To remind people to take their medicine on time, the traditional methods require human effort. Machines can perform that task in the digital era and we aren't bound by those rules. Besides doctors in hospitals and patients at home, Smart Medicine Reminder has many other uses.

When it comes to reminding, there can be many ways to remind it:

- Show it on a display
- Send notification on email or Phone
- Using mobile apps
- Buzz alarm
- Using Bluetooth/ Wi-Fi
- Get a call
- Remind for next medicine time while reminding current time

Depending on the circumstances, we can combine different methods. Our Medicine Reminder has a simple Arduino circuit that reminds us to take our medicines 1 or 2 or 3 times a day. Push buttons allow you to select a time slot. Additionally, it displays the current date and time. This article will be further extended into an IoT project, where a notification will be sent by email or SMS to users. Patient Monitoring Systems can also be used to send medication reminders.

Remembering to take medications may seem like an unnecessary task, but we cannot emphasize its importance enough. Most seniors are prescribed medication to manage illness due to increased visits to the doctor and hospital. Many of the patients find it difficult to remember to take their medication and not just because of their hectic schedules. Some patients have trouble adhering to their medication regimen because of memory loss.

Our loved one's health and quality of life depend on making sure they follow their doctor's orders for prescribed medications. One small change can make all the difference in the effectiveness of a health care plan.

We value patient's health and ensure he or she takes their medication properly. To facilitate this, this project and caregivers are standing by to encourage your loved one to take their medications on time.

Arduino Medicine Reminder Circuit Diagram and Connections

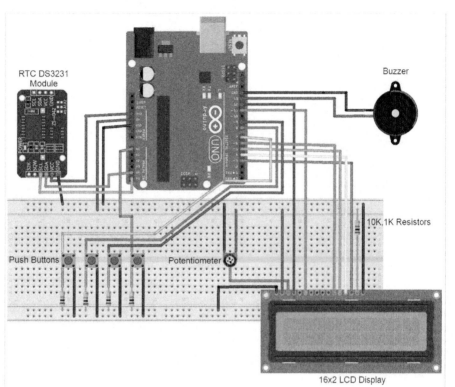

Components Required

- Arduino Uno (We can use other Arduino boards also, like Promini, Nano)
- RTC DS3231 module
- 16x2 LCD Display
- Buzzer
- LED (any color)
- Breadboard
- Push Buttons
- 10K Potentiometer
- 10K,1K Resistors
- Jumper Wires

Arduino Pins		Peripheral Pins
▪ 2	------------------------->	D7 of 16x2 LCD Display
▪ 3	------------------------->	D6 of 16x2 LCD Display
▪ 4	------------------------->	D5 of 16x2 LCD Display
▪ 5	------------------------->	D4 of 16x2 LCD Display
▪ 7	------------------------->	3rd push button
▪ 8	------------------------->	2nd push button
▪ 9	------------------------->	1st push button
▪ 11	------------------------->	EN pin of 16x2 LCD Display
▪ 12	------------------------->	RS pin of 16x2 LCD Display
▪ 13	------------------------->	+Ve Pin of Buzzer and Led
▪ A0	------------------------->	Stop Push Button
▪ A4	------------------------->	SDA of DS3231
▪ A5	------------------------->	SCL of DS3231
▪ 3.3V	------------------------->	Vcc of DS3231
▪ Gnd	------------------------->	Gnd

The DS3231 RTC is interfaced with Arduino Uno over I2C protocol in this Medicine Reminder Project. Also, you can use an RTC IC DS1307 with Arduino to read the time. Also included with the RTC DS3231 is a 32k memory that may be used to store additional information. The RTC module requires 3.3V to be powered from the Arduino uno.

The LCD display occupies a 16x2 area, and it is connected using SPI. It is common for buzzers to be used to remind people before taking medication. Each push button features a distinct feature that allows it to be selected. It brings up a reminder to take your medication once a day using the first push button. There is a second button for reminding twice a day, and a third for reminding three times a day. Once a user has heard the alert, they can press the fourth push button to turn off the buzzer.

Working of Automatic Medicine Reminder System

In order to power the Pill Reminder Alarm, 5V is required. When Circuit Digest is first launched, it displays the welcome message "Welcome to Circuit Digest". Three screens are displayed on the LCD screen at a time. As soon as the screen loads, a message appears saying "Stay Healthy, Get Well Soon". On the next screen, a help screen is displayed that instructs you how to choose a time-slot to remember (once, twice, or three times per day). A time slot can be configured in the program in accordance with the user's preference. The duration has now been reduced to three, which are 8am, 2pm, and 8pm.

There are three modes of dividing up the time slots. When the user presses the first push button, the user is instructed to take medicine once a day at 8am. When the user presses the second push button in mode 2, the system selects to take medicine twice daily at 8am and 8pm. In Mode 3, when the third push button is pressed, the user will take their medication three times daily at 8am, 2pm and 8pm.

Additionally, the buzzer can be snoozed for a period of ten minutes (not included in this project). Push buttons allow the user to choose desired slots, and a RTC is used to determine the current time. The buzzer starts to buzz when the time matches the selected time slot. Users have the option of stopping the buzzer by pressing the STOP button. Similarly, the next reminder is sent by the same method.

Summary

The following chapter should be quite interesting to you, and we presume that you have practiced more than 100 Arduino Project Ideas as they will be useful to you in building your dream project. In upcoming sessions, we will cover How to Troubleshoot and Fix Arduino Issues as well as how to repurpose your old Arduino.

CHAPTER 6

How to Troubleshoot and Fix Arduino Issues

There are times when your Arduino program and your hardware won't function as expected. There are a number of causes to this problem, including software or hardware incompatibility. Using this section, you can troubleshoot Arduino and solve hardware and software related problems.

Can't Load Programs on Arduino

The right board should make it easy for you to load programs once the computer program is configured correctly. There are several reasons for why codes cannot be loaded into the system.

An unknown problem may result from using the incorrect port, using the wrong drivers, or missing the right drivers. Physical connection problems or issues with the device's firmware can give rise to hardware problems.

Solution: Verify that the board model is compatible with the configured model

As a first solution, you should confirm that you have configured the Arduino model on the program properly. The program's users often select the incorrect board type. If you haven't already done so, verify the model used within the Arduino software by going to **Tools > Board.** You can then reload the code to see if it was loaded when you selected the right board type.

Also, make sure the board has the right type of microcontroller. Many Arduino boards, particularly the older ones, feature the ATmega160 microcontroller. In the newer models, an ATmega328 is used. Look at the board's microcontroller and choose it on the device if you aren't sure which one to select.

There are also many reasons why the code can't be loaded, such as driver issues. Make sure the serial port driver is installed by going to **Tools > Serial Port.** Make sure to verify this information with a computer connected to the board.

Your computer's device manager is another place to look. Identify any items in the device that are marked yellow or unidentified. It might be the Arduino-specific driver that is causing the problem if you are unaware of the drivers that are causing the problem. If you need to install a new driver, you can access its properties and install it by accessing its driver installation tab. Review the previous chapter for more information about installing drivers.

Solution: Ensure a Functioning Arduino

When the device isn't powered, it may not be detected by your computer. By viewing its LED, you can determine whether the board itself is receiving power. There must be some sort of problem with the electric system if it isn't working. Check the power supply source to see if it's functioning.

Those boards with dual power options need to be set to receive power from the appropriate source. In the case of USB power, look for a jumper direction that points towards the side of the USB connector, which means the system should be powered by this connector. To fix it, re-plug it after disconnecting it, setting the jumper to ground, and resetting it to power. The LED indicator should turn on to let you know if it is functioning.

Solution: Reset the Device

Arduino boards come with a reset button, which can be useful if you run into problems loading codes. By pressing the reset button, the board can be reset. Hold the button down for several seconds and then reset it. If it doesn't work after waiting for a few minutes, reload the program.

Solution: Diagnose USB Connection Problem

In most cases, the inconsistency is caused by the hardware itself. If the data pathway itself is down, the code transfer will not be completed. Change your USB cable to solve this problem. Diagnosis of the cable problem can be done in a variety of ways. The board may not be detected if it is plugged into your computer with the wrong cable. Verify through the Arduino program whether or not your board has the serial port that should be assigned.

Arduino Software is Not Working

There are times when programs don't perform as expected. Arduino software that doesn't load correctly has probably been installed on the computer with an outdated or incorrect version compared to what the operating system requires. A computer program should not be installed if it is incompatible with your system. For this case, you should uninstall the program, download a newer installer, and reinstall.

There's also the possibility that you're using a third-party Arduino program. Programs developed by third parties should work as advertised by Arduino developers. Install the new third-party application after uninstalling the current one

The official website of the developer. Downloading a file from another source is not recommended. Installation is as simple as extracting and installing.

If the previous solution does not work, you can download the Arduino program. Upon installing the program, make sure it is loaded

Arduino Software is Freezing and Crashing

It is caused by a program inconsistency that causes Arduino software to freeze. Programs installed with peripherals, drivers, or other files can conflict with conflicting programs. By using MSConfig, identify likely conflicting programs. Disable Start-up programs and services by loading this utility. Load Arduino software and restart your computer. You might have an issue with one of your starts up programs, even if the Arduino program loaded flawlessly. Identify the cause of the problem by testing each program and service. The result will be necessary to prevent lagging before you can load Arduino software.

Although the program does not freeze or crash, sometimes it runs slowly. Additionally, a device on your computer may be causing this issue. It is most commonly caused by installation of the COM port interfering with loading. To troubleshoot and disable program causes, use MSConfig again. Connect all of your computers' other devices to your computer before turning it off. Connect the device to the computer once it has been turned on. Try opening the program and taking a look at how it responds.

Don't Throw Damaged Arduino

Beginners have a high risk of damaging an Arduino PCB q43. This is part of the learning process, so don't worry about it.

Never discard a board after it has been damaged. It still has value as a way for you to become familiar with its components. In order to understand how its parts are assembled, it's recommended that you take it apart. When you are ready to build a custom board, this information will come in handy.

Essential Resources

---

1. Arduino Official Home Page https://www.arduino.cc/ Info on hardware, some libraries for sensors, the integrated development environment (IDE) and reference material on commands and structures
2. www.instructables.com : Info on DIY projects prepared by others
3. Arduino Official Project Pages https://create.arduino.cc/projecthub
4. https://learn.adafruit.com Adafruit makes many shields and sensors, and they have tutorials for almost everything they carry
5. http://www.arduinoclassroom.com/index.php/arduino-101 Arduino Classroom is currently doing an intro series on Arduinos. Check it for updates and more topics in the future
6. http://playground.arduino.cc/ Arduino playground is the wiki run by the Arduino Company for its products. There is a lot of helpful information on almost everything imaginable here.
7. Github Arduino Page https://github.com/arduino/Arduino
8. Hackster Arduino Page https://www.hackster.io/arduino
9. Hackster Arduino Projects https://www.hackster.io/arduino/projects
10. Circuit digest Arduino Projects https://circuitdigest.com/arduino-projects
11. Electronics Hub Arduino Project Ideas https://www.electronicshub.org/arduino-project-ideas/
12. Electronics for u Arduino Project Ideas https://www.electronicsforu.com/arduino-projects-ideas
13. Home of Make Magazine, which has lots of Arduino projects www.makezine.com
14. Arduino Projects by All about circuits dot com https://www.allaboutcircuits.com/projects/category/arduino
15. Arduino Projects by How to mechatronics dot com

503

https://howtomechatronics.com/arduino-projects/
16. Arduino Official YouTube Channel
https://www.youtube.com/c/Arduino/videos

Bibliography

---

[1]. Arduino official web site https://www.arduino.cc/

[2]. Exploring Arduino: Tools and Techniques for Engineering Wizardry; 2nd Ed; Jeremy Blum; Wiley; 512 pages; 2019;

[3]. Fritzing. Project web site: http://fritzing.org/

[4]. Programming Arduino Next Steps: Going Further with Sketches; 2nd Ed; Simon Monk; McGraw-Hill Education; 320 pages; 2018;

[5]. Arduino. Project web site: https://www.arduino.cc

[6]. J. Fraden. Handbook of modern sensors. Springer Verlag, Berlin, third edition, 2004.

[7]. Hackster Arduino Page https://www.hackster.io/arduino

[8]. Arduino Workshop: A Hands-On Introduction with 65 Projects; 1st Ed; John Boxall; No Starch Press; 392 pages; 2013;

[9]. Circuit digest Arduino Projects https://circuitdigest.com/arduino-projects

[10]. Arduino For Dummies; 2nd Ed; John Nussey; John Wiley & Sons; 400 pages; 2018;

[11]. Arduino Official YouTube Channel https://www.youtube.com/c/Arduino/videos

[12]. Make: Getting Started with Arduino; 3rd Ed; Massimo Banzi, Michael Shiloh; Make Community; 262 pages; 2014;

[13]. Hackster Arduino Page https://www.hackster.io/arduino

[14]. Programming Arduino: Getting Started With Sketches; 2nd Ed;

[15]. Electronics for u Arduino Project Ideas
https://www.electronicsforu.com/arduino-projects-ideas

 [16]. Simon Monk; McGraw-Hill Education; 192 pages; 2016

[17]. Circuit digest Arduino Projects https://circuitdigest.com/arduino-projects

[18]. Beginning C for Arduino: Learn C Programming for the Arduino; 2nd Ed; Jack Purdum; Apress; 388 pages; 2015;

[19]. Github Arduino Page https://github.com/arduino/Arduino

[20]. Electronics Hub Arduino Project Ideas
https://www.electronicshub.org/arduino-project-ideas/

[21]. Hackster Arduino Projects https://www.hackster.io/arduino/projects

[22]. Arduino: A Quick Start Guide; 2nd Ed; Maik Schmidt; Pragmatic Bookshelf; Pragmatic Bookshelf; 323 pages; 2015;

[23]. Home of Make Magazine, which has lots of Arduino projects
www.makezine.com

[24]. Arduino Projects by How to mechatronics dot com
https://howtomechatronics.com/arduino-projects/

[25]. Make: Sensors; 1st Ed; Tero Karvinen, Kimmo Karvinen, Ville Valtokari; Make Community; 400 pages; 2014;

ABOUT THE AUTHOR

Arsath Natheem is an Indian Biomedical Engineer and YouTuber who works primarily in the field of Data Science, He is best known for his multimedia presentation regard "How Biomedical Engineers Save the lives" displayed at VCET in Tamilnadu, he was honored best project award for Human Interaction Intelligence Robot as Personal Assistance, and IoT Based Voice Recognition Robot for defenses, also presented his project at Adhiyamaan CET and won the first prize. He participated project competition at Madras institute of technology (MIT) in Chennai, He completed his Undergraduate Degree at VCET, and He Enthusiast in R&D at Data Science and Online Content Creation, now he working on Amazon as a Self-Publishing Author and Technical Writer.

ONE LAST THING...

If you enjoyed this book or found it useful, I'd be very grateful if you'd post a short review on Amazon. Your support really does make a difference and I read all the reviews personally so I can get your feedback and make this book even better.

If you'd like to leave a review, then all you need to do is click the review link on this book's page on Amazon.com

Thanks again for your support